CH00941936

Trademark Acknowledgments

All terms mentioned in this book that are known to be trademarks or service marks ....
or Cisco Systems, Inc. cannot attest to the accuracy of this information. Use of a term in this book should not be regarded as affecting
the validity of any trademark or service mark.

Publisher: John Wait

Editor-in-Chief: John Kane

Executive Editor: Brett Bartow

Cisco Representative: Anthony Wolfenden

Cisco Press Program Manager: Jeff Brady

Production Manager: Patrick Kanouse

Development Editor: Andrew Cupp

Senior Project Editor: San Dee Phillips

Editorial Assistant: Raina Han

Copy Editor: John Edwards

Technical Editors: Shawn Boyd, Keith Hutton, Amir Ranjbar

Book and Cover Designer: Louisa Adair

Composition Tolman Creek Design

Indexer: Tim Wright

CISCO SYSTEMS

Corporate Headquarters
Cisco Systems, Inc.
170 West Tasman Drive
San Jose, CA 95134-1706
USA
www.cisco.com
Tel: 408 526-4000
          800 553-NETS (6387)
Fax: 408 526-4100

European Headquarters
Cisco Systems International BV
Haarlerbergpark
Haarlerbergweg 13-19
1101 CH Amsterdam
The Netherlands
www-europe.cisco.com
Tel: 31 0 20 357 1000
Fax: 31 0 20 357 1100

Americas Headquarters
Cisco Systems, Inc.
170 West Tasman Drive
San Jose, CA 95134-1706
USA
www.cisco.com
Tel: 408 526-7660
Fax: 408 527-0883

Asia Pacific Headquarters
Cisco Systems, Inc.
Capital Tower
168 Robinson Road
#22-01 to #29-01
Singapore 068912
www.cisco.com
Tel: +65 6317 7777
Fax: +65 6317 7799

Cisco Systems has more than 200 offices in the following countries and regions. Addresses, phone numbers, and fax numbers are listed on the
Cisco.com Web site at www.cisco.com/go/offices.

Argentina • Australia • Austria • Belgium • Brazil • Bulgaria • Canada • Chile • China PRC • Colombia • Costa Rica • Croatia • Czech Republi
Denmark • Dubai, UAE • Finland • France • Germany • Greece • Hong Kong SAR • Hungary • India • Indonesia • Ireland • Israel • Ital
Japan • Korea • Luxembourg • Malaysia • Mexico • The Netherlands • New Zealand • Norway • Peru • Philippines • Poland • Portuga
Puerto Rico • Romania • Russia • Saudi Arabia • Scotland • Singapore • Slovakia • Slovenia • South Africa • Spain • Swede
Switzerland • Taiwan • Thailand • Turkey • Ukraine • United Kingdom • United States • Venezuela • Vietnam • Zimbabw

About the Authors

Catherine Paquet is a network architect in the field of internetworking and security. Catherine has in-depth knowledge of security systems, remote access, and routing technology. She is a CCSP, a CCNP, and a certified Cisco Systems instructor. Her internetworking career started as a LAN manager, moving to MAN manager, and eventually became a nationwide WAN manager. Catherine teaches network security courses with one of the largest Cisco Learning Partners and has been a guest speaker with the Computer Security Institute (CSI). In 2002 and 2003, Catherine volunteered with the UN mission in Kabul, Afghanistan, to train Afghan public servants in the area of networking. Catherine has a master's degree in business administration with a major in management information systems (MBA MIS). She coauthored the Cisco Press books *Building Scalable Cisco Networks; CCNP Self-Study: Building Scalable Cisco Internetworks (BCSI)* (first and second editions); and *The Business Case for Network Security: Advocacy, Governance, and ROI*; she edited *Building Cisco Remote Access Networks*.

Diane Teare is a consultant in the networking, training, and e-learning fields. Diane has more than 20 years of experience in design, implementation, and troubleshooting of network hardware and software, and has also been involved in teaching, course design, and project management. She has extensive knowledge of network design and routing technologies and is an instructor with one of the largest authorized Cisco Learning Partners. She was recently the director of e-learning for the same company, where she was responsible for planning and supporting all the company's e-learning offerings in Canada, including Cisco courses. Diane has a bachelor's degree in applied science in electrical engineering (BASc) and a master's degree in applied science in management science (MASc). Diane is a certified Cisco Systems instructor and currently holds her CCNP and Cisco Certified Design Professional (CCDP) certifications. She edited *Designing Cisco Networks* and *CCDA Self-Study: Designing for Cisco Internetwork Solutions (DESGN)*, and she coauthored *Building Scalable Cisco Networks* and *CCNP Self-Study: Building Scalable Cisco Internetworks (BSCI)* (first and second editions), all from Cisco Press.

About the Technical Reviewers

Shawn Boyd is a senior network consultant for ARP Technologies Inc. Shawn has worldwide experience consulting on many different projects such as security/VoIP for Cisco Systems Israel, intrusion prevention for Top Layer Networks of Boston, and DSL infrastructure rollout for Telus Canada. Shawn is also active in course development and is a certified Cisco Systems instructor with ARP Technologies Inc., responsible for teaching most of the Cisco curriculum. His background is in network security and design at a service provider level. He has worked for Canada's largest telco providers, performing network designs and implementations, and was lead contact on many large government contracts.

Keith Hutton is a senior network consultant at Bell Canada, where he is responsible for the design of client service solutions. Prior to joining Bell, he held the position of senior Cisco network administrator at Magma Communications Ltd. Keith has also worked as a certified Cisco Systems instructor with Global Knowledge Canada. He is the coauthor of the Cisco Press book *CCDP Self-Study: Designing Cisco Network Architectures (ARCH)*. Keith currently holds the certified Cisco Systems instructor, CCNP, and CCDP certifications.

Amir Ranjbar, CCIE No. 8669, works as a consultant and trainer in the field of information technology in his own corporation, AMIRACAN Inc. AMIRACAN's major client is Global Knowledge Network, where Amir worked as a full-time instructor until October 2005. Amir obtained his Master of Science degree in 1991 from the University of Guelph (Ontario, Canada). He also is a certified Cisco Systems instructor. After spending a few years in the field of computer programming, Amir joined Digital Equipment Corporation's Learning Services to do training on Microsoft's operating systems and back office products. Since 1998, Amir has switched his focus to Cisco Systems products and has been training many professionals from service provider and telecommunications companies on routing protocols, LAN switching, remote access, troubleshooting, MPLS VPNs, MPLS traffic engineering, voice over IP, and other subjects. Amir authored *CCNP Self-Study: CCNP CIT Exam Certification Guide*, Second Edition, and coauthored *CCDP Self-Study: Designing Cisco Network Architectures (ARCH)* for Cisco Press.

Dedications

"Anyone who stops learning is old, whether at twenty or eighty. Anyone who keeps learning stays young. The greatest thing in life is to keep your mind young."

—Henry Ford

From Diane:

This book is dedicated to my loving husband, Allan Mertin, who not only heartily encouraged this project but also provided his insightful comments as our first-level reviewer; to our captivating and delightful son Nicholas, who never ceases to amaze us; to my parents, Syd and Beryl, for their continuous caring and love; and to my friends, including "the Girls," for helping me keep my sanity!

From Catherine:

To Pierre Rivard, my soul mate and husband, the rock I stand on: Your vast knowledge of life and your work ethics are an inspiration for all of us. To our children, Laurence and Simon: Your intrepidity, inquisitive minds, and capacity to think logically delight us.

Acknowledgments

We would like to thank many people for helping us put this book together:

The Cisco Press team: We are very fortunate to be working once again with a great team at Cisco Press . . . we hope someday to actually meet you! Many thanks to Brett Bartow, for initiating this project and guiding us through the process to completion. (We must admit, though, that it is good to be near the end!) Thanks to Drew Cupp, for his usual invaluable suggestions, eye for detail, and quick responses to our many queries. We would also like to thank San Dee Phillips, the project editor, and John Edwards, the copy editor, for their excellent work in steering this book through the editorial process. Also, many thanks to Tim Wright for always doing a great indexing job.

The technical reviewers: We would like to thank the technical reviewers of this book—Amir Ranjbar, Shawn Boyd, and Keith Hutton—for their usual thorough, detailed review and very valuable input. It's great to be working with you all again!

Our families: Of course, this book would not have been possible without the constant understanding, patience, and tolerance of our families. They have always been there to motivate and inspire us. We thank you all.

Each other: Last but not least, this book is a product of work by two friends, which made it even more of a pleasure (or, as Catherine says, less of a pain ☺) to complete.

We would also like to thank Tim Szigeti of Cisco Systems for his QoS work, and his willingness to share it and answer our queries.

This Book Is Safari Enabled

The Safari® Enabled icon on the cover of your favorite technology book means the book is available through Safari Bookshelf. When you buy this book, you get free access to the online edition for 45 days.

Safari Bookshelf is an electronic reference library that lets you easily search thousands of technical books, find code samples, download chapters, and access technical information whenever and wherever you need it.

To gain 45-day Safari Enabled access to this book:

- Go to http://www.ciscopress.com/safarienabled
- Enter the ISBN of this book (shown on the back cover, above the bar code)
- Log in or Sign up (site membership is required to register your book)
- Enter the coupon code ECEH-5YBF-7Q79-U2FC-1PVU

If you have difficulty registering on Safari Bookshelf or accessing the online edition, please e-mail customer-service@safaribooksonline.com.

Contents at a Glance

Contents

Icons Used in This Book

Desktop

Laptop

Router

Workgroup Switch

Multilayer Switch

PIX Firewall

Router with Firewall

Server with IPS

IDS Sensor

IDS Management Station

VPN Concentrator

100TBase Hub

Router with Access Point

Wireless Access Point

Wireless Connection

CallManager

PBX Switch

Phone

Cisco IP Phone

Wireless IP Phone

Content Engine

Content Switch

CDM (Content Distribution Manager)

iptv Server

CiscoWorks Workstation

Enterprise Fibre Channel disk

Voice-Enabled Router

File Server

Introduction

This all-in-one book tells you what you need to know, why you need to know it, and how to apply this knowledge to create a campus network that includes as many or as few of today's technologies as you require. This book starts, in Part I, "Designing Networks," with an introduction to the design process, network design, and some models that can be used as a design is developed. We then describe, in Part II, "Technologies: What You Need to Know and Why You Need to Know It," fundamental technologies in detail, including not only the mechanics of each but also why the technology can be important for your design. Examples are included throughout the book to emphasize how the concepts can be implemented. The book concludes with Part III, "Designing Your Network: How to Apply What You Know," a comprehensive case study about a fictitious company called Venti Systems, a manufacturer of high-end automotive power modules. Venti Systems is in the process of acquiring two other companies: one is located close to Venti, in eastern Canada, and the other is located on the West Coast of the United States. A new headquarters will be home for the combined operations of Venti and for one of the acquired companies, to achieve better synergy and to consolidate personnel and manufacturing facilities. The second acquired company will remain in its current West Coast facilities as a branch office. The design methodologies discussed in Part I and the technologies discussed in Part II are applied to this case study, as appropriate.

Campus Network Design Fundamentals is part of the Cisco Press Fundamentals Series, and therefore focuses on readers who are already in the networking field and who now want to gain a solid understanding of how to design campus networks. We assume that readers understand basic networking concepts and are familiar with basic networking terminology; however, we also provide Appendix B, "Network Fundamentals," so that readers can review any of these basic concepts that they might be less familiar with.

The book comprises three parts, which include 12 chapters, followed by four appendixes.

Part I, "Designing Networks," consists of one chapter about network design:

■ Chapter 1, "Network Design," introduces the network design process and two network design models.

Part II, "Technologies: What You Need to Know and Why You Need to Know It," introduces various technologies, and for each discusses what you need to know, the business case for why you might want to use this technology, and how the technology is used in network designs:

■ Chapter 2, "Switching Design," discusses how switches are used in network design. Topics include the Spanning Tree Protocol (STP), virtual local-area networks (VLANs), two types of Layer 3 switching [multilayer switching [MLS] and Cisco Express Forwarding [CEF]), and security in a switched environment.

- Chapter 3, "IPv4 Routing Design," describes Internet Protocol version 4 (IPv4) addressing and address design considerations. The factors differentiating the available IPv4 routing protocols are also described, followed by a discussion of the specific protocols. The considerations for choosing the routing protocol (or protocols) for your network complete this chapter.

- Chapter 4, "Network Security Design," explains concepts that relate to network security. Attack types, mitigation techniques, and security equipment such as firewalls, authentication systems, intrusion detection systems, traffic-filtering services, and virtual private networks (VPNs) are presented.

- Chapter 5, "Wireless LAN Design," describes wireless LAN (WLAN) technology and how it improves mobility. You discover the concepts that surround wireless networks, with a special emphasis on the technology, design, and security.

- Chapter 6, "Quality of Service Design," discusses how to design quality of service (QoS) into a network. Topics include the QoS-related requirements for various types of traffic and two models for deploying end-to-end QoS in a network: Integrated Services (IntServ) and Differentiated Services (DiffServ). QoS tools, including classification and marking, policing and shaping, congestion avoidance, congestion management, and link-specific tools, are explained. The Cisco Automatic QoS (AutoQoS) tool, which provides a simple, automatic way to enable QoS configurations in conformance with the Cisco best-practice recommendations, is introduced.

- Chapter 7, "Voice Transport Design," introduces how to design a network that will carry voice traffic. The mechanics of voice transport and QoS for voice are explored. The components required in a Voice over IP (VoIP) network and in an IP telephony network are described. The standard for how voice calls are coded and compressed are introduced, and the bandwidth requirements for voice traffic are explored.

- Chapter 8, "Content Networking Design," describes how content networking (CN) can be implemented to provide content to users as quickly and efficiently as possible. The services provided under CN and the components that provide those services—the content engine, content router, content distribution and management device, and content switch—are described.

- Chapter 9, "Network Management Design," introduces how the management of networks can be included in designs. The related International Organization for Standardization (ISO) standard is described, and various protocols and tools available for network management are introduced. The chapter includes a description of network management strategy and how performance measurements can be made to ensure that requirements are being met.

- Chapter 10, "Other Enabling Technologies," briefly discusses IP multicast, increasing network availability, storage networking, and IP version 6 (IPv6).

Part III, "Designing Your Network: How to Apply What You Know," comprises a case study, first providing the background information and context and then providing a solution. The design methodologies discussed in Part I and the technologies discussed in Part II are applied to this case network, as appropriate:

■ Chapter 11, "Case Study Context: Venti Systems," introduces a case study of a fictitious company called Venti Systems. The chapter also presents background information on Venti Systems and the two companies acquired by Venti. The requirements for the network after the acquisitions are complete are also developed.

■ Chapter 12, "Case Study Solution: Venti Systems," provides a comprehensive network design solution for Venti Systems after the acquisition is complete, based on the requirements identified in Chapter 11.

The following four appendixes complete the book:

■ Appendix A, "References," lists websites and other external readings that are referred to throughout this book.

■ Appendix B, "Network Fundamentals," introduces some fundamental concepts and terminology that are the foundation for the other sections of the book.

■ Appendix C, "Decimal–Binary Conversion," describes how to convert between the binary and decimal numbering systems.

■ Appendix D, "Abbreviations," identifies key abbreviations, acronyms, and initialisms in the book.

NOTE The website references in this book were accurate at the time of writing; however, they might have since changed. If a URL is unavailable, you might try conducting a search using the title as key words in a search engine such as Google (http://www.google.com).

The notes and sidebars found in this book provide extra information on a subject.

KEY POINT Key Points highlight crucial and fundamental information that is important for understanding the topic at hand.

Part I: Designing Networks

Part I of this book is composed of this chapter. It describes the network design process and two network design models, and includes the following sections:

- What Is Design?

- Design Principles

- Modular Network Design

CHAPTER 1

Network Design

This chapter discusses design and the various methodologies for designing today's networks.

> **NOTE** Appendix B, "Network Fundamentals," is a refresher of topics that you should understand before reading this chapter—and the rest of the book. Appendix B includes the following topics:
>
> - Introduction to networks
> - Protocols and the OSI model
> - LANs and WANs
> - Network devices
> - Introduction to the TCP/IP suite
> - Routing
> - Addressing
>
> You are encouraged to review any of the material in Appendix B that you are not familiar with before reading the rest of this chapter.

What Is Design?

Before delving into the details of network design, consider what design is and, in particular, what you expect from a *good* design.

Dictionaries generally define design as planning how to create something, or the actual plans themselves. However, when you think of designing something, whether it is a product, an addition to a house, or a network, you likely contemplate a broader use of the word *design.*

For example, if you hire an architect to design an addition to your house, you expect her to produce detailed plans and engineering drawings that can be used to create the space that you want. What is the process that an architect uses to get to this final product, plans that can be used to create what you want and need? Crucial inputs are the dimensions, the state, and the use of the existing house, and your requirements for the addition (including your budget), as illustrated in Figure 1-1. The former are much easier to solidify than the latter. For the existing house, the architect must measure all the rooms and spaces, and take notes of the existing use and function—for example, the layout of the existing kitchen, where the family usually eats, and so forth.

Figure 1-1   *When Designing an Addition to a House, an Architect Needs to Have Knowledge of the Existing Structure and the Requirements for the Addition—Along with Skills and Creativity*

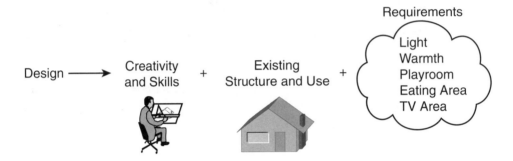

<table>
<tr><td>**KEY POINT**</td><td>To determine the requirements for the addition, a good architect should ask probing questions. Determining the *actual requirements*, rather than your *perceived solutions,* is a key skill for a good architect.</td></tr>
</table>

For example, assume that you tell the architect that you want three skylights and a fireplace in the room. Rather than just including these items, a good architect should ask *why* you want them and what you see their function to be. You might want skylights to provide more light to the room and a fireplace to provide heat. The ability to determine the *actual requirements* (light and heat), rather than your *perceived solutions* (skylights and fireplace), is a critical skill for a good architect. The architect can then recommend different solutions to what you perceive the problems to be—lack of light and lack of heat. For example, a heated floor can provide warmth, while a wall of opaque glass blocks can provide light. (Of course, you might just want a fireplace and skylights, in which case, these would also be requirements.)

The architect then takes all the requirements together as inputs to the design. Using her creativity and training, the architect typically prepares several options, which are then presented to you. At this stage, the options are not fully developed, but will probably be at a conceptual level, and might include sketches and cost estimates. A meeting is normally held to review the options and to choose one option or a combination of them, to note changes and additions, and so forth. The architect then develops the final design, which must be approved by you before the engineering drawings are created, permits obtained, contractors selected, and so forth. The architect can also provide continuity and quality control for the project by reviewing the progress while the addition is being built.

Thus, as is true for any project, a good design requires good inputs—clear requirements are critical. The design process must, of course, allow requirements to change; however, spending time up-front clarifying requirements goes a long way toward reducing major problems later. For example, many government projects include a mandatory requirements document that must be reviewed and signed off before any design or implementation work can be started. Finalizing this requirements document can be a lengthy process—for example, one large project had a requirements definition phase that was years long (thankfully, it has now been implemented successfully).

Understanding the existing structure, if one exists, is also important because it can introduce constraints (for example, in the house-addition project, the window area allowed on a side wall might be restricted by a building code), but it can also provide opportunity (for example, you might be able to reuse some doors that will be removed from the existing house in the new addition).

Good design also requires creativity and skills. For a residential architect, these traits come from both training and experience.

A network design is no different. Understanding the requirements for the network, as well as knowing how the existing network is structured and used, is key to understanding how the new or updated network should function and which features should be included. Understanding how the features operate, what they do, what their constraints are, and what alternative approaches are available comes from both training and experience. Part II of this book, "Technologies: What You Need to Know and Why You Need to Know It," introduces you to some of the fundamental networking technologies available today, while Part III, "Designing Your Network: How to Apply What You Know," explores the use of these technologies in the context of a case study. This chapter introduces you to network design principles and design models.

Design Principles

Cisco has developed the Plan-Design-Implement-Operate-Optimize (PDIOO) network life cycle to describe the multiple phases through which a network passes. This life cycle is illustrated in Figure 1-2, and the phases are briefly described as follows:

- **Plan phase**—The detailed network requirements are identified, and the existing network is reviewed.

- **Design phase**—The network is designed according to the initial requirements and additional data gathered during analysis of the existing network. The design is refined with the client.

- **Implement phase**—The network is built according to the approved design.

- **Operate phase**—The network is operational and is being monitored. This phase is the ultimate test of the design.

- **Optimize phase**—During this phase, issues are detected and corrected, either before problems arise or, if no problems are found, after a failure has occurred. Redesign might be required if too many problems exist.

- **Retirement phase**—Although not part of the PDIOO acronym, this phase is necessary when part of the network is outdated or is no longer required.

Figure 1-2 *PDIOO Network Life Cycle Includes Many Design Aspects[1]*

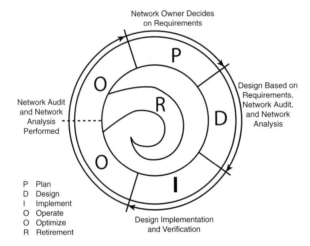

The PDIOO cycle describes all the phases of a network's life. The task of designing a network is obviously an integral part of this life cycle and influences all phases. For example, the implementation phase might involve a prototype, which can help validate the design.

Network design should include the following tasks, as illustrated in Figure 1-3:

- Determine requirements

- Analyze the existing network, if one exists

- Prepare the preliminary design

- Complete the final design development

- Deploy the network

- Monitor, and redesign if necessary

- Maintain documentation (as a part of all the other tasks)

Figure 1-3 *Network Design Is an Ongoing Process*

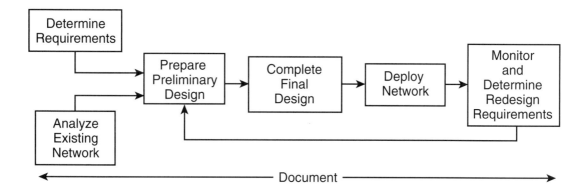

These tasks, and their relationship to the PDIOO phases, are examined in the following sections.

Determining Requirements

Determining the network requirements is a part of the PDIOO Plan phase. Many types of requirements must be considered, including those that are related to technical and business issues. Any factors that might restrict the design must also be identified. In the case where an existing network is in place, these constraints can be related to what is already there and how the new network must be phased in to allow continuous operation.

Technical requirements and restraints can include the following items:

■ Applications that are to run on the network

■ Internet connections required

■ Addressing restrictions, for example, the use of private Internet Protocol (IP) version 4 (IPv4) addresses

■ Support for IP version 6 (IPv6) addresses

■ Other protocols that are to run on the network (for example, routing protocols)

■ Cabling requirements

■ Redundancy requirements

■ Use of proprietary equipment and protocols

■ Existing equipment that must be supported

■ Network services required, including quality of service (QoS) and wireless

- How security is to be integrated into the network

- Network solutions required (for example, voice traffic, content networking, and storage networking)

- Network management

- Support for existing applications while new ones are being phased in

- Bandwidth availability

KEY POINT An intelligent network service supports network applications. For example, security and QoS are not ultimate goals of or applications on a network; rather, they are necessary services that enable other applications. Note that some of these services, such as security, are now integral parts of any well-designed network.

Intelligent network solutions are network-based applications. These network solutions require the support of the network services. Voice communication is an example of an intelligent network solution; it requires QoS for optimal operation.

Requirements and restrictions related to business issues can include the following:

- **Budget**—Capital (for new equipment) and operating (for ongoing expenses).

- **Schedule**—This could include the phasing out of older applications, hiring of new personnel, and so forth.

- **People**—Considerations include who will install and operate the network, what skills they have, whether they require training, whether any of these tasks will be outsourced, and so forth.

- **Legal**—Issues include any restrictions on the use and storage of data collected, whether the organization has contractual obligations or opportunities related to the network (for example, long-term maintenance or lease contracts), and so forth.

- **History**—Factors include examining the existing network's structure and determining whether any person or group will block changes or additions.

- **Policies**—Consider whether current organizational policies might restrict the network design.

As discussed earlier in the house-addition analogy, extracting requirements is a difficult task.

KEY POINT | Requirements must be clear and deterministic (verifiable); in other words, at the end of the project, you should easily be able to determine whether a requirement has been met.

For example, a customer might say that the new network must help reduce overall costs. This goal must be translated into requirements that can be implemented and measured. For example, reducing costs could mean that a web-based ordering system replaces call-center ordering, or it could mean that unreliable equipment is replaced. Each of these options has its own initial and operating costs, so you must understand what the network owner means when he states his goals.

Each of the requirements should also be assessed for its importance, and a weighting factor should be assigned so that if conflicts arise (for example, an inadequate budget), the most important requirements can be met.

Analyzing the Existing Network

If this is a redesign of an existing network, the current network must be analyzed and understood. As noted earlier, an existing network is likely to restrict the network design in some manner; for example, the existing cabling might not be optimal but might have to be kept for cost reasons. Analyzing the existing network is typically done during the Optimize phase of the existing network; it could also be considered as part of the Plan phase for the new network.

You should analyze the network to determine both what is good and what should be changed. For example, the network might include virtual private network (VPN) connections so that employees can access corporate files through the Internet (VPN is discussed in Chapter 4, "Network Security Design"). If the organization is satisfied with this feature, this portion of the network might not have to be changed.

KEY POINT | While examining documentation about the existing network and discussing it with users, administration staff, and other stakeholders is important, you should also do an audit of the network. The audit can identify items such as the protocols that are running (both those that are known to be running and those that have not been reported), the devices installed and their configurations, the utilization of these devices, and the bandwidth on key WANs).

Many operating systems include commands that display information about device hardware and software. For example, the **show version** command in the Cisco Internet Operating System (IOS) displays information related to the version of the software and the amount of memory available. Additional tools, such as protocol analyzers, might be necessary to gather other information.

Preparing the Preliminary Design

Preliminary design involves considering all the network requirements and constraints (including the budget), and determining viable alternative solutions. The network owner is then consulted, and together an optimal solution is chosen; this solution is later developed into the final design. Both the preliminary design and final design are done during the PDIOO Design phase.

Two models that can be used for network design are examined in the "Modular Network Design" section, later in this chapter. Whichever model is used, a top-down approach (rather than a bottom-up approach) is recommended.

KEY POINT

A *top-down approach* to network design means that requirements are considered first, with the applications and network solutions that will run on the network driving the design.

A *bottom-up approach* would first select devices, features, cabling, and so on, and then try to fit the applications onto this network. A bottom-up approach can lead to redesign if the applications are not accommodated properly. This approach can also result in increased costs by including features or devices that are not required and would have been excluded had the network requirements analysis been completed.

After the alternative solutions have been developed, the optimal solution must be chosen. A systematic approach works best—all the options should be listed along with how well they meet (or don't meet) the design requirements and constraints. If no clear winner exists, the importance of the requirements (as determined in the requirements-gathering process) should be considered to select the optimal design.

Completing the Final Design Development

Developing the final design involves producing detailed drawings, configuration specifications, costing, addressing plans, and any other information required for implementation.

KEY POINT

You can verify the design by implementing a prototype network, separate from the existing network. Alternatively, a pilot network can be implemented within a portion of the existing network to verify that the design is feasible.

Deploying the Network

Deployment of the network must start with a plan and a schedule. Deployment planning starts in the PDIOO Design phase and continues into the Implement phase.

The deployment plan must include details of what is to be done and how it is to be done. For example, if new cabling is required, the procedure to run the cable and the location where it is needed must be fully documented. Scheduling is important, not only to identify when things will be done but also to determine who will do them, and what impact the deployment will have on the existing network. For example, if current applications must still work while the new network is being implemented, the schedule must show any times during which the applications will be unavailable.

Contingency plans, that is, plans for what happens if a problem occurs during the implementation, should also be included. These contingency plans should address how the network will be returned to a known working state, if possible. Testing should be incorporated into the deployment plan to ensure that the functions are working as they are implemented.

Any training required for personnel should be planned during this time. For example, if you are deploying a Voice over IP (VoIP) solution, the network administrators might require some instruction on the technology before they can implement and maintain it.

Any contracts required should be negotiated during this time. Examples include outsourcing, Internet connectivity, maintenance, and so forth.

When the plans, schedules, contracts, and so on are in place, the network can be implemented. Any problems found in the design during this phase must be corrected and documented.

KEY POINT | Implementation is the final verification of the design.

Monitoring and Redesigning

After the network is operating, baseline operational statistics should be gathered so that values for a working network are known. The network should then be monitored for anomalies and problems. If problems that require redesign occur, or if requirements change or are added, the appropriate design changes must be made and the entire design process should be repeated for that portion of the network. Monitoring and redesign take place in the PDIOO Operate and Optimize phases, and can lead back into the Plan and Design phases.

Maintaining Design Documentation

The design should be documented throughout the process. Documentation should include the following items:

- All the agreed-to requirements and constraints

- The state of the existing network, if any

- Preliminary design options and a brief review of why the final design was chosen

- Final design details

- Results of any pilot or prototype testing

- Deployment plans, schedules, and other implementation details

- Monitoring requirements

- Any other pertinent information

Documentation should be started in the PDIOO Design phase but might not be complete until well into the Implement phase. Updates to the design documentation can be made in the Operate and Optimize phases if redesign is required.

Modular Network Design

The following sections explore modular network design and then introduce two models that can be used for modular network design.

What Is Modular Design?

KEY POINT   A *module* is a component of a composite structure. Modular network design involves creating modules that can then be put together to meet the requirements of the entire network.

Modules are analogous to building blocks of different shapes and sizes; when creating a building, each block has different functions. Designing one of these blocks is a much easier task than designing the entire building. Each block might be used in multiple places, saving time and effort in the overall design and building process. The blocks have standard interfaces to each other so that they fit together easily. If the requirements for a block change, only that block needs to change—other blocks are not affected. Similarly, a specific block can be removed or added without affecting other blocks.

As when used for a building, a modular design for a network has many benefits, including the following:

- It is easier to understand and design smaller, simpler modules rather than an entire network.

- It is easier to troubleshoot smaller elements compared to the entire network.

■ The reuse of blocks saves design time and effort, as well as implementation time and effort.

■ The reuse of blocks allows the network to grow more easily, providing network scalability.

■ It is easier to change modules rather than the entire network, providing flexibility of design.

NOTE The Open Systems Interconnection (OSI) model, described in Appendix B, is an example of a modular framework for the communication protocols used between computers.

The following sections introduce two models that can be used for network design: the hierarchical model and the Cisco Enterprise Composite Network Model. You will see that both of these models involve creating modules, and that hierarchical design can in fact be part of the modules of the Enterprise Composite Network Model.

Hierarchical Network Design

The hierarchical network design model is illustrated in Figure 1-4.

Figure 1-4 *The Hierarchical Network Design Model Separates the Network into Three Functions*

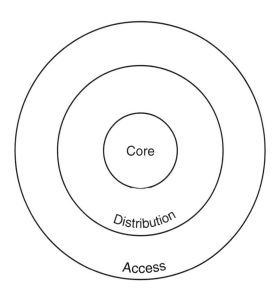

The three functions that comprise the hierarchical network design model are as follows:

- **Access layer**—Provides user and workgroup access to the resources of the network

- **Distribution layer**—Implements the organization's policies, and provides connections between workgroups and between the workgroups and the core

- **Core layer**—Provides high-speed transport between distribution-layer devices and to core resources

These three layers can also be thought of as modules; each module has specific functions and can therefore be designed using the optimal devices and features to meet the specific requirements of the module.

Figure 1-5 illustrates a simple network and shows how it maps to the hierarchical model. (Later chapters in this book detail the functions of the devices shown in this figure.)

Figure 1-5 *The Hierarchical Network Design Model as Mapped to a Simple Network*

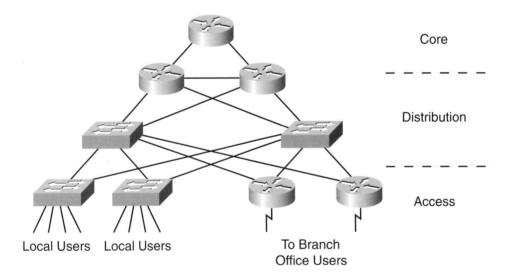

Do you always need to have separate devices for each layer? No. Consider how the Transmission Control Protocol/Internet Protocol (TCP/IP) suite is an *implementation* of the OSI model. The TCP/IP model combines some of the OSI layers; for example, the TCP/IP application layer represents the OSI model application, presentation, and session layers. Similarly, your implementation of the hierarchical model can combine some of the functions into one physical device, especially if you have a smaller network.

Some factors to consider when designing each of the hierarchical layers are described in the following sections.

Access Layer

The access layer is where users access the network. Users can be local or remote.

Local users typically access the network through connections to a hub or a switch. Recall that hubs operate at OSI Layer 1, and all devices connected to a hub are in the same collision (or bandwidth) domain. Switches operate at Layer 2, and each port on a switch is its own collision domain, meaning that multiple conversations between devices connected through the switch can be happening simultaneously. Using a LAN switch rather than a hub has a performance advantage: A LAN switch forwards unicast traffic only out of the port through which the traffic's destination is considered reachable. However, a hub forwards all traffic out of all its ports. For this reason, most of today's networks have LAN switches rather than hubs. (Switching, including Layer 3 switching, is discussed in Chapter 2, "Switching Design.")

Remote users might access the network through the Internet, using VPN connections, for example. Connections to the Internet can be through dial-up, digital subscriber line (DSL), cable, and so forth. Other access possibilities include WANs such as Frame Relay, leased lines, and Integrated Services Digital Network (ISDN).

The access layer must also ensure that only users who are authorized to access the network are admitted.

Distribution Layer

The distribution layer interfaces between the core and access layers, and between access layer workgroups.

The distribution layer functions and characteristics include the following:

- Implementing policies by filtering, and prioritizing and queuing traffic.

- Routing between the access and core layers. If different routing protocols are implemented at these other two layers, the distribution layer is responsible for redistributing (sharing) among the routing protocols, and filtering if necessary (as discussed in Chapter 3, "IPv4 Routing Design").

- Performing route summarization (as also discussed in Chapter 3). When routes are summarized, routers have only summary routes in their routing tables, instead of unnecessary detailed routes. This results in smaller routing tables, which reduces the router memory required. Routing updates are also smaller and therefore use less bandwidth on the network. As discussed in Chapter 3, route summarization is only possible if the IP addressing scheme is designed properly.

- Providing redundant connections, both to access devices and to core devices.

- Aggregating multiple lower-speed access connections into higher-speed core connections and converting between different media types (for example, between Ethernet and Frame Relay connections), if necessary.

Core Layer

The core layer provides a high-speed backbone. Functions and attributes of the core layer include the following:

- Providing high-speed, low-latency links and devices for quick transport of data across the backbone.

- Providing a highly reliable and available backbone. This is accomplished by implementing redundancy in both devices and links so that no single points of failure exist.

- Adapting to network changes quickly by implementing a quick-converging routing protocol. The routing protocol can also be configured to load-balance over redundant links so that the extra capacity can be used when no failures exist.

Filtering is not performed at this layer, because it would slow processing. Filtering is done at the distribution layer.

Limitations of the Hierarchical Model

The hierarchical model is useful for smaller networks, but it does not scale well to larger, more complex networks. With only three layers, the model does not allow the modularity required to efficiently design networks with many devices and features. The Enterprise Composite Network Model, introduced in the following section, provides additional modularity and functions.

The Cisco Enterprise Composite Network Model

Cisco has developed a SAFE blueprint, the principle goal of which is to provide best practices information on designing and implementing secure networks. The SAFE architecture uses a modular approach, providing the advantages previously discussed. (The SAFE model is discussed further in Chapter 4.)

The Cisco Enterprise Composite Network Model is the name given to the architecture used by the SAFE blueprint. This model supports larger networks than those designed with only the hierarchical model and clarifies the functional boundaries within the network.

The Enterprise Composite Network Model first divides a network into three functional areas, as illustrated in Figure 1-6.

Figure 1-6   *Functional Areas of the Enterprise Composite Network Model*[2]

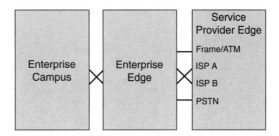

The three functional areas are as follows:

- **Enterprise Campus**—This area contains all the functions required for independent operation within one campus location; it does not provide remote connections. You can have multiple campuses.

- **Enterprise Edge**—This area contains all the functions required for communication between the Enterprise Campus and remote locations, including the Internet, remote employees, other campuses, partners, and so forth.

- **Service Provider Edge**—This functional area is not implemented by the organization; rather, it is included to represent WANs and Internet connections provided by service providers.

Each of these functional areas contains network modules, which in turn can include the hierarchical core, distribution, and access layer functionality.

Figure 1-7 displays the modules within each of these functional areas. The following sections provide details on each of these modules.

Figure 1-7 *Each Functional Area Contains Modules[3]*

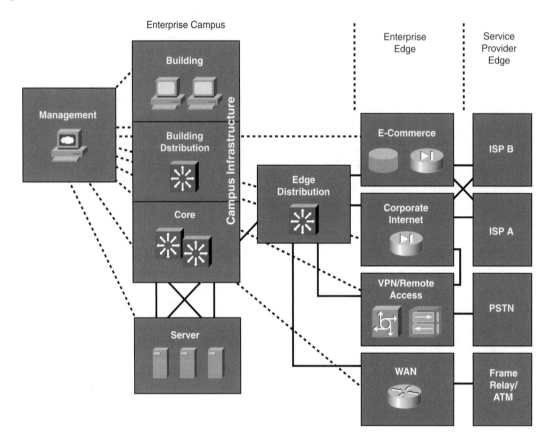

Enterprise Campus Functional Area

The modules within the Enterprise Campus functional area are as follows:

- Campus Infrastructure module

- Management module

- Server module

- Edge Distribution module

NOTE   These module names are consistent with those in the SAFE blueprint. However, slight variations exist between these names and those in the following Cisco Press books: *CCDA Self-Study: Designing for Cisco Internetwork Solutions (DESGN)* and *CCDP Self-Study: Designing Cisco Network Architectures (ARCH).*

Campus Infrastructure Module

The Campus Infrastructure module represents one or more buildings connected to a backbone. This module is comprised of three submodules: Building, Building Distribution, and Core. These submodules map directly onto the hierarchical model's access, distribution, and core layers.

The combination of a Building and a Building Distribution submodule represents each building within a campus. Each of these buildings is connected to the Core, to provide connectivity between buildings and to the Server and Edge Distribution modules.

The Building submodule contains all the devices to allow users in the building to access the network. This includes end-user devices, such as IP phones and PCs, as well as devices to interconnect the end users to the services they require. This latter functionality is typically provided by Layer 2 switches, but it can also include Layer 3 switches if more advanced features are required. This submodule is responsible for ensuring that only users who are authorized to access the network are admitted. The Building submodule also performs functions such as marking the QoS level of the traffic (for example, to distinguish voice traffic from file transfer traffic so that it can be handled appropriately throughout the network).

The Building Distribution submodule provides access between workgroups and to the Core. This functionality is typically provided by Layer 3 switches or routers. Routing is implemented in this submodule; route filtering might also be required. Summarizing of routes should also be implemented here so that the routing overhead is minimal. This submodule controls access to services by implementing filters or access lists. Redundant switches and redundant links to both the access and backbone should also be implemented in this submodule.

The Core submodule typically uses Layer 3 switching to provide a high-speed connection between the campus buildings and the Server and Edge Distribution modules. Redundancy is implemented to ensure a highly available and reliable backbone.

Management Module

The Management module houses monitoring, logging, security, and other management features within an enterprise.

A network-monitoring server monitors devices in the network and reports any events that occur (such as an interface error on a router). This can be combined with a system administration server to configure network devices.

Some of the management security features that can be implemented in this module are as follows:

■ An authentication, authorization, and accounting (AAA) server to provide security checks of users. Authentication determines who the user is and whether he is allowed on the network. Authorization determines what the user can do on the network. Accounting records the time of day and time spent, for example, so that the user can be billed for the network services used. The AAA server can also record a user's location.

■ Intrusion detection system (IDS) and intrusion prevention system (IPS) management. IDSs scan network traffic for malicious activity, while IPSs can protect the network if an attack is detected. An IDS and IPS management server logs suspicious activities that are detected by IDS and IPS sensors deployed throughout the network.

■ System logging, for example, using a syslog server to log events and traps.

Network management traffic can traverse through an out-of-band or an in-band connection. Out-of-band management provides access to devices on a connection dedicated to management data (different from the connections on which network data flows), for example, through the console port of a Cisco router. In-band management provides access to devices through the same path as data traffic; for example, you can use Telnet to access a router over an IP network.

NOTE   Chapter 9, "Network Management Design," describes the Management module in detail.

Server Module
The centralized Server module contains internal campus servers. These servers can include e-mail, file, and print servers, or any other servers that are necessary for the network solutions (for example, a Cisco CallManager server if IP telephony is implemented in the network). Redundancy is typically implemented within this module and to the Core so that users always have access to the servers they need. Layer 3 switches are typically used in this module to provide both the high performance of Layer 2 switching and the Layer 3 routing and filtering capabilities.

Edge Distribution Module
The Edge Distribution module is the interface between the Enterprise Campus (through the Core submodule) and the Enterprise Edge functional areas.

This module typically uses Layer 3 switching to provide high-performance routing, similar to the Server module. Redundancy is again implemented in this module to ensure that the campus users always have access to the Enterprise Edge.

Enterprise Edge Functional Area

The Enterprise Edge functional area is the interface between the Enterprise Campus functional area (through the Edge Distribution module) and the Service Provider Edge functional area. It is comprised of the following four modules:

- E-commerce module

- Corporate Internet module

- VPN/Remote Access module

- WAN module

The E-commerce module includes the devices and services necessary for an organization to support e-commerce applications, such as online ordering. The devices in this module usually include web servers, application servers, and security devices such as firewalls and IDS appliances.

The Corporate Internet module provides Internet access for the users and passes VPN traffic from remote users to the VPN/Remote Access module. Typical servers in this module include e-mail, File Transfer Protocol (FTP), and Domain Name System (DNS) servers. Security systems, such as firewalls and IDSs/IPSs, are also present here to ensure that only legitimate Internet traffic is allowed into the enterprise.

The VPN/Remote Access module terminates VPN traffic and dial-in connections from external users. Typical devices in this module include dial-in access and VPN concentrators to terminate the remote user connections, and firewalls and IDS appliances to provide security.

The WAN module provides connectivity between remote sites and the main site over various WAN technologies. This module does not include the WAN connections; rather, it provides the *interfaces* to the WANs. The WAN connections themselves are supplied by the service providers, which are represented in the Service Provider Edge modules. Example WAN interfaces provided by this module are Frame Relay, Asynchronous Transfer Mode (ATM), cable, and leased lines.

Service Provider Edge Functional Area

The three modules within the Service Provider Edge functional area are as follows:

■ Internet Service Provider (ISP) module

■ Public Switched Telephone Network (PSTN) module

■ Frame Relay/ATM module

Recall that these modules are not implemented within the Enterprise itself but are provided by the service providers.

The ISP module represents connections to the Internet. Redundant connections to multiple ISPs can be made to ensure service availability. The actual connection type is dictated by the ISPs.

The PSTN module represents all dial-up connectivity, including analog phone, cellular phone, and ISDN connections.

The Frame Relay/ATM module represents all permanent connections to remote locations, including Frame Relay and ATM, but also leased lines and cable, DSL, and wireless connections.

Summary

In this chapter, you learned about design in general and specifically about network design principles. You also learned about modular network design and the hierarchical and Enterprise Composite Network models for designing networks.

As a summary of the network design process presented here, consider the following checklist:

❑ Did you ask probing questions to really understand the requirements?

❑ Have you determined the requirements and constraints related to technical issues? Are the requirements clear and deterministic (verifiable)?

❑ Have you determined the requirements and constraints related to business issues, including the budget? Are the requirements clear and deterministic?

❑ Have you prioritized, or assigned weights to, each of the requirements?

❑ Do you understand the network solutions/applications that are called for, and which network services are required to support them?

❑ Have you analyzed and audited the existing network, if one exists, to determine any restrictions on the new network as well as what portions of the existing network should be retained?

❑   Did you create some preliminary design options, using a top-down approach, so that all the network requirements are considered?

❑   Did you create a modular design?

❑   Did you identify the hierarchical network design layers in your design, and did you consider the appropriate devices and links for each layer?

❑   Did you use the Enterprise Composite Network Model in your design? Did you identify the relevant functional areas and modules of this model that will be used in your network, and did you consider the appropriate devices and links for each module?

❑   Did you and the network owner agree on the optimal solution, based on your preliminary design options?

❑   Did you implement a prototype or pilot network to verify all or a portion of the design?

❑   Did you create a detailed deployment plan and schedule, including implementation, testing, training, and contracts?

❑   Do you have a plan for what is to be monitored in the operating network and how errors are to be handled?

❑   Have you thoroughly documented the details of the design and the design process?

Network design is an art as well as a science. Just as there are many different ways to design an addition to a house, there are a variety of ways to design a network. It is critical to keep going back to the agreed-to requirements and their importance to the network owner; this helps ensure that the final network will be a success.

The technologies used in the network are constantly—and in some cases quickly—evolving. Because it is impossible to be an expert on all the technologies, we encourage you to seek help during your design from experts in specific fields. A good up-front design reduces the likelihood of catastrophes during the implementation or operation phases of the network life cycle.

Endnotes

[1]Teare, *CCDA Self-Study: Designing for Cisco Internetwork Solutions (DESGN),* Indianapolis, Cisco Press, 2004, p. 45.

[2]Adapted from "SAFE: A Security Blueprint for Enterprise Networks," http://www.cisco.com/go/safe.

[3]Ibid.

Part II: Technologies: What You Need to Know and Why You Need to Know It

This chapter discusses switching network design and includes the following sections:

- Making the Business Case

- Switching Types

- Spanning Tree Protocol

- Virtual LANs

- Multilayer Switching and Cisco Express Forwarding

- Switching Security

- Switching Design Considerations

CHAPTER 2

Switching Design

This first chapter in Part II, "Technologies: What You Need to Know and Why You Need to Know It," discusses switching network design. After introducing why switches are an important part of a network, we examine the different types of switching and then discuss the Spanning Tree Protocol (STP), which is key in Layer 2 switched environments to ensure that redundancy does not cause the network performance to deteriorate. Virtual local-area networks (VLANs) are then described. Two types of Layer 3 switching, multilayer switching (MLS) and Cisco Express Forwarding (CEF), are then introduced. Security in a switched environment is examined next. The chapter concludes with considerations and examples of switched designs.

> **NOTE** Appendix B, "Network Fundamentals," includes material that we assume you understand before reading the rest of the book. Thus, you are encouraged to review any of the material in Appendix B that you are not familiar with before reading the rest of this chapter.

Making the Business Case

Switches can enhance the performance, flexibility, and functionality of your network.

The first networks were LANs; they enabled multiple users in a relatively small geographical area to exchange files and messages, and to access shared resources such as printers and disk storage. A hub—an Open Systems Interconnection (OSI) Layer 1 device—interconnected PCs, servers, and so forth as the number of devices on the network grew. However, because all devices connected to a hub are in the same bandwidth (or collision) domain—they all share the same bandwidth—using hubs in anything but a small network is not efficient.

To improve performance, LANs can be divided into multiple smaller LANs, interconnected by a Layer 2 LAN switch. Because each port of the switch is its own collision domain, multiple simultaneous conversations between devices connected through the switch can occur.

By default, all ports of a switch are in the same broadcast domain. Recall (from Appendix B) that a broadcast domain includes all devices that receive each other's broadcasts (and multicasts). A *broadcast* is data meant for all devices; it uses a special broadcast address to indicate this. A *multicast* is data destined for a specific group; again, a special address indicates this. Note that

Layer 3 broadcast packets are typically encapsulated in Layer 2 broadcast frames, and Layer 3 multicast packets are typically encapsulated in Layer 2 multicast frames (assuming that the packets are going over a data-link technology that supports these types of frames, such as Ethernet).

The implications of this for modern networks are significant—a large switched OSI Layer 2 network is one broadcast domain, so any broadcasts or multicasts traverse the entire network. Examples of broadcast traffic include Internet Protocol (IP) Address Resolution Protocol (ARP) packets, and routing protocol traffic such as Routing Information Protocol (RIP) version 1 (RIPv1). Multicast traffic includes packets from more advanced routing protocols such as Open Shortest Path First (OSPF) and applications such as e-learning and videoconferencing. As network use increases, the amount of traffic—including multicast and broadcast traffic—will also increase.

Today's switches support VLANs so that physically remote devices can appear to be on the same (virtual) LAN. Each VLAN is its own broadcast domain. Traffic within a VLAN can be handled by Layer 2 switches. However, traffic between VLANS, just like traffic between LANs, must be handled by an OSI Layer 3 device. Traditionally, routers have been the Layer 3 device of choice. Today, Layer 3 switches offer the same functionality as routers but at higher speeds and with additional functionality.

The rest of this chapter explains how switches—Layer 2 and Layer 3—and the protocols associated with them work, and how they can be incorporated into network designs.

Switching Types

Switches were initially introduced to provide higher-performance connectivity than hubs, because switches define multiple collision domains.

Switches have always been able to process data at a faster rate than routers, because the switching functionality is implemented in hardware—in Application-Specific Integrated Circuits (ASICs)—rather than in software, which is how routing has traditionally been implemented. However, switching was initially restricted to the examination of Layer 2 frames. With the advent of more powerful ASICs, switches can now process Layer 3 packets, and even the contents of those packets, at high speeds.

The following sections first examine the operation of traditional Layer 2 switching. Layer 3 switching—which is really routing in hardware—is then explored.

Layer 2 Switching

KEY POINT   Layer 2 switches segment a network into multiple collision domains and interconnect devices within a workgroup, such as a group of PCs.

The heart of a Layer 2 switch is its Media Access Control (MAC) address table, also known as its content-addressable memory (CAM). This table contains a list of the MAC addresses that are reachable through each switch port. (Recall that the physical MAC address uniquely identifies a device on a network. When a network interface card is manufactured, the card is assigned an address—called a burned-in address [BIA]—which doesn't change when the network card is installed in a device and is moved from one network to another. Typically, this BIA is copied to interface memory and is used as the MAC address of the interface.) The MAC address table can be statically configured, or the switch can learn the MAC addresses dynamically. When a switch is first powered up, its MAC address table is empty, as shown in the example network of Figure 2-1.

Figure 2-1 *The MAC Address Table Is Initially Empty*

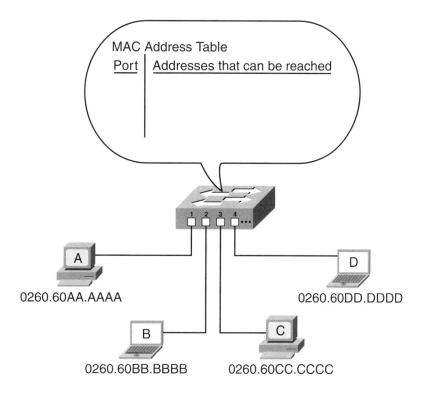

In this example network, consider what happens when device A sends a frame destined for device D. The switch receives the frame on port 1 (from device A). Recall that a frame includes the MAC address of the source device and the MAC address of the destination device. Because the switch does not yet know where device D is, the switch must *flood* the frame out of all the other ports; therefore, the switch sends the frame out of ports 2, 3, and 4. This means that devices B, C, and D all receive the frame. Only device D, however, recognizes its MAC address as the destination address in the frame; it is the only device on which the CPU is interrupted to further process the frame.

In the meantime, the switch now knows that device A can be reached on port 1 (because the switch received a frame from device A on port 1); the switch therefore puts the MAC address of device A in its MAC address table for port 1. This process is called *learning*—the switch is learning all the MAC addresses that it can reach.

At some point, device D is likely to reply to device A. At that time, the switch receives a frame from device D on port 4; the switch records this information in its MAC address table as part of its learning process. This time, the switch knows where the destination, device A, is; the switch therefore forwards the frame only out of port 1. This process is called *filtering*—the switch is sending the frames only out of the port through which they need to go—when the switch knows which port that is—rather than flooding them out of all the ports. This reduces the traffic on the other ports and reduces the interruptions that the other devices experience.

Over time, the switch learns where all the devices are, and the MAC address table is fully populated, as shown in Figure 2-2.

Figure 2-2 *The Switch Learns Where All the Devices Are and Populates Its MAC Address Table*

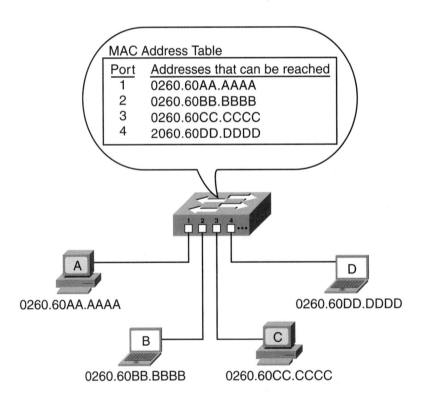

The filtering process also means that multiple simultaneous conversations can occur between different devices. For example, if device A and device B want to communicate, the switch sends their data between ports 1 and 2; no traffic goes on ports 3 or 4. At the same time, devices C and

D can communicate on ports 3 and 4 without interfering with the traffic on ports 1 and 2. Thus, the overall throughput of the network has increased dramatically.

The MAC address table is kept in the switch's memory and has a finite size (depending on the specific switch used). If many devices are attached to the switch, the switch might not have room for an entry for every one, so the table entries will time out after a period of not being used. For example, the Cisco Catalyst 2950 switch defaults to a 300-second timeout. Thus, the most active devices are always in the table.

NOTE Cisco LAN switches are also known as *Catalyst switches.*

KEY POINT Broadcast and multicast frames are, by default, flooded to all ports of a Layer 2 switch, other than the incoming port. The same is true for unicast frames that are destined to any device that is not in the MAC address table.

MAC addresses can also be statically configured in the MAC address table, and you can specify a maximum number of addresses allowed per port.

One advantage of static addresses is that less flooding occurs, both when the switch first comes up and because of not aging out the addresses. However, this also means that if a device is moved, the switch configuration must be changed. A related feature available in some switches is the ability to *sticky-learn* addresses—the address is dynamically learned, as described earlier, but is then automatically entered as a static command in the switch configuration. Limiting the number of addresses per port to one and statically configuring those addresses can ensure that only specific devices are permitted access to the network; this feature is particularly useful when addresses are sticky-learned.

Layer 3 Switching

KEY POINT A Layer 3 switch is really a router with some of the functions implemented in hardware to improve performance. In other words, some of the OSI model network layer routing functions are performed in high-performance ASICs rather than in software.

In Appendix B and Chapter 3, "IPv4 Routing Design," we describe the following various functions and characteristics of routers:

- Learning routes and keeping the best path to each destination in a routing table.

- Determining the best path that each packet should take to get to its destination, by comparing the destination address to the routing table.

- Sending the packet out of the appropriate interface, along the best path. This is also called *switching the packet,* because the packet is encapsulated in a new frame, with the appropriate framing header information, including MAC addresses.

- Communicating with other routers to exchange routing information.

- Allowing devices on different LANs to communicate with each other and with distant devices.

- Blocking broadcasts. By default, a router does not forward broadcasts, thereby helping to control the amount of traffic on the network.

These tasks can be CPU intensive. Offloading the switching of the packet to hardware can result in a significant increase in performance.

A Layer 3 switch performs all the previously mentioned router functions; the differences are in the physical implementation of the device rather than in the functions it performs. Thus, functionally, the terms *router* and *Layer 3 switch* are synonymous.

Layer 4 switching is an extension of Layer 3 switching that includes examination of the contents of the Layer 3 packet. For example, as described in Appendix B, the protocol number in the IP packet header indicates which transport layer protocol (for example, Transmission Control Protocol [TCP] or User Datagram Protocol [UDP]) is being used, and the port number in the TCP or UDP segment indicates the application being used. Switching based on the protocol and port numbers can ensure, for example, that certain types of traffic get higher priority on the network or take a specific path.

Depending on the switch, Layer 3 switching can be implemented in two different ways within Cisco switches—through multilayer switching and Cisco Express Forwarding. These terms are described in the section "Multilayer Switching and Cisco Express Forwarding," later in this chapter (after we discuss VLANs, which you must understand before you read that section).

Spanning Tree Protocol

KEY POINT | STP is a Layer 2 protocol that prevents logical loops in switched networks that have redundant links.

In the following sections, we first examine why such a protocol is needed in Layer 2 networks. We then introduce STP terminology and operation.

NOTE In the following sections, we are only concerned with Layer 2 switching; as you see in Chapter 3, routed (Layer 3) networks inherently support networks with multiple paths, so a protocol such as STP is not required.

Redundancy in Layer 2 Switched Networks

Redundancy in a network, such as that shown in Figure 2-3, is desirable so that communication can still take place if a link or device fails. For example, if switch X in this figure stopped functioning, devices A and B could still communicate through switch Y. However, in a switched network, redundancy can cause problems.

Figure 2-3 *Redundancy in a Switched Network Can Cause Problems*

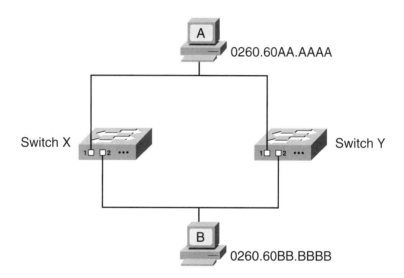

The first type of problem occurs if a broadcast frame is sent on the network. (Recall that a switch floods broadcast frames to all ports other than the one that it came in on.) For example, consider what happens when device A in Figure 2-3 sends an ARP request to find the MAC address of device B. The ARP request is sent as a broadcast. Both switch X and switch Y receive the broadcast; for now, consider just the one received by switch X, on its port 1. Switch X floods the broadcast to all its other connected ports; in this case, it floods it to port 2. Device B can see the broadcast, but so can switch Y, on its port 2; switch Y floods the broadcast to its port 1. This broadcast is received by switch X on its port 1; switch X floods it to its port 2, and so forth. The broadcast continues to loop around the network, consuming bandwidth and processing power. This situation is called a *broadcast storm*.

The second problem that can occur in redundant topologies is that devices can receive multiple copies of the same frame. For example, assume that neither of the switches in Figure 2-3 has learned where device B is located. When device A sends data destined for device B, switch X and switch Y both flood the data to the lower LAN, and device B receives two copies of the same frame. This might be a problem for device B, depending on what it is and how it is programmed to handle such a situation.

The third difficulty that can occur in a redundant situation is within the switch itself—the MAC address table can change rapidly and contain wrong information. Again referring to Figure 2-3, consider what happens when neither switch has learned where device A or B are located, and device A sends data to device B. Each switch learns that device A is on its port 1, and each records this in its MAC address table. Because the switches don't yet know where device B is, they flood the frame, in this case on their port 2. Each switch then receives the frame, from the other switch, on its port 2. This frame has device A's MAC address in the source address field; therefore, both switches now learn that device A is on their port 2. The MAC address table is therefore overwritten. Not only does the MAC address table have incorrect information (device A is actually connected to port 1, not port 2, of both switches), but because the table changes rapidly, it might be considered to be unstable.

To overcome these problems, you need a way to logically disable part of the redundant network for regular traffic while still maintaining the redundancy for the case when an error occurs. The Spanning Tree Protocol does just that.

STP Terminology and Operation

The following sections introduce the Institute of Electrical and Electronics Engineers (IEEE) 802.1d STP terminology and operation.

STP Terminology

STP terminology can best be explained by examining how an example network, such as the one in Figure 2-4, operates.

Figure 2-4 *STP Chooses the Port to Block*

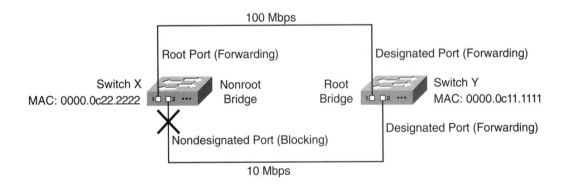

NOTE   Notice that STP terminology refers to the devices as *bridges* rather than *switches*. Recall (from Appendix B) that bridges are previous-generation devices with the same logical functionality as switches; however, switches are significantly faster because they switch in hardware, whereas bridges switch in software. Functionally, the two terms are synonymous.

Within an STP network, one switch is elected as the *root bridge*—it is at the root of the spanning tree. All other switches calculate their best path to the root bridge. Their alternate paths are put in the blocking state. These alternate paths are logically disabled from the perspective of regular traffic, but the switches still communicate with each other on these paths so that the alternate paths can be unblocked in case an error occurs on the best path.

All switches running STP (it is turned on by default in Cisco switches) send out bridge protocol data units (BPDUs). Switches running STP use BPDUs to exchange information with neighboring switches. One of the fields in the BPDU is the bridge identifier (ID); it is comprised of a 2-octet bridge priority and a 6-octet MAC address. STP uses the bridge ID to elect the root bridge—the switch with the lowest bridge ID is the root bridge. If all bridge priorities are left at their default values, the switch with the lowest MAC address therefore becomes the root bridge. In Figure 2-4, switch Y is elected as the root bridge.

NOTE   The way that STP chooses the root bridge can cause an interesting situation if left to the default values. Recall that the MAC address is a 6-octet or 48-bit value, with the upper 24 bits as an Organizational Unique Identifier (OUI) (representing the vendor of the device) and the lower 24 bits as a unique value for that OUI, typically the serial number of the device. A lower MAC address means a lower serial number, which likely means an older switch. Thus, because STP by default chooses a switch with a lower MAC address, the oldest switch is likely to be chosen. This is just one reason why you should explicitly choose the root bridge (by changing the priority), rather than getting the STP default choice.

All the ports on the root bridge are called *designated ports,* and they are all in the *forwarding state*—that is, they can send and receive data. (The STP states are described in the next section of this chapter.)

On all *nonroot bridges,* one port becomes the *root port,* and it is also in the forwarding state. The root port is the one with the lowest cost to the root. The cost of each link is by default inversely proportional to the bandwidth of the link, so the port with the fastest total path from the switch to the root bridge is selected as the root port on that switch. In Figure 2-4, port 1 on switch X is the root port for that switch because it is the fastest way to the root bridge.

NOTE If multiple ports on a switch have the same fastest total path costs to the root bridge, STP considers other BPDU fields. STP looks first at the bridge IDs in the received BPDUs (the bridge IDs of the next switch in the path to the root bridge); the port that received the BPDU with the lowest bridge ID becomes the root port. If these bridge IDs are also equal, the port ID breaks the tie; the port with the lower port ID becomes the root port. The port ID field includes a port priority and a port index, which is the port number. Thus, if the port priorities are the same (for example, if they are left at their default value), the lower port number becomes the root port.

Each LAN segment must have one designated port. It is on the switch that has the lowest cost to the root bridge (or if the costs are equal, the port on the switch with the lowest bridge ID is chosen), and it is in the forwarding state. In Figure 2-4, the root bridge has designated ports on both segments, so no more are required.

NOTE The root bridge sends configuration BPDUs on all its ports periodically, every 2 seconds by default. (These configuration BPDUs include the STP timers, therefore ensuring that all switches in the network use the same timers.) On each LAN segment the switch that has the designated port forwards the configuration BPDUs to the segment; all switches in the network therefore receive these BPDUs, on their root port.

All ports on a LAN segment that are not root ports or designated ports are called *nondesignated ports* and transition to the *blocking state*—they do not send data, so the redundant topology is logically disabled. In Figure 2-4, port 2 on switch X is the nondesignated port, and it is in the blocking state. Blocking ports do, however, listen for BPDUs.

If a failure happens—for example, if a designated port or a root bridge fails—the switches send topology change BPDUs and recalculate the spanning tree. The new spanning tree does not include the failed port or switch, and the ports that were previously blocking might now be in the forwarding state. This is how STP supports the redundancy in a switched network.

STP States

Figure 2-5 illustrates the various STP port states.

Figure 2-5 *A Port Can Transition Among STP States*

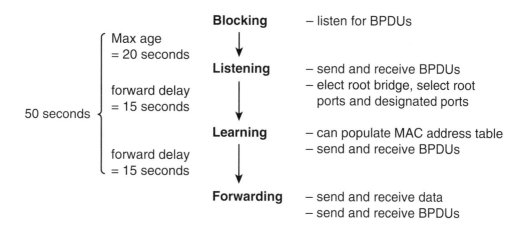

When a port initially comes up, it is put in the blocking state, in which it listens for BPDUs and then transitions to the listening state. A blocking port in an operational network can also transition to the listening state if it does not hear any BPDUs for the *max-age time* (a default of 20 seconds). While in the listening state, the switch can send and receive BPDUs but not data. The root bridge and the various final states of all the ports are determined in this state. If the port is chosen as the root port on a switch or as a designated port on a segment, the port transitions to the learning state after the listening state. In the learning state, the port still cannot send data, but it can start to populate its MAC address table if any data is received. The length of time spent in each of the listening and learning states is dictated by the value of the *forward-delay* parameter, which is 15 seconds by default. After the learning state, the port transitions to the forwarding state, in which it can operate normally. Alternatively, if in the listening state the port is not chosen as a root port or designated port, it becomes a nondesignated port and it transitions back to the blocking state.

KEY POINT   Do not confuse the STP learning state with the learning process that the switch goes through to populate its MAC address table. The STP learning state is a transitory state. While a switch can learn MAC addresses from data frames received on its ports that are in the STP learning state, it does not forward those frames. In a stable network, switch ports are in either the forwarding or blocking state. Ports in the blocking state do not listen to data frames and therefore do not contribute to the switch's MAC address table. Ports in the forwarding state do, of course, listen to (and forward) data frames, and those frames populate the switch's MAC address table.

STP Options

Figure 2-5 illustrates that it could take up to 50 seconds for a blocked port to transition to the forwarding state after a failure has occurred in the forwarding path. This lengthy time is one of the drawbacks of STP.

Several features and enhancements to STP can help to reduce the convergence time, that is, the time it takes for all the switches in a network to agree on the network's topology after that topology has changed. The following are some of these features that are implemented in Cisco switches:

- **PortFast**—This feature should be used for ports that have only end-user stations or servers attached to them, in other words, for ports that are not attached to other switches (so that no BPDUs are received on the port). Because no other switches are attached, the port cannot be part of a loop, so the switch immediately puts the port in the forwarding state. Thus, the port transitions to the forwarding state much faster than it otherwise would.

- **UplinkFast**—This feature is intended to be used on redundant ports on access layer switches.[1] If the root port (pointing to the root bridge) on a switch goes down, the nondesignated port (the redundant blocking port) on the switch is quickly put in the forwarding state, rather than going through all the other states.

- **BackboneFast**—This feature helps to reduce the convergence time when links other than those directly connected to a switch fail. This feature must be deployed on all switches in the network if it is to be used.

Rapid STP (RSTP)

RSTP is defined by IEEE 802.1w. RSTP incorporates many of the Cisco enhancements to STP, resulting in faster convergence. Switches in an RSTP environment converge quickly by communicating with each other and determining which links can be forwarding, rather than just waiting for the timers to transition the ports among the various states. RSTP ports take on different roles than STP ports. The RSTP roles are root, designated, alternate, backup, and disabled. RSTP port states are also different than STP port states. The RSTP states are discarding, learning, and forwarding. RSTP is compatible with STP.

Virtual LANs

As noted earlier, a broadcast domain includes all devices that receive each other's broadcasts (and multicasts). All the devices connected to one router port are in the same broadcast domain. Routers block broadcasts (destined for *all* networks) and multicasts by default; routers only forward *unicast* packets (destined for a specific device) and packets of a special type called *directed broadcasts*. Typically, you think of a broadcast domain as being a physical wire, a LAN. But a broadcast domain can also be a VLAN, a logical construct that can include multiple physical LAN segments.

NOTE   IP multicast technology, which enables multicast packets to be sent throughout a network, is described in Chapter 10, "Other Enabling Technologies."

NOTE   An IP directed broadcast is a packet destined for all devices on an IP subnet, but which originates from a device on another subnet. A router that is not directly connected to the destination subnet forwards the IP directed broadcast in the same way it would forward unicast IP packets destined to a host on that subnet.

On Cisco routers, the **ip directed-broadcast** interface command controls what the last router in the path, the one connected to the destination subnet, does with the packet. If **ip directed-broadcast** is enabled on the interface, the router changes the directed broadcast to a broadcast and sends the packet, encapsulated in a Layer 2 broadcast frame, onto the subnet. However, if the **no ip directed-broadcast** command is configured on the interface, directed broadcasts destined for the subnet to which that interface is attached are dropped. In Cisco Internet Operating System (IOS) version 12.0, the default for this command was changed to **no ip directed-broadcast**.

KEY POINT   We found the Cisco definition of VLANs to be very clear: "[A] group of devices on one or more LANs that are configured (using management software) so that they can communicate as if they were attached to the same wire, when in fact they are located on a number of different LAN segments. Because VLANs are based on logical instead of physical connections, they are extremely flexible."[2]

Figure 2-6 illustrates the VLAN concept. On the left side of the figure, three individual physical LANs are shown, one each for Engineering, Accounting, and Marketing. (These LANs contain workstations—E1, E2, A1, A2, M1, and M2—and servers—ES, AS, and MS.) Instead of physical LANs, an enterprise can use VLANs, as shown on the right side of the figure. With VLANs, members of each department can be physically located anywhere, yet still be logically connected with their own workgroup. Thus, in the VLAN configuration, all the devices attached to VLAN E (Engineering) share the same broadcast domain, the devices attached to VLAN A (Accounting) share a separate broadcast domain, and the devices attached to VLAN M (Marketing) share a third broadcast domain. Figure 2-6 also illustrates how VLANs can span across multiple switches; the link between the two switches in the figure carries traffic from all three of the VLANs and is called a *trunk*.

Figure 2-6 *A VLAN Is a Logical Implementation of a Physical LAN*

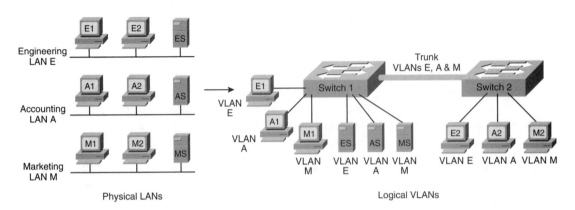

VLAN Membership

**KEY
POINT** | A switch port that is not a trunk can belong to only one VLAN at a time. You can configure which VLAN a port belongs to in two ways: statically and dynamically.

Static port membership means that the network administrator configures which VLAN the port belongs to, regardless of the devices attached to it. This means that after you have configured the ports, you must ensure that the devices attaching to the switch are plugged into the correct port, and if they move, you must reconfigure the switch.

Alternatively, you can configure dynamic VLAN membership. Some static configuration is still required, but this time, it is on a separate device called a *VLAN Membership Policy Server (VMPS)*. The VMPS could be a separate server, or it could be a higher-end switch that contains the VMPS information. VMPS information consists of a MAC address-to-VLAN map. Thus, ports are assigned to VLANs based on the MAC address of the device connected to the port. When you move a device from one port to another port (either on the same switch or on another switch in the network), the switch dynamically assigns the new port to the proper VLAN for that device by consulting the VMPS.

Trunks

As mentioned earlier, a port that carries data from multiple VLANs is called a trunk. A trunk port can be on a switch, a router, or a server.

A trunk port can use one of two protocols: Inter-Switch Link (ISL) or IEEE 802.1q.

ISL is a Cisco-proprietary trunking protocol that involves encapsulating the data frame between an ISL header and trailer. The header is 26 bytes long; the trailer is a 4-byte cyclic redundancy check (CRC) that is added after the data frame. A 15-bit VLAN ID field is included in the header to identify the VLAN that the traffic is for. (Only the lower 10 bits of this field are used, thus supporting 1024 VLANs.)

The 802.1q protocol is an IEEE standard protocol in which the trunking information is encoded within a Tag field that is inserted inside the frame header itself. Trunks using the 802.1q protocol define a native VLAN. Traffic for the native VLAN is not tagged; it is carried across the trunk unchanged. Thus, end-user stations that don't understand trunking can communicate with other devices directly over an 802.1q trunk, as long as they are on the native VLAN. The native VLAN must be defined to be the same VLAN on both sides of the trunk. Within the Tag field, the 802.1q VLAN ID field is 12 bits long, allowing up to 4096 VLANs to be defined. The Tag field also includes a 3-bit 802.1p user priority field; these bits are used as class of service (CoS) bits for quality of service (QoS) marking. (Chapter 6, "Quality of Service Design," describes QoS marking.)

The two types of trunks are not compatible with each other, so both ends of a trunk must be defined with the same trunk type.

NOTE   Multiple switch ports can be logically combined so that they appear as one higher-performance port. Cisco does this with its Etherchannel technology, combining multiple Fast Ethernet or Gigabit Ethernet links. Trunks can be implemented on both individual ports and on these Etherchannel ports.

STP and VLANs

Cisco developed per-VLAN spanning tree (PVST) so that switches can have one instance of STP running per VLAN, allowing redundant physical links within the network to be used for different VLANs and thus reducing the load on individual links. PVST is illustrated in Figure 2-7.

Figure 2-7 *PVST Allows Redundant Physical Links to Be Used for Different VLANs*

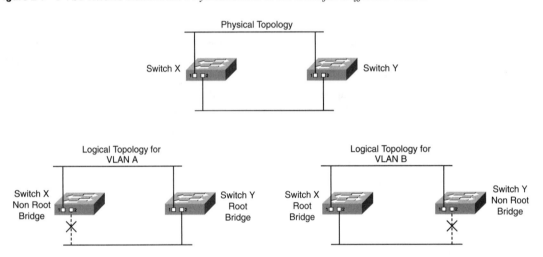

The top diagram in Figure 2-7 shows the physical topology of the network, with switches X and Y redundantly connected. In the lower-left diagram, switch Y has been selected as the root bridge for VLAN A, leaving port 2 on switch X in the blocking state. In contrast, the lower-right diagram shows that switch X has been selected as the root bridge for VLAN B, leaving port 2 on switch Y in the blocking state. With this configuration, traffic is shared across all links, with traffic for VLAN A traveling to the lower LAN on switch Y's port 2, while traffic for VLAN B traveling to the lower LAN goes out switch X's port 2.

PVST only works over ISL trunks. However, Cisco extended this functionality for 802.1q trunks with the PVST+ protocol. Before this became available, 802.1q trunks only supported Common Spanning Tree (CST), with one instance of STP running for all VLANs.

Multiple-Instance STP (MISTP) is an IEEE standard (802.1s) that uses RSTP and allows several VLANs to be grouped into a single spanning-tree instance. Each instance is independent of the other instances so that a link can be forwarding for one group of VLANs while blocking for other VLANs. MISTP therefore allows traffic to be shared across all the links in the network, but it reduces the number of STP instances that would be required if PVST/PVST+ were implemented.

VLAN Trunking Protocol

KEY POINT | The VLAN Trunking Protocol (VTP) is a Cisco-proprietary Layer 2 protocol that allows easier configuration of VLANs on multiple switches. When VTP is enabled in your network, you define all the VLANs on one switch, and that switch sends the VLAN definitions to all the other switches. On those other switches, you then have to only assign the ports to the VLANs; you do not have to configure the VLANs themselves. Not only is configuration easier, but it is also less prone to misconfiguration errors.

A switch in a VTP domain (a group of switches communicating with VTP) can be in one of three modes: server (which is the default mode), client, or transparent mode. The VTP server is the one on which you configure the VLANs; it sends VTP advertisements, containing VLAN configuration information, to VTP clients in the same VTP domain, as illustrated in Figure 2-8. Note that VTP advertisements are only sent on trunks.

Figure 2-8   *VTP Eases VLAN Definition Configuration*

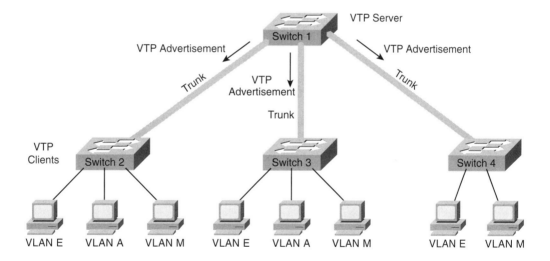

You cannot create, modify, or delete VLANs on a VTP client; rather, a VTP client only accepts VLAN configuration information from a VTP server. A VTP client also forwards the VTP advertisements to other switches.

You can create, modify, or delete VLANs on a switch that is in VTP transparent mode; however, this information is not sent to other switches, and the transparent-mode switch ignores advertisements from VTP servers (but does pass them on to other switches).

VTP pruning is a VTP feature that helps reduce the amount of flooded traffic (including broadcast, multicast, and unicast) that is sent on the network. With VTP pruning enabled, the switches communicate with each other to find out which switches have ports in which VLANs; switches that have no ports in a particular VLAN (and have no downstream switches with ports in that VLAN) do not receive that VLAN's traffic. For example, in Figure 2-8, switch 4 has no need for VLAN A traffic, so VTP pruning would prevent switch 1 from flooding VLAN A traffic to switch 4. VTP pruning is disabled by default.

Inter-VLAN Routing

You have learned how devices on one VLAN can communicate with each other using switches and trunks. But how do networked devices on different VLANs communicate with each other?

KEY POINT | Just like devices on different LANs, those on different VLANs require a Layer 3 mechanism (a router or a Layer 3 switch) to communicate with each other.

A Layer 3 device can be connected to a switched network in two ways: by using multiple physical interfaces or through a single interface configured as a trunk. These two connection methods are shown in Figure 2-9. The diagram on the left in this figure illustrates a router with three physical connections to the switch; each physical connection carries traffic from only one VLAN.

Figure 2-9 *A Router, Using Either Multiple Physical Interfaces or a Trunk, Is Required for Communication Among VLANs*

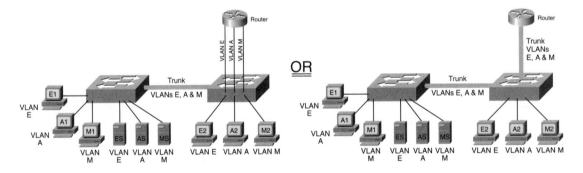

The diagram on the right in Figure 2-9 illustrates a router with one physical connection to the switch. The interfaces on the switch and the router have been configured as trunks; therefore, multiple logical connections exist between the two devices. When a router is connected to a switch through a trunk, it is sometimes called a "router on a stick," because it has only one physical interface (a stick) to the switch.

Each interface between the switch and the Layer 3 device (whether physical interfaces or logical interfaces within a trunk) is in a separate VLAN (and therefore in a separate subnet for IP networks).

Multilayer Switching and Cisco Express Forwarding

Now that you have an understanding of VLANs, the following sections introduce the two different ways that Layer 3 switching is implemented within Cisco switches—multilayer switching and Cisco Express Forwarding.

Multilayer Switching

Multilayer switching, as its name implies, allows switching to take place at different protocol layers. Switching can be performed only on Layers 2 and 3, or it can also include Layer 4.

MLS is based on network flows.

KEY POINT | A *network flow* is a unidirectional sequence of packets between a source and a destination. Flows can be very specific. For example, a network flow can be identified by source and destination IP addresses, protocol numbers, and port numbers as well as the interface on which the packet enters the switch.

The three major components of MLS are as follows[3]:

- **MLS Route Processor (MLS-RP)**—The MLS-enabled router that performs the traditional function of routing between subnets

- **MLS Switching Engine (MLS-SE)**—The MLS-enabled switch that can offload some of the packet-switching functionality from the MLS-RP

- **Multilayer Switching Protocol (MLSP)**—Used by the MLS-RP and the MLS-SE to communicate with each other

MLS can be implemented in the following two ways:

- **Within a Catalyst switch**—Here both the MLS-RP and the MLS-SE are resident in the same chassis. An example of an internal MLS-RP is a Route Switch Module (RSM) installed in a slot of a Catalyst 5500 Series switch.

- **Using a combination of a Catalyst switch and an external router**—An example of a router that can be an external MLS-RP router is a Cisco 3600 Series router with the appropriate IOS software release and with MLS enabled.

NOTE   Not all Catalyst switches and routers support MLS. Refer to specific product documentation on the Cisco website for device support information for switches[4] and routers.[5]

KEY POINT | MLS allows communication between two devices that are in different VLANs (on different subnets) and that are connected to the same MLS-SE and that share a common MLS-RP. The communication bypasses the MLS-RP and instead uses the MLS-SE to relay the packets, thus improving overall performance.[6]

Figure 2-10 is an example network that illustrates MLS operation.

Figure 2-10 *The MLS-SE Offloads Work from the MLS-RP*

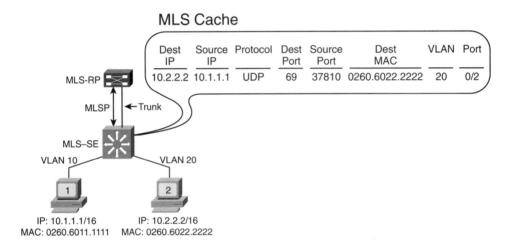

In Figure 2-10, the MLS-RP and MLS-SE communicate using MLSP. The SE learns the MAC addresses of the RP (one for each VLAN that is running MLS). When device 1 (10.1.1.1/16) wants to send a packet to device 2 (10.2.2.2/16), device 1 creates a frame with the destination MAC address of its default gateway, the router, which in this case is the RP. The SE receives the frame, sees that it is for the RP, and therefore examines its MLS cache to see whether it has a match for this flow. In the case of the first packet in the flow, no match exists, so the SE forwards the frame to the RP. The SE also puts the frame in its MLS cache and marks the frame as a *candidate entry*.

The MLS-RP receives the frame, decapsulates (unwraps) the frame, and examines the packet. The RP then examines its routing table to see whether it has a route to the destination of the packet; assuming that it does, the RP creates a new frame for the packet after decrementing the IP header

Time to Live (TTL) field and recalculating the IP header checksum. The source MAC address of this frame is the MAC address of the RP; the destination MAC address of this frame is the MAC address of the destination device (or next-hop router). The RP then sends the frame through the SE.

The MLS-SE receives the frame and compares it to its MLS cache; the SE recognizes that the frame is carrying the same packet as a candidate entry and is on its way back from the same RP. The SE therefore completes the MLS cache entry using information from the frame; this entry is now an *enabler entry*. The SE also forwards the frame out of the appropriate port toward its destination.

When a subsequent packet in the same flow enters the switch, the SE examines its MLS cache to see whether it has a match. This time it does have a match, so it does not forward the frame to the RP. Instead, the SE rewrites the frame using the information in the MLS cache, including decrementing the TTL field, recalculating the IP header checksum, and using the MAC address of the RP as the source MAC address; the resulting frame looks as though it came from the RP. The SE then forwards the frame out of the appropriate port toward its destination.

NOTE   Network flows are unidirectional. Therefore, if device 1 and device 2 both send packets to each other, two flows would be recorded in the MLS cache, one for each direction.

NOTE   In Figure 2-10, the MLS cache is shown as having a "protocol" field. In the output of the display on the Catalyst switches this field is called a "port" field, even though it represents the protocol field in the IP header.

The MLS-SE also keeps traffic statistics that can be exported to other utilities to be used, for example, for troubleshooting, accounting, or other functions.

Cisco Express Forwarding

Cisco Express Forwarding (CEF), like MLS, aims to speed the data routing and forwarding process in a network. However, the two methods use different approaches.

CEF uses two components to optimize the lookup of the information required to route packets: the Forwarding Information Base (FIB) for the Layer 3 information and the adjacency table for the Layer 2 information.[7]

CEF creates an FIB by maintaining a copy of the forwarding information contained in the IP routing table. The information is indexed so that it can be quickly searched for matching entries as packets are processed. Whenever the routing table changes, the FIB is also changed so that it always contains up-to-date paths. A separate routing cache is not required.

The adjacency table contains Layer 2 frame header information, including next-hop addresses, for all FIB entries. Each FIB entry can point to multiple adjacency table entries, for example, if two paths exist between devices for load balancing.

After a packet is processed and the route is determined from the FIB, the Layer 2 next-hop and header information is retrieved from the adjacency table and a new frame is created to encapsulate the packet.

Cisco Express Forwarding can be enabled on a router (for example, on a Cisco 7500 Series router) or on a switch with Layer 3 functionality (such as the Catalyst 8540 switch).

NOTE Not all Catalyst switches support Cisco Express Forwarding. Refer to specific product documentation on the Cisco website[8] for device support information.

Switching Security

In the past few years, switches have become equipped with features that make them more intelligent, allowing them to provide an active role in network security.

Cisco documentation refers to Catalyst integrated security (CIS). However, the term CIS refers only to built-in functionality that is native to the Catalyst switches, not to the security features inherent in the modules that can be installed in the switches (for example, firewall blades and so forth). Thus, in this book, we have categorized these two types of switch security as follows:

■ **Catalyst native security**—Those features built into the switch itself

■ **Catalyst hardware security**—Features of hardware that can be installed in the switch

These categories are described in the following sections.

NOTE Refer to Chapter 4, "Network Security Design," for general information on network security.

Catalyst Native Security

Cisco switches have many native attributes that can be used to secure a network.

Some attributes are related to the secure management of the switch itself. One example is the use of secure shell (SSH), rather than Telnet, when remotely managing the switch. Another example is disabling unused switch ports so that the network cannot be accessed through them.

Secure Shell

SSH is a protocol that is similar to Telnet, but SSH uses encryption for security. SSH usually uses TCP port 22.

Catalyst native security can protect networks against serious threats originating from the exploitation of MAC address vulnerabilities, ARP vulnerabilities, and Dynamic Host Configuration Protocol (DHCP) vulnerabilities. (Both ARP and DHCP are covered in Appendix B.) Table 2-1 shows some examples of the protection provided by the built-in intelligence in Catalyst switches.

Table 2-1   *Examples of Built-In Intelligence to Mitigate Attacks*

Attack	Native Security (Built-In Intelligence) to Mitigate Attacks
DHCP Denial of Service (DoS) A DHCP DoS attack can be initiated by a hacker. As well as taking down the DHCP server, the attack could also be initiated from a server that is pretending to be a legitimate DHCP server. This rogue server replies to DHCP requests with phony DHCP information.	**Trusted-State Port** The switch port to which the DHCP server is attached can be set to a "trusted" state. Only trusted ports are allowed to pass DHCP replies. Untrusted ports are only allowed to pass DHCP requests.
MAC Flooding A hacker targets the switch's MAC address table, to flood it with many addresses.	**MAC Port Security** The switch can be configured with a maximum number of MAC addresses per port. The switch can also be configured with static MAC addresses that identify the specific addresses that it should allow, further constraining the devices allowed to attach to the network.

Table 2-1 *Examples of Built-In Intelligence to Mitigate Attacks (Continued)*

Attack	Native Security (Built-in Intelligence) to Mitigate Attacks
Redirected Attack A hacker wanting to cover his tracks and complicate the network forensics investigation might decide to compromise an intermediary target first. The hacker would then unleash his attack to the intended target from that intermediary victim.	**Private VLAN (PVLAN)** The flow of traffic can be directed by using PVLANs. In the example shown in Figure 2-11, a PVLAN is defined so that traffic received on either switch port 2 or 3 can exit only by switch port 1. Should a hacker compromise server A, he would not be able to directly attack server B because the traffic can only flow between port 1 and port 2, and between port 1 and port 3. Traffic is not allowed to flow between port 2 and port 3.

Figure 2-11 *Using a Switch to Create a PVLAN*

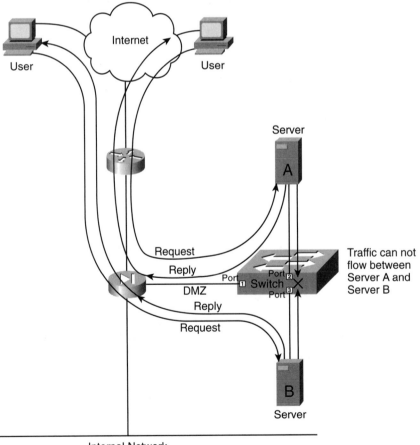

Catalyst Hardware Security

Cisco switches can provide security, flexibility, and expandability to networks. As an example, the Catalyst 6500 Series switches can be equipped with modules that are full-fledged security devices themselves. Some example security modules are as follows:

- Cisco Firewall service module

- Cisco Internet Protocol security (IPsec) virtual private network (VPN) service module

- Cisco Intrusion Detection System (IDS)

- Cisco Secure Socket Layer (SSL)

> **NOTE**   Refer to Chapter 4 for information on IPsec, VPNs, IDSs, and SSLs.

As an example of the flexibility provided by these modules, consider that when using a Cisco Firewall service module, any port on a Catalyst 6500 switch can operate as a firewall. An example of the expandability of the modules is the use of the IPsec VPN module. This module can terminate up to 8000 VPN connections (known as *VPN tunnels*) simultaneously and can create 60 new tunnels per second; up to 10 of these modules can be installed in a Catalyst 6500 switch.

Switching Design Considerations

Chapter 1, "Network Design," introduces the hierarchical network design model and the Enterprise Composite Network Design model. Recall that the three functions that comprise the hierarchical network design model are the access layer, the distribution layer, and the core layer. The Enterprise Composite Network Model is the name given to the architecture used by the Cisco SAFE blueprint; it supports larger networks than those designed with only the hierarchical model and clarifies the functional boundaries within the network. Three functional areas exist within this model: Enterprise Campus, Enterprise Edge, and Service Provider Edge. Each of these functional areas contains network modules, which in turn can include the hierarchical layers.

Switches within the Enterprise Campus are in all three of the hierarchical layers. Layer 2 and/or Layer 3 switches can be used, depending on a number of factors.

For the access layer, design considerations include the following:

- The number of end-user devices to be supported

- The applications that are being used—this defines some of the features required in the switches, as well as the performance and bandwidth needed

- The use of VLANs, including whether trunks are required between switches

- Redundancy requirements

For the distribution layer, design factors include the following:

- The number of access switches to be aggregated

- Redundancy requirements

- Features required for specific applications to be supported

- Required interfaces to the core layer

- For Layer 3 switches, the routing protocols to be supported and whether sharing of information among multiple routing protocols is required. (Routing protocols are discussed in detail in Chapter 3.)

The role of the core layer is to provide a high-speed backbone. Thus, the key requirement is the performance needed to support all the access and distribution data. The number of ports to the distribution layer, and the protocols (for example, routing protocols) that need to be supported on those ports, are also important considerations. Redundancy in the core is a typical requirement, to meet the availability needs of the network.

Cisco current campus design recommendations include the following:[9]

- Layer 2 switches can be used at the access layer, with Layer 3 switches at the distribution and core layers.

- VLANs should not spread across the campus, because this can slow network convergence.

- The core and distribution layers can be combined into one layer (called a *collapsed backbone*) for smaller networks. Larger campuses should have a separate distribution layer to allow the network to grow easily.

- Redundancy in the core, between the core and distribution layers, and between the distribution and access layers is also recommended. Redundancy can also be used within these layers as required.

Figure 2-12 illustrates a sample small network design that uses Layer 2 switches in the access layer of the campus Building and Server modules. This network features a collapsed backbone in Layer 3 switches. Redundancy is incorporated between all layers.

Figure 2-12   *A Small Network Can Include a Collapsed Backbone*

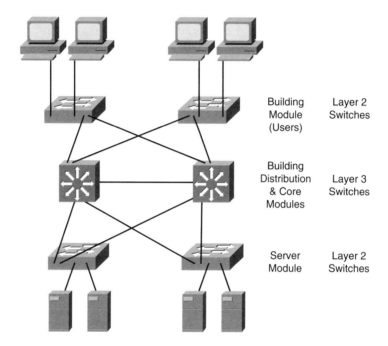

Figure 2-13 illustrates an example of a larger network design. Two buildings are shown, each with Layer 2 access switches and Layer 3 distribution switches. These buildings are then redundantly connected to the Layer 3 core. The Server module is shown with Layer 2 access switches connected directly to the core; distribution switches can be added if additional functionality or performance is required.

Figure 2-13 *A Larger Network Has Separate Core and Distribution Switches*

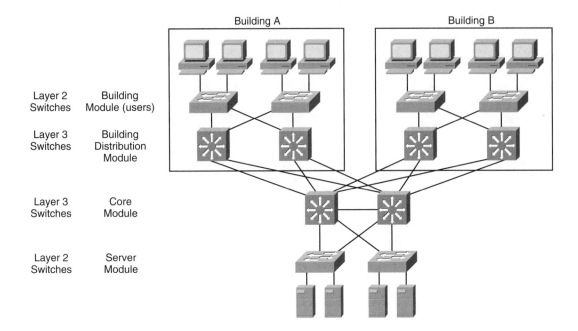

Summary

In this chapter, you learned about Layer 2 and Layer 3 switching network design, including the following topics:

■ How switches improve the performance of your network

■ The two types of switches: Layer 2 and Layer 3

■ The two implementations of Layer 3 switching within Cisco switches: multilayer switching and Cisco Express Forwarding

■ How the STP is critical in a Layer 2 switched environment to prevent loops

■ The usefulness of VLANs in defining logical broadcast domains

■ The features in switches that can be used to increase the security of your network

■ How switches fit into the design models

Endnotes

[1]Webb, *Building Cisco Multilayer Switched Networks,* Indianapolis, Cisco Press, 2001, p. 165.

[2]"Virtual LANs/VLAN Trunking Protocol (VLANs/VTP)," http://www.cisco.com/en/US/tech/tk389/tk689/tsd_technology_support_protocol_home.html.

[3]"Troubleshooting IP Multilayer Switching," http://www.cisco.com/en/US/products/hw/switches/ps700/products_tech_note09186a00800f99bc.shtml.

[4]Cisco switch products home page, http://www.cisco.com/en/US/products/hw/switches/index.html.

[5]Cisco router products home page, http://www.cisco.com/en/US/products/hw/routers/index.html.

[6]"Troubleshooting IP Multilayer Switching," http://www.cisco.com/en/US/products/hw/switches/ps700/products_tech_note09186a00800f99bc.shtml.

[7]"Cisco Express Forwarding Overview," http://www.cisco.com/univercd/cc/td/doc/product/software/ios122/122cgcr/fswtch_c/swprt1/xcfcef.htm.

[8]Cisco switch products home page, http://www.cisco.com/en/US/products/hw/switches/index.html.

[9]"Hierarchical Campus Design At-A-Glance," http://www.cisco.com/application/pdf/en/us/guest/netsol/ns24/c643/cdccont_0900aecd800d8129.pdf.

This chapter describes IP addressing and routing protocols, and includes the following sections:

■ Making the Business Case

■ IPv4 Address Design

■ IPv4 Routing Protocols

■ IPv4 Routing Protocol Selection

CHAPTER **3**

Pv4 Routing Design

This chapter discusses Internet Protocol (IP) version 4 (IPv4) addressing design and routing protocol selection. After introducing why these topics are important, the address design considerations are explored. The factors that differentiate the available IPv4 routing protocols are described, followed by a discussion of the specific protocols. The considerations for choosing the routing protocol (or protocols) for your network complete this chapter.

> **NOTE** In this book, the term *IP* refers to IPv4. IP version 6 (IPv6), a successor to IPv4 not yet in common use, is introduced in Chapter 10, "Other Enabling Technologies."

> **NOTE** Appendix B, "Network Fundamentals," includes material that we assume you understand before reading the rest of the book. Thus, you are encouraged to review any of the material in Appendix B that you are not familiar with before reading the rest of this chapter.

Making the Business Case

Each chapter in the technologies section of this book discusses not only what you need to know but also why you need to know it. For IP addressing and routing, consider the following items:

■ **The importance of IP**—IP is used throughout the public Internet and on most organizations' networks, and is therefore the most important routed protocol to the majority of businesses today. IP is not limited to sending traditional data such as files and e-mails—it forms the basis for many other technologies and solutions, as described in later chapters in this book. For example, IP telephony uses an IP network for voice traffic, eliminating many of the costs associated with long-distance calls and at the same time introducing other capabilities to your telephone network. (IP telephony is described in Chapter 7, "Voice Transport Design.")

Toronto's Pearson International Airport's new terminal is a further example of how IP is being used as the foundation for an intelligent system. At this terminal, a variety of communications systems and applications were put onto a single, secure, IP-based network. For example, when a gate at the airport is used by one airline, the system provides access to that airline's applications for check-in, baggage tracking, and so forth, and the IP phones provide that airline's telephone service. When another airline uses the same gate later in the day, the configuration changes so that the new airline's applications and telephone service can be accessed instead.[1] Cisco calls this a *common-use network*—a single communications infrastructure shared by all tenants of the terminal.[2]

■   **The importance of proper IP addressing**—Correct IP addressing is crucial to making an IP network work, and if done properly, addresses can be summarized. Summarization ensures that the routing tables are smaller and therefore use less router memory, that the routing updates are smaller and use less network bandwidth, and that network problems can be localized (changes are sent to fewer routers). All of these benefits can result in a more stable network that adjusts faster to changes.

■   **The importance of proper routing protocol selection**—Routers learn about paths to destinations from other routers by using a routing protocol. Many IP routing protocols are available to choose from, each with its own advantages and disadvantages. The key is to understand the requirements for your network, understand how the routing protocols work, and match the network requirements to the routing protocol specifications. In some cases, it might be appropriate to run multiple routing protocols. Understanding how they will interact and how to avoid problems in a mixed routing protocol environment is important to the successful operation of your network.

IPv4 Address Design

This section discusses IP addressing design. First, we examine how to determine how many IP addresses are needed in a network. We next discuss the use of private addresses. If private addresses are used in a network that also requires Internet connectivity, Network Address Translation (NAT) is also needed, so the various features of NAT are described. This is followed by a discussion of how routers use IP subnet masks. We next show you how to determine the subnet mask to use within a network. Assigning IP addresses in a hierarchical way allows them to be summarized, which has many benefits. These benefits are examined, and route summarization calculations are illustrated. The use of variable-length subnet masks (VLSMs) can help you to use your available IP address space more efficiently—an explanation of VLSMs concludes this section.

NOTE   Appendix B, "Network Fundamentals," includes an introduction to IP addresses.

Determining How Many IP Addresses Are Required

To determine how many IP addresses are required in your network, you should consider[3] the many different locations in your network that need addresses, including headquarters, branch and regional offices, telecommuters, and so forth. The number of devices in each location must be counted, including the network devices such as routers, switches, and firewalls; workstations; IP phones; network management stations; servers; and so forth. For each of these devices, determine how many interfaces need to be addressed and whether private or public addresses will be used.

A reserve for future growth should be added to the total number of addresses required. A 10 to 20 percent reserve is typically sufficient, but the reserve should be based on your knowledge of the organization. If you do not reserve enough space for future growth, you might have to reconfigure some of your routers (for example, to add new subnets or networks into route summarization calculations); in the worst case, you might have to re-address your entire network.

Using Private and Public Addresses and NAT

Recall that Requests For Comments (RFC) 1918, "Address Allocation for Private Internets," defines the private IPv4 addresses as follows:

- 10.0.0.0 to 10.255.255.255

- 172.16.0.0 to 172.31.255.255

- 192.168.0.0 to 192.168.255.255

NOTE   RFC 3330, "Special-Use IPv4 Addresses," describes IPv4 address blocks that have been assigned by the Internet Assigned Numbers Authority (IANA) for specialized purposes, and includes reference to the private addresses defined in RFC 1918.

The remaining Class A, B, and C addresses are public addresses. Private addresses are for use only within a company's network; public addresses must be used when communicating on the public Internet. Internal private addresses must be translated to public addresses when data is sent out to the Internet, and these public addresses must be translated back to the private addresses when packets come in from the Internet.

Because only a finite number of public addresses are available, they are becoming scarce. Using private addresses internally on your network means that you will require fewer public addresses. However, public addresses are required for the Internet connections and for servers that must be accessible from the Internet—for example, File Transfer Protocol (FTP) servers that contain publicly accessible data, and web servers. Other devices internal to the network can use private addresses—they can connect to the Internet through a NAT device.

RFC 1631, "The IP Network Address Translator," defines NAT. NAT can be provided by a variety of devices, including routers and firewalls.

KEY POINT | To configure NAT, you first define *inside* and *outside* interfaces on the NAT device. The inside interface connects to the internal network, while the outside interface connects to the Internet. You also define the addresses that are to be translated on each side.

For example, in the network in Figure 3-1, a person at PC 172.16.1.1 wants to access data on the FTP server at 192.168.7.2. A NAT device (in this case, a router) translates addresses on the inside network 172.16.0.0 to addresses on the outside network 10.1.0.0.

Figure 3-1 *NAT Translates Between Inside and Outside Addresses*

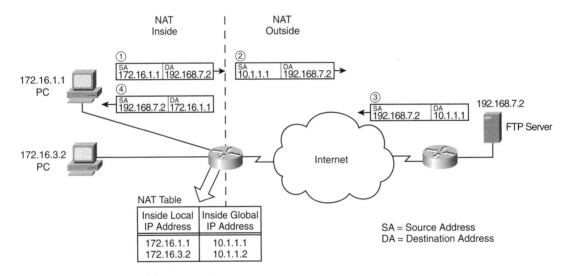

NOTE Recall that the IP addresses shown in the examples in this book are private addresses. In practice, public addresses would be used on the Internet.

A NAT device has a NAT table, created either dynamically or with static entries configured by the network administrator. In Figure 3-1, the simple NAT table in the NAT router includes the following:

- **Inside local IP address**—The address used by a host on the inside network

- **Inside global IP address**—The address that represents an inside host on the outside network

When a packet is sent from 172.16.1.1 to 192.168.7.2 (at 1 in Figure 3-1), it goes to the NAT router, which translates the source address (SA) 172.16.1.1 to 10.1.1.1 (at 2 in the figure). The packet then goes through the Internet and arrives at its destination, the FTP server. The server replies to 10.1.1.1 (at 3 in the figure). When the NAT router receives this packet, the router looks in its NAT table and translates the destination address (DA) from 10.1.1.1 to 172.16.1.1 (at 4 in the figure). The packet is then sent to its destination, the PC.

More complex translations might be necessary, for example, if some addresses in the inside network overlap addresses in the outside network. In this case, the NAT table would be expanded to include the following:

- **Outside global IP address**—The address that represents an outside host on the outside network

- **Outside local IP address**—The address that represents an outside host on the inside network

The example in Figure 3-1 shows a one-to-one translation from inside to outside addresses. NAT can also support address overloading, in which many inside addresses are translated into one outside address. In this case, the Transmission Control Protocol (TCP) and User Datagram Protocol (UDP) port numbers distinguish between the connections; the TCP and UDP port numbers are added to the NAT translation table.

How Routers Use Subnet Masks

When you configure the IP address of a router's interface, you include the address and the subnet mask. The router uses this information not only to address the interface but also to determine the address of the subnet to which the interface is connected. The router then puts this subnet address in its routing table, as a connected network on that interface.

KEY POINT

To determine the network or subnet address to which a router is connected, the router performs a *logical AND* of the interface address and the subnet mask. Logically "ANDing" a binary 1 with any number yields that number; logically "ANDing" a binary 0 with any number yields 0.

Because subnet mask bits set to binary 0 indicate that the corresponding bits in the IP address are host bits, the result of this AND operation is that the host portion of the address is removed (zeroed out), and the subnet address (also called the subnet number) remains.

Table 3-1 illustrates an example of logically ANDing an IP address and subnet mask. The router puts the remaining subnet address in its routing table as the subnet to which the interface is connected.

Table 3-1 *Example Calculation of Subnet Address*

	Network	Subnet	Subnet	Host
Interface IP Address 10.5.23.19	00001010	00000101	00010111	00010011
Subnet Mask 255.255.255.0	11111111	11111111	11111111	00000000
Subnet Address 10.5.23.0	00001010	00000101	00010111	00000000

When a packet arrives at the router, the router analyzes the destination address of the packet to determine which network or subnet it is on. The router looks up this network or subnet in its routing table to determine the interface through which it can best be reached; the packet is then sent out of the appropriate router interface. [If the router does not have a route to the destination subnet, the packet is rejected and an Internet Control Message Protocol (ICMP) error message is sent to the source of the packet.]

Determining the Subnet Mask to Use

When addressing your network, you must determine the subnet mask to use. Because the subnet mask represents the number of bits of network, subnet, and host available for addressing, the subnet mask selected depends on the number of subnets required and the number of host addresses required on each of these subnets.

For example, consider the network shown in Figure 3-2. A total of 12 subnets exist in this network; each has a maximum of 10 device addresses. Some of the addresses are for router interfaces and some are for hosts (not shown in the figure); each device on each subnet needs to have its own IP address. You decide to use the private Class C network 192.168.3.0 to address this network.

Figure 3-2   *The Number of Subnets and Hosts Required Determines the Subnet Mask to Use*

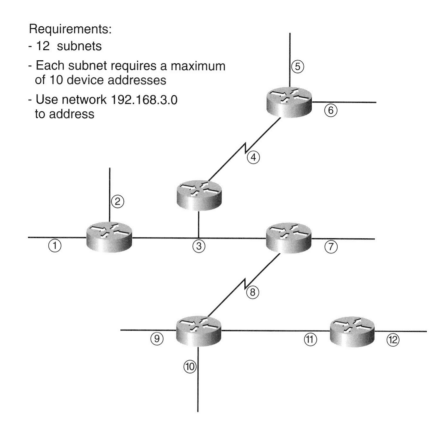

Requirements:
- 12 subnets
- Each subnet requires a maximum of 10 device addresses
- Use network 192.168.3.0 to address

In a Class C address, only the last octet contains host bits, and therefore this is the only octet from which bits can be borrowed for subnets.

KEY POINT

Because IP addresses are binary, they are used in blocks of powers of 2 (2, 4, 8, and so on).

To determine the size of the block needed for the subnets, round the number of subnets required up to the next higher power of 2 (if it is not already a power of 2).

To determine the size of the block needed for the hosts, add 2—one for the subnet address (also referred to as the wire address) and one for the broadcast address—to the maximum number of hosts required per subnet, and round this number up to the next higher power of 2 (again, if it is not already a power of 2).

In the example in Figure 3-2, 12 subnets are needed; rounding up to the next power of 2 gives 16. Because $2^4 = 16$, 4 bits are needed for the subnets. A maximum of 10 device addresses per subnet are needed; adding 2 and rounding up to the next power of 2 gives 16. Because $2^4 = 16$, 4 bits are needed for the hosts. The subnet mask to use is therefore 255.255.255.240.

To determine the available subnet addresses, first write the network address in binary. Then, keeping the network bits as they are, use all combinations of the subnet bits. Remember that all the host bits are 0 in the subnet address, so leave the host bits set to 0. Finally, convert the binary number back to decimal. Figure 3-3 illustrates this process. (Note that any octets not changed in this process are left as decimal numbers, to save converting them twice.)

Figure 3-3 *Calculating Subnet Addresses*

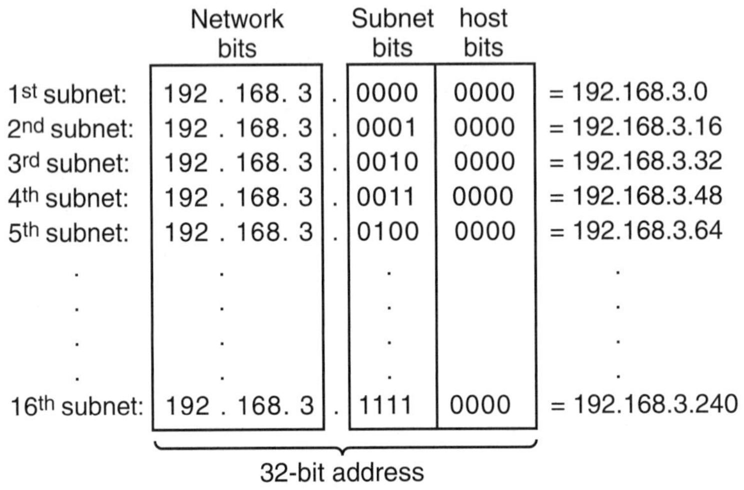

Thus, the first subnet address that can be used with a mask of 255.255.255.240 is 192.168.3.0; this can also be written as 192.168.3.0/28. The second subnet is 192.168.3.16/28, and so on.

To determine the device addresses on each subnet, first write the subnet address in binary. Next, keeping the network and subnet bits as they are, use all the combinations of the host bits. Remember that the address in which all host bits are 0 is the subnet address, and the address in which all host bits are 1 is the broadcast address. Finally, convert the binary number back to decimal. Figure 3-4 illustrates this process for the third subnet, 192.168.3.32/28. (Again, note that any octets not changed in this process are left as decimal numbers, to save converting them twice.)

Figure 3-4   *Calculating Device Addresses*

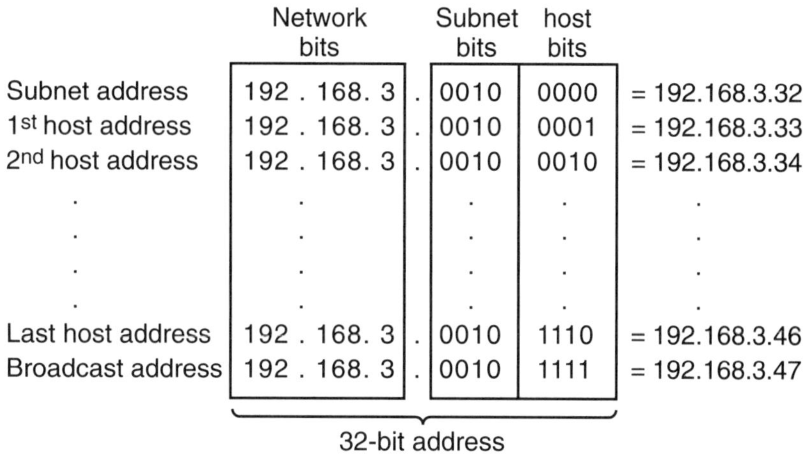

Thus, the first device address on this subnet is 192.168.3.33/28, the second device address is 192.168.3.34/28, and so on. The last host address is 192.168.3.46/28. The broadcast address is 192.168.3.47/28. For example, the network marked as "3" in Figure 3-2 could be assigned the 192.168.3.32/28 subnet. The interfaces of the three routers on that subnet could be assigned addresses 192.168.3.33/28, 192.168.3.34/28, and 192.168.3.35/28.

Hierarchical IP Address Design and Summarization

A hierarchical IP address design means that addresses are assigned in a hierarchical manner, rather than randomly. The telephone network provides a good analogy. This network is divided into countries, which in turn are divided into areas and local exchanges. Phone numbers are assigned based on location. For example, in North America, 10-digit phone numbers represent a 3-digit area code, a 3-digit central office code, and a 4-digit line number. So if you are in Europe and you want to call someone in Canada, you dial his country code followed by his area code, central office, and line number. The telephone network switches in Europe recognize the country code and send the call to Canada; they don't have to worry about the details of the phone number. The switches in Canada send the call to the appropriate area code, to the central office, and finally to the correct line.

This hierarchical structure allows the telephone switches to keep less detailed information about the network. For example, a central office (CO) switch only needs to know how to get to the numbers served by its equipment, and how to get to other COs and other area codes, but it doesn't need to know how to get to the specific numbers in other COs. For example, 416 is the area code for downtown Toronto. Switches outside of Toronto only need to know how to get to 416; they don't need to know how to get to each number in Toronto. Area code 416 can be considered to be a summary of Toronto.

An IP network can use a similar hierarchical structure to get comparable benefits. When routers only have summary routes instead of unnecessary details, their routing tables are smaller. Not only does this save memory in the routers, but it also means that routing updates are smaller and therefore use less bandwidth on the network. Hierarchical addressing can also result in a more efficient allocation of addresses. With some routing protocols (known as *classful routing protocols*), addresses can be wasted if they are assigned randomly (as explained further in the "Classifying Routing Protocols" section, later in this chapter.)

To illustrate, consider the network shown in Figure 3-5. Subnet addresses were assigned sequentially as the subnets were created, regardless of architecture, resulting in a random pattern. Consequently, when Router A sends its routing table to the other routers, it has no choice but to send all its routes.

Figure 3-5 *Router A Cannot Summarize Its Routes Because of Random Address Assignment*

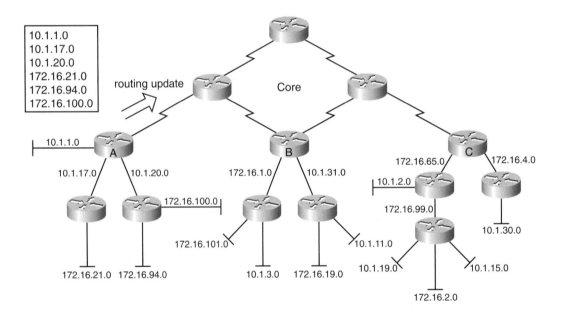

Contrast this to the network in Figure 3-6, in which subnets were assigned in a hierarchical manner. Notice, for example, that all the subnets under Router A start with 10.1, while all under Router B start with 10.2. Therefore, the routers can summarize the subnets. When they communicate to other routers, they don't send all the detailed routes; they just send the summary route. Not only does this save bandwidth on the network (because smaller updates are sent), but it also means that the routing tables in the core are smaller, which eases processing requirements. It also means that small local problems don't need to be communicated network-wide. For example, if network 10.1.1.0 under Router A goes down, the summary route 10.1.0.0/16 does not change, so the routers in the core and other areas are not told about it. They do not need to process the route change, and the update does not use bandwidth on the network. (If traffic is routed to a device on that network that is down, Router A will respond with an error message, so the network can continue to function normally.)

Figure 3-6   *Router A Can Summarize Its Routes, Resulting in Smaller Routing Tables*

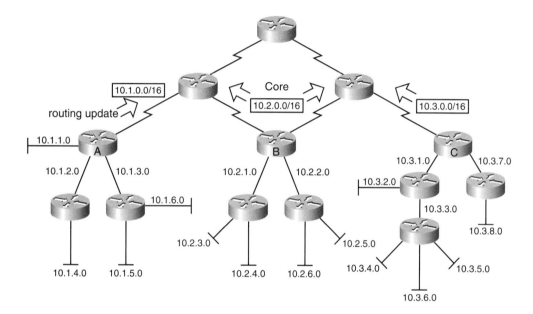

The summary routes shown in Figure 3-6 are obvious—all the subnets under Router A start with 10.1 and thus the summary route is 10.1.0.0/16. It isn't always this easy.

For example, consider a network in which Router A has the following subnet routes in its routing table: 192.168.3.64/28, 192.168.3.80/28, 192.168.3.96/28, and 192.168.3.112/28. Router B in the same network has the following subnet routes in its routing table: 192.168.3.0/28, 192.168.3.16/28, 192.168.3.32/28, and 192.168.3.48/28. What is the summary route for Router A's subnets? While you might be tempted to use 192.168.3.0/24 because they all have the first three octets in common, this won't work. If both Routers A and B reported the same 192.168.3.0/24 summary route, traffic would not necessarily go to the correct router, resulting in a nonfunctioning network. Instead, you have to determine the summary routes on nonoctet boundaries. Figure 3-7 illustrates how this is done.

Figure 3-7 *Route Summarization on a Nonoctet Boundary*

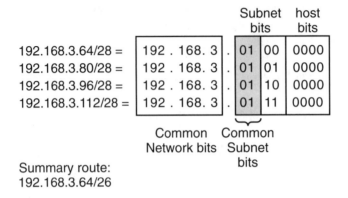

To calculate the summary route, first write the subnet addresses in binary. Then, determine which network and subnet bits the addresses have in common—it can be helpful to draw a line at the end of the common bits. (Notice that the network portions of the addresses are all common, because they are all subnets of the same network.) In this case, the addresses have the first two subnet bits in common. The addresses should also encompass all combinations of the remaining subnet bits so that the summary route covers only these subnets; in this example, the addresses do cover all combinations of the remaining two subnet bits. Thus, if an address matches the network bits and the first two subnet bits of these addresses, it is on one of these four subnets. The summary route is written as the first address in the list with a prefix equal to the total number of common bits. In this example, the summary is 192.168.3.64/26. Similarly, the summary route for Router B is 192.168.3.0/26.

KEY POINT | Another way to think of the summary route 192.168.3.64/26 is that Router A is saying "I have all routes that match the first 26 bits of the address 192.168.3.64."

Variable-Length Subnet Masks

Consider the network in the upper portion of Figure 3-8. All the subnets are configured with a /24 mask, meaning that up to $2^8 - 2 = 254$ hosts can be addressed. This can be useful on the LAN links. However, only two addresses will ever be required on each of the point-to-point serial WAN connections between the two routers, one for each of the routers. Therefore, the other 252 addresses available on each of these WAN subnets are wasted.

Figure 3-8   *Using the Same Mask on LAN and WAN Links Can Waste Addresses; Using Different Masks Can Be a More Efficient Use of the Available Addresses*

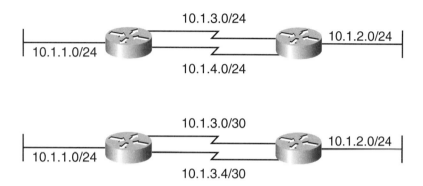

KEY POINT block:

KEY POINT   A major network is a Class A, B, or C network.

A fixed-length subnet mask (FLSM) is when all subnet masks in a major network must be the same size.

A VLSM is when subnet masks within a major network can be different sizes.

The routing protocol in use in the network influences whether VLSMs can be used—we discuss why in the "Classifying Routing Protocols" section, later in this chapter. If a routing protocol supports VLSMs, IP addresses can be allocated more efficiently. For example, in the network shown in the lower portion of Figure 3-8, the LAN subnets use a /24 mask, while the WAN subnets use a more appropriate /30 mask. With a /30 mask, only 2 host bits exist, and therefore $2^2 - 2 = 2$ host addresses are available. This is the exact number of addresses required, one for each of the routers.

Using VLSMs also means that the addressing plan can have more levels of hierarchy, resulting in routes that can be summarized easily. This in turn results in smaller routing tables and more efficient updates.

To see how VLSM addresses are calculated, consider the network in the upper portion of Figure 3-9, with one LAN requiring 150 addresses, two LANs requiring 100 addresses each, and two point-to-point WANs. You have been given the 10.5.16.0/20 address space to use in this network, and you have been asked to conserve as many addresses as possible (which also makes this exercise as challenging as possible).

Figure 3-9 *The Number of Addresses Required Determines the Subnet to Use*

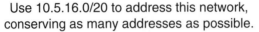

Use 10.5.16.0/20 to address this network,
conserving as many addresses as possible.

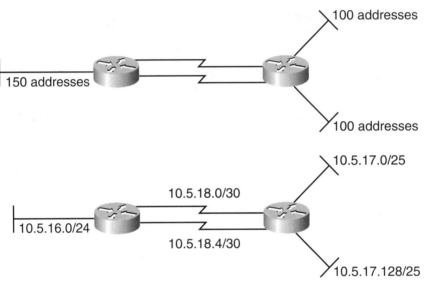

100 addresses

150 addresses

100 addresses

10.5.17.0/25

10.5.18.0/30

10.5.16.0/24

10.5.18.4/30

10.5.17.128/25

For the left LAN, 150 addresses are needed; rounding up to the next power of 2 gives 256. Because $2^8 = 256$, 8 host bits are needed. For the other two LANs, 100 addresses are needed; rounding up to the next power of 2 gives 128. Because $2^7 = 128$, 7 host bits are needed for each LAN. The WANs require 2 host bits each.

Because at most 8 host bits are needed, the 10.5.16.0/20 address can be further subnetted into sixteen /24 subnets (leaving 8 host bits): 10.5.16.0/24, 10.5.17.0/24, and so on, up to 10.5.31.0/24, as shown at the top of Figure 3-10. Subnet 10.5.16.0/24 can be used to address the left LAN.

Figure 3-10   *Calculating the VLSM Subnetting for the Network in Figure 3-9*

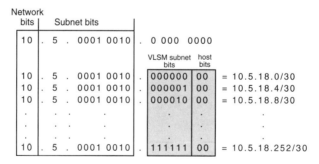

One of the unused /24 subnets, 10.5.17.0/24, can be further subnetted by 1 bit, resulting in $2^1 = 2$ subnets, each with 7 host bits, as shown in the middle of Figure 3-10. The 10.5.17.0/25 and 10.5.17.128/25 subnets can be used to address the LANs on the right.

Another of the unused /24 subnets, 10.5.18.0/24, can be further subnetted by 6 bits, resulting in $2^6 = 64$ subnets, each with 2 host bits, as shown at the bottom of Figure 3-10. Two of these subnets can be used to address the WANs. The resulting addresses are shown in the lower portion of Figure 3-9.

**KEY
POINT** Remember that only *unused* subnets should be further subnetted. In other words, if you use any addresses from a subnet, that subnet should not be further subnetted. In the example in the lower portion of Figure 3-9, one subnet, 10.5.16.0/24, is used on the left LAN. One of the unused subnets, 10.5.17.0/24, is further subnetted for use on the other two LANs. Another, as yet unused, subnet, 10.5.18.0/24, is further subnetted for use on the WANs.

> **NOTE**   Because only two devices exist on point-to-point links, a specification has been developed (as documented in RFC 3021, "Using 31-Bit Prefixes on IPv4 Point-to-Point Links") to allow the use of only 1 host bit on such links, resulting in a /31 mask. The two addresses created—with the host bit equal to 0 and with the host bit equal to 1—are to be interpreted as the addresses of the interfaces on either end of the link rather than as the subnet address and the directed broadcast address. Support for /31 masks is provided on some Cisco devices running IOS Release 12.2 and later; details regarding the support for this (and other features) on specific platforms and IOS releases are identified at the Cisco feature navigator site (http://www.cisco.com/go/fn).

IPv4 Routing Protocols

Recall that routers work at the Open Systems Interconnection (OSI) model network layer, and that the main functions of a router are first to determine the best path that each packet should take to get to its destination, and second to send the packet on its way.

To determine the best path on which to send a packet, a router must know where the packet's destination network is. Routers learn about networks by being physically connected to them or by learning about them either from other routers or from a network administrator. Routes configured by network administrators are known as *static routes* because they are hard-coded in the router and remain there—static—until the administrator removes them. Routes to which a router is physically connected are known as *directly connected routes*. Routers learn routes from other routers by using a *routing protocol*.

**KEY
POINT** A router uses a *routing protocol* to learn routes which it then puts in a routing table. A *routed protocol* is the type of packet forwarded, or routed, through a network.[4]

IP is a routed protocol; this section explores routing protocols that can be used for IP. First, we examine ways in which routing protocols are classified. We then discuss the different metrics that routing protocols use to determine the best way to get to each destination network. This is followed by a discussion of how convergence time and the ability to summarize routes are affected by the choice of routing protocol. The final portion of this section describes the specific IP routing protocols.

Classifying Routing Protocols

You can classify routing protocols in many ways. In the following sections, we describe four ways: interior versus exterior, distance vector versus link state versus hybrid, flat versus hierarchical routing, and classful versus classless routing.

Interior and Exterior Routing Protocols

An autonomous system (AS) is a network controlled by one organization; it uses interior routing protocols, called interior gateway protocols (IGPs) within it, and exterior routing protocols, called exterior gateway protocols (EGPs), to communicate with other autonomous systems.

Distance Vector, Link-State, and Hybrid Routing Protocols

When a network is using a *distance vector routing protocol,* all the routers send their routing tables (or a portion of their tables) to only their neighboring routers. The routers then use the received information to determine whether any changes need to be made to their own routing table (for example, if a better way to a specific network is now available). The process repeats periodically.

In contrast, when a network is using a *link-state routing protocol,* each of the routers sends the state of its own interfaces (its links) to all other routers (or to all routers in a part of the network, known as an area) only when there is a change to report. Each router uses the received information to recalculate the best path to each network and then saves this information in its routing table.

As its name suggests, a *hybrid protocol* borrows from both distance vector and link-state protocols. Hybrid protocols send only changed information (similar to link-state) but only to neighboring routers (similar to distance vector).

KEY POINT In summary, link-state protocols send small updates everywhere only when a change occurs, while distance vector protocols send larger updates periodically only to neighboring routers. Hybrid routing protocols send small updates only to neighboring routers and only when a change occurs.

Link-state routers have knowledge of the entire network, while distance vector routers only know what their neighbors tell them.

Routers running distance vector routing protocols typically send updates in broadcast packets, while those running link-state and hybrid routing protocols send the updates in multicast packets. Recall that broadcast packets are received and processed by all devices on a network, so even servers and PCs that have no need to see routing updates are interrupted by those sent in broadcast packets. In contrast, special multicast addresses are defined for each routing protocol that uses them. Only routers that are configured for that routing protocol and therefore need to receive the updates receive and process them; other devices are not interrupted.

Routers running distance vector routing protocols have rules in place to help prevent *routing loops.*

KEY POINT   A *routing loop* occurs when packets bounce back and forth between routers because the routers are confused as to the best way to reach a destination network. These loops can occur if a network has changed but the routers have not yet all agreed on what the changed network looks like.

One of these rules for distance vector routing protocols is known as the *split-horizon rule*. This rule states that if a router has a route in its routing table (in other words, if a router is using a route) that it learned through an interface, it must not advertise that route out of that same interface (even to a different device on that interface). This works fine unless the routing protocol is being used in a nonbroadcast multiaccess (NBMA) network, such as Frame Relay. In an NBMA environment, multiple routers are connected to each other using multiple virtual circuits on one interface. For example, in the network in Figure 3-11, when Router A learns a route from Router B, it wants to pass it to Router C. However, the split-horizon rule prevents it from doing this, because Router A has only one physical interface, connected to both Routers B and C. (You can find ways around this problem, including defining multiple virtual subinterfaces, one for each virtual circuit, on the physical interface.)

Figure 3-11   *The Distance Vector Split-Horizon Rule Prevents Router A from Passing Routes Learned from Routers B to C*

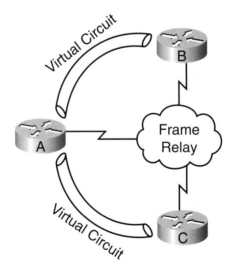

Distance vector routing protocols also use a hold-down mechanism to help prevent routing loops. When a router running a distance vector routing protocol receives information that a route to a destination has changed with the same or worse metric, it marks the route as being in a hold-down state; the new route is not put into the routing table until the hold-down timer expires, to give time for the other routers in the network to learn the new information.

Flat and Hierarchical Routing Protocols

Flat routing protocols have no way to restrict routes from being propagated within a major network (a Class A, B, or C network). In contrast, hierarchical routing protocols allow the network administrator to separate the network into areas and limit how routes are propagated between areas. This in turn reduces the routing table size and amount of routing protocol traffic in the network.

Classful and Classless Routing Protocols

Routing protocols can be categorized as *classful* or *classless.*

KEY POINT

Routing updates sent by a classful routing protocol do not include the subnet mask.

Routing updates sent by a classless routing protocol include the subnet mask.

Because classful routing updates do not come with a subnet mask, devices must assume what the subnet mask associated with a received route is. If a router has an interface in the same major network as the received route, it assumes the same mask; otherwise, it assumes the default mask, based on the class of the address. The IP address design implications of using a classful routing protocol are as follows:

■   FLSMs must be used; in other words, all subnets of the same major network must use the same subnet mask.

■   All subnets of the same major network must be contiguous; in other words, all subnets of the same major network must be reachable from each other without going through a part of any other major network.

■   Classful routing protocols automatically summarize routes on the major network boundary.

Figure 3-12 uses subnet addresses from three major networks. The upper portion of the figure illustrates routes sent through a network using a classful routing protocol. Router B assumes that the mask of the 10.1.1.0 route sent by Router A must be the same as the mask on the 10.1.2.0 subnet to which it is connected, because the mask is not sent along with the route. Router B summarizes all subnets of network 10.0.0.0 when it sends routing information to Router C because it is sending the route on an interface that is in a different major network. For the same reason, Router C summarizes network 172.16.0.0 when it sends routing information to Router D.

Figure 3-12 *Classful Routing Protocols Automatically Summarize on Major Network Boundaries; Classless Routing Protocols Do Not Have To*

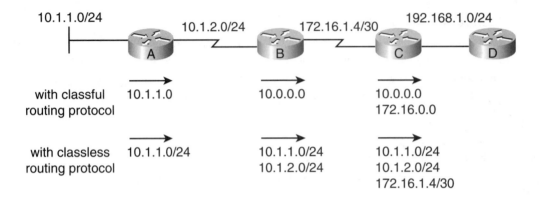

Classless routing protocols include the subnet mask information with routing updates, so devices do not have to make any assumptions about the mask that is being used. Therefore, classless routing protocols support VLSMs, and subnets of the same major network can be discontiguous. Classless routing protocols also allow route summarization to be manually configured and to be turned off if it is automatic on the major network boundary. The lower portion of Figure 3-12 illustrates the routing information that could be sent when using a classless routing protocol.

Figure 3-13 illustrates a discontiguous network. Three subnets of the major network 10.0.0.0 are allocated to the three LANs, and the three WANs are using subnets from the major network 172.16.0.0. If a classful routing protocol was used, Routers A, B, and C would all automatically summarize when sending routes to Router D—Router D would have three routes to network 10.0.0.0. Router D would therefore send traffic for any of the subnets of 10.0.0.0 to any of the other three routers, thinking that any of them can get to any of the available subnets; however, you can see from the topology that this is not true.

Figure 3-13 *Classful Routing Protocols Do Not Support Discontiguous Networks; Classless Routing Protocols Do*

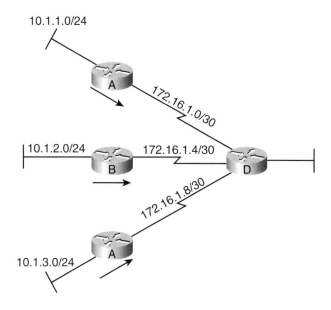

Instead, if a classless routing protocol is used, the following could be configured on the routers:

- Router A could report the route 10.1.1.0/24.

- Router B could report the route 10.1.2.0/24.

- Router C could report the route 10.1.3.0/24.

Router D could then send traffic for destinations on the three subnets to the correct router.

Metrics

One of a router's jobs is to determine the best path to each destination network. The routing protocol *metric* is the value that the routing protocol uses to evaluate which path is best. Metrics can include the following factors:

- **Hop count**—The number of hops, or other routers, to the destination network; the path with the least number of hops is preferred.

- **Bandwidth**—The path with the lowest bandwidth segment is the least preferred path.

- **Delay**—The path with the lowest accumulated delay (also called *latency*) is the preferred path.

- **Cost**—Usually inversely related to bandwidth; in other words, the path with the slowest links has the highest cost and is the least preferred path.

- **Load**—The utilization of the path (in other words, how much of the bandwidth is currently being used). For example, in the Cisco Interior Gateway Routing Protocol (IGRP) and Enhanced Interior Gateway Routing Protocol (EIGRP) metrics, load can be included as a number from 0 to 255, representing a 5-minute exponentially weighted average load. Load is not included by default in these calculations because it can be constantly changing.

- **Reliability**—The likelihood of successful packet transmission. For example, in IGRP and EIGRP metrics, reliability can be included as a number from 0 to 255, with 255 meaning 100 percent reliability and 0 meaning no reliability. Reliability is not included by default in these calculations because it can change often (for example, with heavy traffic load).

Some routing protocols use a composite metric, which is a combination of various factors. For example, IGRP and EIGRP use a metric that can include the bandwidth, delay, load, and reliability of the path. (However, by default, these protocols only use the bandwidth and delay in their metric calculations, as described in the "Routing Protocol Comparison" section, later in this chapter.)

KEY POINT

A lower metric value indicates a better path. For example, a path with a hop count of 2 is preferred over a path with a hop count of 5.

Note, however, that comparisons can only be made between the same metric type; for example, you cannot compare a hop count of 2 to a cost of 10.

On Cisco routers, all IP routing protocols support *equal-cost* (or *equal-metric*) *load balancing,* the ability to keep multiple paths, with the same metric, to the same destination network, and balance (or share) the load between those paths. By default, Cisco routers can keep up to four equal-cost paths and can be configured to keep up to six such paths.

Convergence Time

KEY POINT

A network is *converged* when the routing tables in all the routers are synchronized so that they all contain a usable route to every available network.

Convergence time is the time it takes all the routers in a network to agree on the network's topology, after that topology has changed.

Network design impacts convergence time significantly; in fact, proper network design is a must, or else the network might never converge.[5] Other factors that affect the convergence time include the routing protocol used, the size of the network (the number of routers), and various configurable timers.

For example, consider the type of routing protocol used. Assuming a proper design, link-state routing protocols usually converge quicker than distance vector routing protocols, because they immediately send the change to all other routers. Link-state routing protocols have a timer that prevents them from calculating the new routes immediately (so that many changes can be incorporated into one calculation); thus, they tend to converge within a few seconds.

Distance vector algorithms send updates periodically (every 30, 60, or 90 seconds is typical), so you might think that it takes a long time for changes to propagate. Fortunately, the distance vector routing protocols in use today are usually more intelligent and send flash updates. *Flash updates,* also called *triggered updates,* are sent as soon as something changes so that the routers are notified quickly. However, another mechanism prevents these routing protocols from converging fast—the hold-down mechanism (to prevent routing loops). When a router running a distance vector routing protocol receives information that a route to a destination has changed with the same or worse metric, it marks the route as being in a hold-down state; the new route is not put into the routing table until the hold-down timer expires. The hold-down timer is typically set to three times the periodic update timer; this gives time for the other routers in the network to learn the new information. Note, however, that a route in the hold-down state is still used to forward traffic. Therefore, if a link goes down and then comes up before the hold-down timer expires, it will be reachable. If the link remains down for the hold-down period, though, the router connected to the link will reply to any packets destined for devices on the link with an error message.

EIGRP is a hybrid routing protocol; it therefore has different convergence characteristics. EIGRP does not use periodic updates or hold-down timers; it does send flash updates to its neighboring routers, but only when necessary. EIGRP not only keeps the best routes in its routing table, but it also keeps all the routes to all destinations in another table, called a *topology table.* If the best route to a destination goes down, a router running EIGRP simply has to get the next-best route from the topology table, if one exists, and put it in its routing table; thus EIGRP can converge extremely fast. The router only has to talk to its neighboring routers if a suitable next-best route in its topology table doesn't exist. This can occur, for example, if the downed link has resulted in a significant change in the network, or if specific routes are no longer reachable through any paths.

NOTE   The "Routing Protocol Comparison" section, later in this chapter, details the operation of each IP routing protocol.

Route Summarization

The routing protocol choice affects summarization. As noted in the "Classful and Classless Routing Protocols" section earlier in this chapter, classful routing protocols automatically summarize on the major network boundary; this automatic behavior cannot be turned off. Some classless routing protocols also automatically summarize, but do allow summarization to be turned off and also allow summarization to be turned on at other boundaries.

Routing Protocol Comparison

The following routing protocols can be used for IP:

- Routing Information Protocol (RIP), versions 1 and 2 (RIPv1 and RIPv2)

- IGRP

- EIGRP

- Open Shortest Path First (OSPF)

- Integrated Intermediate System-to-Intermediate System (IS-IS)

- Border Gateway Protocol (BGP) Version 4 (BGP4)

Table 3-2 shows where these routing protocols fit in the various categories discussed earlier in this chapter. Each of the routing protocols is further described in the following sections. Later in this chapter, the "IPv4 Routing Protocol Selection" section describes how to choose which routing protocols you should use in your network, and what you need to consider if you decide to use more than one routing protocol.

Table 3-2   *Routing Protocol Comparison Chart[6]*

Characteristic	RIPv1	RIPv2	IGRP	EIGRP	OSPF	Integrated IS-IS	BGP-4
Interior	✓	✓	✓	✓	✓	✓	
Exterior							✓
Distance vector	✓	✓	✓	✓*			✓**
Link-state				✓*	✓	✓	
Hierarchical topology required					✓	✓	
Hierarchical topology supported				✓	✓	✓	
Classless		✓		✓	✓	✓	✓
Classful	✓		✓				
VLSMs supported		✓		✓	✓	✓	✓

Table 3-2   *Routing Protocol Comparison Chart[6] (Continued)*

Characteristic	RIPv1	RIPv2	IGRP	EIGRP	OSPF	Integrated IS-IS	BGP-4
Metric	Hops	Hops	Com-posite	Com-posite	Cost	Cost	Path Attributes
Convergence time	Slow	Slow	Slow	Very Fast	Fast	Fast	Slow
Automatic route summarization at classful network boundary	✓	✓	✓	✓			✓
Ability to turn off automatic summarization		✓		✓			✓
Ability to summarize at other than classful network boundary		✓***		✓	✓	✓	✓
Size of network supported	Small	Small	Medium	Large	Large	Very Large	Very Large

*EIGRP is a hybrid routing protocol, with some distance vector and some link-state characteristics.

**BGP is a path vector routing protocol.

***RIPv2 summarization has some restrictions; for details, refer to "IP Summary Address for RIPv2" at http://www.cisco.com/en/US/products/sw/iosswrel/ps1830products_feature_ guide09186a0080087 ad1.html

Routing Information Protocol, Versions 1 and 2

RIP is the original IP distance vector routing protocol. RIPv1 is classful and RIPv2 is classless. RIP's metric is hop count; for each destination, it selects the path with the least number of routers. The hop count is limited to 15, so RIP is only suitable for small networks.

RIPv1 is not as popular as it once was. However, RIPv2 can still be used for small networks. The main advantage of using RIP is its simplicity, as explained in the following list:

■ It is easy to understand how it works.

■ It is easy to predict which way traffic will flow because RIP only uses hop count for its metric.

■ It is relatively easy to configure.

■ It is relatively easy to troubleshoot.

Both RIPv1 and RIPv2 automatically summarize at the major network boundary; RIPv2 allows this functionality to be turned off, so it supports discontiguous addressing. Other RIPv2 improvements over RIPv1 include its support for VLSMs, its use of multicast rather than broadcast for sending routing updates, and its support for authenticating routing updates to ensure that routes are only exchanged with authorized routers.

The main disadvantages of using RIP are its slow convergence (because it is a distance vector routing protocol) and the fact that it only uses hop count as its metric—it selects the path with the least number of routers to the destination, without regard to the speed of the links on the path. For example, RIP would choose a route that is two hops through a slow WAN connection rather than going three hops over Ethernet.

RIP's *snapshot routing* feature allows it to be used on a dial-up network. This feature allows the router on each side of the connection to take a snapshot of the routing table while the link is up, and use that snapshot to update any other routers on its side of the connection while the link is down. The link is only brought up when necessary, for example, when data needs to be sent across it—during that time, the routing table can be updated.

Interior Gateway Routing Protocol

IGRP is a Cisco-proprietary routing protocol developed by Cisco to include many improvements over RIP. As a classful distance vector routing protocol though, IGRP has relatively slow convergence, does not support VLSMs, and automatically summarizes routes at the classful network boundary. The distance vector split-horizon feature also restricts its ability to work on NBMA networks, such as Frame Relay.

However, IGRP's metric provides a more useful gauge of a path's suitability in most networks. IGRP uses a composite metric, with bandwidth, delay, load, and reliability all factored into the metric equation. Some constants are used in the metric calculation; with their default values, the IGRP metric formula is as follows:

metric = bandwidth + delay

The terms in this formula are defined as follows:

- The *bandwidth* is 1,000,000 divided by the smallest bandwidth along the path—in other words, the slowest link—in kilobits per second (kbps).

- The *delay* is the sum of all the outgoing delays along the path in microseconds, divided by 10.

NOTE   The hop count and the maximum transmission unit (MTU) are also carried along with IGRP routing updates. The MTU is the maximum packet size that can be sent without fragmentation.

A lower metric value indicates a better path—faster with the least amount of delay.

IGRP allows the network to be divided into what it calls autonomous systems, although this is a different use of the term than in the previous discussion of interior and exterior routing protocols. You can think of IGRP's use of the term as being similar to groups: You can have different groups of routers running IGRP, and routing information is not shared among the groups unless you explicitly configure the routers to do so. For example, if your network is running IGRP and your organization acquires another organization that is also running IGRP, you might want to keep the two networks separate initially, and just share specific routes. The autonomous system numbers allow this to be accomplished easily.

Another feature introduced in IGRP is the ability to load-balance, or load-share, over unequal-cost paths, not just over equal-cost paths, as other routing protocols can do. For example, consider the network shown in Figure 3-14. From Router A's perspective, network 172.16.2.0 can be reached in two ways—through the serial 0 (S0) interface at 64 kbps or through the serial 1 (S1) interface at 128 kbps. Ordinarily, the 128-kbps link would be chosen as the preferred path because it is faster, and all traffic would flow over that link. The 64-kbps link would not be used (unless and until the faster link became unavailable). IGRP allows unequal-cost load balancing so that traffic can flow across both links, in proportion to their speed. This makes better use of the available bandwidth.

Figure 3-14 *GRP (and EIGRP) Can Load-Balance over Both Equal- and Unequal-Cost Paths*

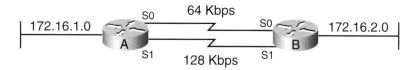

Like RIP, IGRP is easy to configure and troubleshoot. However, because of its classful distance vector behavior, IGRP is seldom used in today's networks; EIGRP is a better choice because it retains all of IGRP's advantages and overcomes its disadvantages. In fact, Cisco will be discontinuing IGRP in future software releases, and recommends EIGRP in its place.[1]

NOTE   Cisco has made it easy to change from running IGRP to EIGRP on a network. The conversion can be made gradually, because routes between the two routing protocols are automatically shared if the same autonomous system number is used when configuring both protocols.

Enhanced Interior Gateway Routing Protocol

EIGRP, as its name indicates, is an enhanced version of IGRP and is also Cisco-proprietary. EIGRP is a classless hybrid routing protocol that combines the best features of distance vector and link-state routing protocols. EIGRP performs well on LANs and WANs, including in NBMA environments; unlike distance vector routing protocols, EIGRP's split-horizon feature can be turned off if necessary for use on an NBMA network.

> **NOTE** EIGRP is not appropriate for use on a dial-up network because it maintains the relationship with its neighboring routers by sending hello messages periodically. Doing this on a dial-up connection would mean that the link would have to remain up all the time.

EIGRP can be used to route not just IP but also Internetwork Packet Exchange (IPX) and AppleTalk routed protocols. Each of these routed protocols is handled completely independently. In this book, we only discuss the operation of EIGRP with respect to IP.

As a classless routing protocol, EIGRP supports VLSMs. It automatically summarizes on the classful network boundary, but this summarization can be turned off and summarization can be done at any other boundary in the network, by any of the EIGRP routers. This allows a hierarchical topology to be supported. Although this is good design practice, it is not required by EIGRP.

EIGRP is based on the Diffusing Update Algorithm (DUAL), which provides its very fast convergence. The following list of EIGRP terms helps to explain how EIGRP operates:

- **Neighbor table**—Each EIGRP router keeps a neighbor table to list the adjacent routers with which it has formed a neighbor relationship.

- **Topology table**—All routes learned to each destination, from all neighbors, are kept in the topology table.

- **Routing table**—Each EIGRP router chooses the best routes to each destination from its topology table and puts them in its routing table.

> **NOTE** EIGRP keeps a separate neighbor table, topology table, and routing table for each routed protocol for which it is running.

- **Successor**—A successor, also called a current successor, is a neighbor router that has the best route to a destination. Successor routes are kept in the routing table as well as in the topology table.

- **Feasible successor**—A feasible successor is a neighbor router that has a backup route to a destination. Feasible successor routes are chosen at the same time that successor routes are chosen, but they are only kept in the topology table. The DUAL algorithm only selects feasible successor routes that are loop-free; in other words, routes that do not loop back and go through the current router.

EIGRP routers exchange routes only with their neighboring routers—neighbor relationships are established and maintained with periodic, small, *hello messages*. Routing updates are only sent when a change occurs, and only the changed information from the routing table is sent. All EIGRP messages use multicast, rather than broadcast, to reduce interruptions of other network devices.

When an EIGRP router learns that a path it was using in its routing table (a successor route) has gone down, it looks in its topology table to see whether a usable backup route is available, through a feasible successor. If a route is available, the router copies that route to its routing table and starts using it—no further calculation or communication with other routers is required. As mentioned earlier, this can result in extremely fast convergence after a change in the network. An EIGRP router only has to send *query messages* to its neighbors—trying to find alternate routes to the destination now that the network has changed—if it doesn't have a suitable backup route in its topology table.

Convergence Time

Remember that network design is a critical factor in convergence times; the design should take advantage of all the routing protocol's features. In general, though, EIGRP networks typically have the fastest convergence times of all IP routing protocols if a feasible successor exists—the network can converge in much less than 1 second. If no feasible successor exists, query messages must be sent to neighboring routers, which might have to send them to their neighbors, and so on, resulting in longer convergence times. Link-state routing protocols typically converge faster than EIGRP without a feasible successor.[8]

The DUAL algorithm uses the same metric calculation as that used by IGRP, but the value is multiplied by 256 for EIGRP (because EIGRP uses 32 bits, instead of IGRP's 24 bits, for the metric). EIGRP, like IGRP, supports both equal- and unequal-cost load balancing.

EIGRP uses much less bandwidth than IGRP because it only sends the routing table entries that have changed only when a change occurs, rather than sending the entire table periodically. The bandwidth used by the periodic hello messages can be a concern on slower WAN links with many neighbors (as can occur on an NBMA network), but normally this is not an issue.

EIGRP, like IGRP, is easy to configure. It uses the same autonomous system numbers as IGRP, and in fact can automatically share information with IGRP routers configured with the same autonomous system number. No special configuration is required for different types of Layer 2 media (as is the case for OSPF, as described in the next section).

Open Shortest Path First

OSPF is a standard (not Cisco-proprietary) routing protocol, developed to overcome RIP's limitations. As a classless link-state routing protocol, it supports VLSMs and convergences quickly.

> **NOTE** The latest version of OSPF for IPv4, OSPF version 2, is described in RFC 2328, "OSPF Version 2."

OSPF requires a hierarchical design. The OSPF network is called a domain or an autonomous system and is divided into areas. One backbone area exists, area 0, to which all other areas must be connected and through which all traffic between other areas must flow. Figure 3-15 illustrates an OSPF network. Traffic between Routers E and F in this figure, for example, must flow from area 1 through Router A, through the backbone area 0, and then into area 3 through Router C. (Even if another physical link existed between the routers in these areas, it could not be used.)

Figure 3-15 *Traffic Between OSPF Areas Must Go Through the Backbone Area 0*

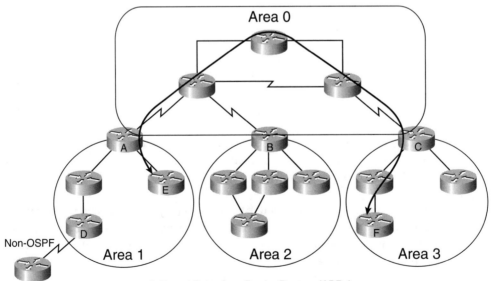

A, B, and C are Area Border Routers (ABRs)
D is an Autonumous System Boundary Router (ASBR)

The routers that are on the boundary between area 0 and another area are called Area Border Routers (ABRs); Routers A, B, and C in Figure 3-15 are ABRs. ABRs are responsible for passing traffic to and from the backbone. Routers that are the interface between the current OSPF domain and other domains (for example, using static routes) are called Autonomous System Boundary Routers (ASBRs). Router D in the figure is an ASBR. The ASBR takes care of exchanging routing information between the current OSPF domain and the external domain.

An OSPF router communicates and maintains relationships with other routers using a hello protocol, similar to the one used by EIGRP. OSPF routing updates are sent in link-state advertisements (LSAs), describing the state of links (interfaces); LSAs are sent in multicast packets called link-state updates (LSUs). An OSPF router exchanges LSAs about all its links with all the routers in its area so that all routers in an area have the same information. Each router puts this information in its topology table and then runs the shortest path first (SPF) algorithm to calculate its shortest path to each destination network. These shortest paths are put in the routing table.

Different types of LSAs are sent, depending on the type of router (ABR, ASBR, and so on) that is sending the advertisement. An OSPF router sends an LSA whenever it detects a change; this can result in a lot of bandwidth being used if the network is not stable. OSPF routers receive LSAs and run the SPF algorithm whenever a change occurs in the network. Timers ensure that OSPF waits for a few seconds after receiving an LSA before running SPF so that multiple changes can be incorporated into one SPF calculation. This helps to limit the resources used by OSPF, but it also means that the convergence time is increased.

NOTE   The OSPF incremental SPF feature, introduced in Cisco Internet Operating System (IOS) Release 12.0(24)S, allows OSPF to converge faster when a network topology changes. Information on this feature is available in the "OSPF Incremental SPF" document.[9]

OSPF routers do not automatically summarize routes. By default, all routing information is sent to all OSPF routers in the domain, although it might be sent in a different LSA type. Manual summarization can be configured, but only on ABRs and ASBRs. Thus, a sound IP addressing design is important, to ensure that the ABR can summarize routes so that the routing protocol traffic between areas is kept to a minimum.

OSPF also supports defining different types of areas to limit the amount of routing traffic passing into areas. For example, on Cisco routers an OSPF area can be configured as a *totally stubby area* so that only a default route is passed into the area; traffic for any destinations external to the area is sent out on the default route. This configuration is useful for areas that do not connect to non-OSPF networks. The routers within the area then only have to keep minimal routing information, but can still get to all destinations.

OSPF treats different Layer 2 media differently, and special configuration is required for some Layer 2 media. For example, OSPF can run on NBMA networks, but it requires special configuration to do so. For use over dial-up links, an OSPF feature called demand circuit (DC) can be configured; it suppresses the hello messages.

The metric used by OSPF is called the *cost,* and it is inversely proportional to the bandwidth of the interface—in other words, slower links have a higher cost. On Cisco routers, the default cost calculation is as follows:

$$\text{Cost} = \text{Reference bandwidth in Mbps} / \text{Bandwidth}$$

The default reference bandwidth is 100 Mbps. The bandwidth in this formula is the bandwidth defined on the interface, which can be configured differently than its default. Using the default reference bandwidth value in the formula assumes a maximum bandwidth of 100 Mbps (resulting in a cost of 1). You can change the reference bandwidth value on the routers in the network if you have faster interfaces (it should be set to the same value on all routers to ensure a consistent calculation). You can also manually set the cost on each interface.

OSPF does not limit the number of hops that a routing update can travel in the network.

In "Designing Large-Scale IP Internetworks,"[10] Cisco recommends the following guidelines:

■   An area should have no more than 50 routers.

■   Each router should have no more than 60 OSPF neighbors.

■   A router should not be in more than three areas.

These values are recommended to ensure that OSPF calculations do not overwhelm the routers. Of course, the network design and link stability can also affect the load on the routers.

Integrated Intermediate System-to-Intermediate System

Integrated IS-IS is a link-state classless routing protocol that has the following similarities with OSPF:

■   It supports VLSMs.

■   It requires a hierarchical topology and defines areas.

■   It converges fast.

■   It does not summarize automatically but does allow manual summarization.

■   It uses the SPF algorithm to compute the best paths.

NOTE   Integrated IS-IS is defined in RFC 1195, "Use of OSI IS-IS for Routing in TCP/IP and Dual Environments."

Many differences also exist between the two protocols. The main difference relates to the fact that IS-IS is the routing protocol for the OSI protocol suite, specifically to route Connectionless Network Protocol (CLNP) data. CLNP is a routed protocol of the OSI suite, just as IP is the routed protocol for the TCP/IP suite. Integrated IS-IS is an extended version of IS-IS used for IP. Recall that EIGRP also supports multiple routed protocols (IP, IPX, and AppleTalk); with EIGRP, each of these routed protocols is handled independently. With Integrated IS-IS, the IP routing information is included as part of the CLNP routing information. Therefore, OSI protocol suite addresses must be configured even if IS-IS is only being used for routing IP.

OSI protocol suite addresses, which are a maximum of 20 bytes long, are called network service access points (NSAPs). Each device, rather than each interface, has an address. Although Integrated IS-IS is used extensively by ISPs, OSI addresses are not widely understood, and therefore this routing protocol is not widely used outside of ISPs.

Another difference between IS-IS and OSPF is how areas are defined and used. The following OSI terminology and Figure 3-16 help to explain how Integrated IS-IS operates:

- A *domain* is any part of an OSI network that is under a common administration; this is the equivalent of an autonomous system or domain in OSPF.

- Within any OSI domain, one or more *areas* can be defined. An area is a logical entity formed by a set of contiguous routers and the links that connect them. All routers in the same area exchange information about all the hosts that they can reach.

- The areas are connected to form a *backbone.* All routers on the backbone know how to reach all areas.

- An *end system* (ES) is any nonrouting host or node.

- An *intermediate system* (IS) is a router.

- OSI defines Level 1, Level 2, and Level 3 routing. Level 1 (L1) ISs (routers) communicate with other L1 ISs in the same area. Level 2 (L2) ISs route between L1 areas and form a contiguous routing backbone. L1 ISs only need to know how to get to the nearest L2 IS. Level 3 routing occurs between domains.

- L1 routers (ISs) are responsible for routing to ESs inside an area. They are similar to OSPF routers inside a totally stubby area.

- L2 ISs only route between areas, similar to backbone routers in OSPF.

- Level-1-2 (L1-2) routers can be thought of as a combination of an L1 router communicating with other L1 routers and an L2 router communicating with other L2 routers. L1-2 routers communicate between L2 backbone routers and L1 internal routers; they are similar to ABRs in OSPF. The backbone consists of both L2 and L1-2 routers.

Figure 3-16 *Integrated IS-IS Level 2 and Level-1-2 Routers Form a Contiguous Backbone*

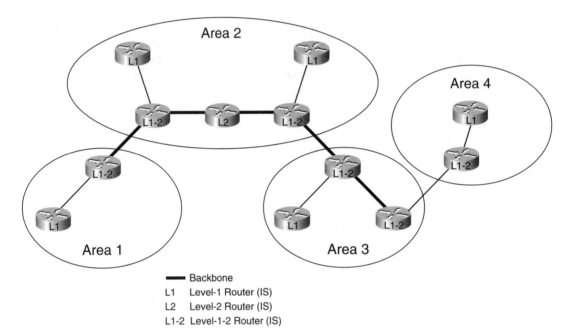

Notice that the edge of an IS-IS area is on a link, rather than inside of a router, as is the case for OSPF. Also notice that it is easy to extend the IS-IS backbone and add on more areas. You just need to configure a router as L2 or L1-2 and connect it to another L2 or L1-2 router, and it is part of the backbone. This flexibility means that IS-IS is much easier to expand than OSPF. IS-IS also sends out less update packets than OSPF, resulting in less traffic and therefore allowing more routers per area.

IS-IS routes can only be summarized by L1-2 routers as they are sent into Level 2. All L1-2 routers in an area should perform the same summarization so that the other areas see only the summary routes; otherwise, traffic will flow to the router that is not summarizing, because it advertises more specific routes.

> **NOTE**   If more than one entry in the routing table matches a particular destination, the longest prefix match—the most specific route that matches—in the routing table is used. Several routes might match one destination, but the one with the longest matching prefix is used.

Integrated IS-IS does not inherently support NBMA point-to-multipoint networks; in this case, multiple subinterfaces must be used to create multiple point-to-point networks.

IS-IS on Cisco routers assigns all interfaces a metric value of 10; it does not take into account the bandwidth of the link. This obviously is not appropriate in networks with varying link speed; in fact, it behaves similar to RIP's hop count metric. The metric for IS-IS can be changed manually on each interface, and should be done so for proper routing behavior.

Border Gateway Protocol Version 4

BGP4 is the exterior routing protocol, the EGP, for the TCP/IP suite and is used extensively throughout the Internet.

BGP is based on distance vector operation and uses a path vector as its metric. A *path vector* is a set of attributes of a path to a destination, including a list of AS numbers that the path goes through. The number of autonomous systems in this list can be thought of as being similar to a hop count, and can be used to affect the choice of which path is considered to be the best.

BGP is needed if an organization has more than one Internet connection and needs to determine which information should flow through each connection. BGP is also required if the AS allows packets to transit through it, from one AS to another AS; in this case, it is called a *transit AS*. An ISP is an example of a transit AS. Another reason to use BGP is if the AS must manipulate the flow of traffic entering or leaving the AS. In this latter case, BGP is being used as a *policy-based* protocol—policies can be defined to affect the way traffic flows through the AS.

In BGP, each AS is assigned an AS number. AS numbers are 16 bits, with values from 1 to 65535. Private AS numbers are 64512 through 65535; these are much like the private IP addresses and are not to be used on the Internet. (We only use private AS numbers in this book, just as we only use private IP addresses.)

BGP uses TCP to communicate. Any two routers that have formed a TCP connection to exchange BGP routing information—in other words, that have formed a BGP connection—are called *BGP peers* or *neighbors*.

BGP peers can be either internal or external to the AS. When BGP is running between routers within one AS, it is called internal BGP (IBGP). IBGP exchanges BGP information within the AS so that it can be passed to other autonomous systems. As long as they can communicate with each other, routers running IBGP do not have to be directly connected to each other. For example, if

EIGRP is running within the AS, the routers will have routes to all destinations within the AS; they use this EIGRP routing information to send the BGP information to the routers that need it. You can think of IBGP running on top of the interior routing protocol (EIGRP in this example)—it uses the interior routing protocol to send its BGP information.

When BGP is running between routers in different autonomous systems, it is called external BGP (EBGP). Routers running EBGP are usually connected directly to each other.

> **NOTE**   Understanding BGP operation is crucial to implementing it successfully. Many BGP parameters can be changed, and many BGP features can be configured—configuring and troubleshooting BGP can be complex. Because BGP typically involves connections to the Internet, errors can be catastrophic.

BGP4 is a classless routing protocol, so both the route and the prefix information are included in the routing updates. Thus, BGP4 supports VLSMs. It also supports classless interdomain routing (CIDR) addressing—blocks of multiple addresses (for example, blocks of Class C addresses) can be summarized, resulting in fewer entries in the routing tables.

IPv4 Routing Protocol Selection

This section describes the process of choosing routing protocols for your network and discusses the concepts of redistribution, filtering, and administrative distance.

Choosing Your Routing Protocol

To decide which routing protocol is best for your network, you need to first look at your requirements. You can then compare your requirements to the specifications for the available routing protocols, as detailed in the previous sections and summarized earlier in Table 3-2, and choose the routing protocol that best meets your needs.

Recall that Chapter 1, "Network Design," described the hierarchical model in which a network is divided into three layers: core, distribution, and access. Because each layer provides different services, they typically have different routing requirements and therefore use different routing protocols. The specific network function performed at each of these layers is as follows:

■   **Access layer**—Provides end-user and workgroup access to the resources of the network.

■   **Distribution layer**—Implements the organization's policies (including filtering of traffic) and provides connections between workgroups and between the workgroups and the core.

■   **Core layer**—Provides high-speed links between distribution-layer devices and to core resources. The core layer typically uses redundancy to ensure high network availability.

Thus, the different routing protocols suitable at each layer are as follows:

■ In the core layer, a fast-converging routing protocol is required: EIGRP, OSPF, and IS-IS are the possible choices. OSPF and IS-IS require a hierarchical topology with areas defined; EIGRP supports a hierarchical topology but doesn't require it. EIGRP is Cisco-proprietary, so it can only be supported if all routers are Cisco routers. IS-IS requires OSI addresses to be configured, which is not a common skill.

■ In the distribution layer, any of the interior routing protocols are suitable, depending on the specific network requirements. For example, if it is an all-Cisco network and has a mixture of link types so that VLSMs would be appropriate, EIGRP would be the logical choice. Because the distribution layer routes between the core and access layers, it might also have to redistribute (share with) and/or filter between the routing protocols running in those layers, as described in the next section.

■ The access layer typically includes RIPv2, IGRP, EIGRP, OSPF, or static routes. The devices in this layer are typically less powerful (in terms of processing and memory capabilities) and therefore support smaller routing tables—thus, the distribution layer should filter routes sent to this layer. Remember that EIGRP is not suitable for use in a dial-up network and that distance vector routing protocols have issues in NBMA networks.

Redistribution, Filtering, and Administrative Distance

KEY POINT | If two (or more) routing protocols are run in the same network, information from one routing protocol can be *redistributed* with, or shared with, another routing protocol. Routers that participate in more than one routing protocol perform the redistribution.

Redistribution can be bidirectional—the information from each routing protocol is shared with the other. It can also be performed in only one direction, with default routes used in the other direction. You must be careful not to introduce routing loops when you use redistribution.

KEY POINT | Routes can be filtered to prevent specific routes from being advertised. In other words, the router can exclude specific routes from the routing updates it sends to other specific routers.

Route filtering is useful when redistribution is being used, to help prevent routing loops.

For example, consider the network in Figure 3-17, with IGRP running in the upper part and RIPv2 running in the lower part. Both Routers A and B are configured to pass IGRP information into the

RIPv2 network, and RIPv2 into the IGRP network, with the intention that all devices can reach all networks.

Figure 3-17   *Routers A and B Are Redistributing Between IGRP and RIPv2*

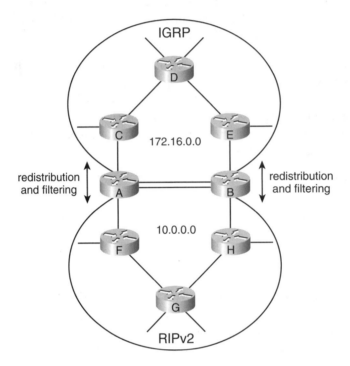

A problem can occur if both Routers A and B redistribute the full content of their routing tables, because more than one path exists between the IGRP and RIPv2 networks. For example, Router B can pass information about network 10.0.0.0 to Router E, which can pass it to Router D, which can pass it to Router C, which can pass it to Router A. Router A is connected to network 10.0.0.0, but depending on how the redistribution is configured, Router A might think that the path to some of the subnets of network 10.0.0.0 through Router C is better—through the IGRP network. If Router A passed this information to Router F, and so on, traffic from the RIPv2 part of the network might loop around the entire network before ending up where it started—in other words, the potential exists for a routing loop. Specific route filtering can be configured to avoid this—you must know your network and ensure that you are not introducing problems.

Because each routing protocol uses different metrics, you can't compare one metric with another—for example, how do you compare whether 3 RIP hops are better than an OSPF cost of 10? Thus, when multiple routing protocols are run on Cisco routers, another parameter, called the *administrative distance,* compares the routing protocols.

KEY POINT | Cisco routers use the administrative distance in the path selection process when they learn two or more routes to the same destination network or subnet from different sources of routing information, such as different routing protocols. The administrative distance rates the *believability* of the sources of routing information.

The administrative distance is a value between 0 and 255; the lower the value, the higher the believability of the source of the routing information.

Table 3-4 lists the default administrative distance of the sources of routing information, including routing protocols, supported by Cisco routers.

Table 3-3   *Administrative Distance of Routing Protocols*

Route Source	Default Distance
Connected interface, static route out an interface	0
Static route to an address	1
EIGRP summary route	5
EBGP	20
Internal EIGRP	90
IGRP	100
OSPF	110
IS-IS	115
RIPv1, RIPv2	120
External EIGRP	170
Internal BGP	200
Unknown	255

For example, consider a router that receives a route to network 10.0.0.0 from RIPv2 (with an administrative distance of 120) and also receives a route to the same network from IGRP (with an administrative distance of 100). The router uses the administrative distance to determine that IGRP is more believable; the router therefore puts the IGRP route into its routing table.

The administrative distance can be changed from its default value, either for all routes from a routing protocol or for specific routes. This can help to eliminate routing loops.

NOTE   Many details about routing protocol operation and configuration, including redistribution, filtering, and administrative distances, are provided in the book *CCNP Self-Study: Building Scalable Cisco Internetworks (BSCI), Second Edition,* by Paquet & Teare, Cisco Press, 2003.

Summary

In this chapter, you learned about IPv4 address design and routing protocol selection.

The following topics were explored:

- Why proper IP addressing and protocol selection are critical to your business

- IP address design issues, including private addresses and NAT, how subnet masks are used and selected, hierarchical addressing and summarization, and VLSMs

- The various features of routing protocols in general, and the specifics for the IP routing protocols RIPv1, RIPv2, IGRP, EIGRP, OSPF, Integrated IS-IS, and BGP4

- The process that chooses IP routing protocols for your network and the concepts of redistribution, filtering, and administrative distance

Endnotes

[1]Redford, R., "Intelligent Information Networks," Keynote Address at the Cisco Technical Symposium 2004, Oct. 5, 2004, Toronto.

[2]"Potential of IP Communications Takes Off at Toronto Pearson International Airport," http://newsroom.cisco.com/dlls/partners/news/2004/f_hd_03-30.html.

[3]Adapted from Teare, *CCDA Self-Study: Designing for Cisco Internetwork Solutions (DESGN),* Indianapolis, Cisco Press, 2004, Chapter 6.

[4]Odom, *CCNA Self-Study: CCNA INTRO Exam Certification Guide,* Indianapolis, Cisco Press, 2004, p. 120.

[5]Linegar, D. and Savage, D., Advanced Routing Protocol Deployment session, Cisco Technical Symposium 2004, Oct. 5, 2004, Toronto.

[6]Adapted from Paquet and Teare, *CCNP Self-Study: Building Scalable Cisco Internetworks (BSCI), Second Edition,* Indianapolis, Cisco Press, 2003, pp. 32 and 118.

[7]Linegar, D. and Savage, D., Advanced Routing Protocol Deployment session, Cisco Technical Symposium 2004, Oct. 5, 2004, Toronto.

[8]Ibid.

[9]"OSPF Incremental SPF," http://www.cisco.com/univercd/cc/td/doc/product/software/ios120/120newft/120limit/120s/120s24/ospfispf.htm.

[10]"Designing Large-Scale IP Internetworks," http://www.cisco.com/univercd/cc/td/doc/cisintwk/idg4/nd2003.htm.

This chapter describes the concepts that relate to network security and includes the following sections:

- Making the Business Case

- Hacking

- Vulnerabilities

- Threats

- Mitigating Technologies

- SAFE Campus Design

CHAPTER 4

Network Security Design

Not long ago, the campus network's sole purpose was to provide connectivity. Nowadays, the campus network is an intricate part of business success, providing productivity tools in every part of the infrastructure. Therefore, sound security must protect the network to ensure high availability, integrity, and confidentiality of the data.

You can deal with risk in four ways: you accept it, you reduce it, you ignore it, or you transfer it. In network security, you seek to reduce the risk with the help of sound technologies and policies. This chapter focuses on reducing the risk and on the security technologies available in campus network design to mitigate vulnerabilities and threats.

Network security can be a complicated but exhilarating subject. Prior to jumping into the design aspects of network security, we review the basics of hacking and the equipment available to mitigate threats.

> **NOTE** Appendix B, "Network Fundamentals," includes material that we assume you understand before reading the rest of the book. Thus, we encourage you to review any of the material in Appendix B that you are not familiar with before reading the rest of this chapter.

Making the Business Case

Not a week goes by without news of another network attack. CERT, a U.S. federally funded center coordinating communication during security emergencies, estimated that security breaches in the United States totaled 153,000 in 2003, almost double that of the prior year and more than a sevenfold increase in three years.

Virsus, Worms, and Trojan Horses

A *virus* is a program that triggers a damaging outcome. Viruses often disguise themselves as executables with clever filenames like "You won." A virus requires a human action, such as opening an e-mail attachment, to be activated.

A *worm* is a virus that can self-duplicate. A worm might have the capability of scanning the network and infecting neighboring workstations.

A *Trojan horse* pretends to be an inoffensive application when in fact it might contain a destructive payload. An example of a Trojan horse could be an attachment that, after being opened, shows a picture of a cute puppy, but in the background, the code is reading the e-mail addresses of the user's address book and forwarding those addresses to a hacker's repository for future spam use. Trojan horses are not considered viruses because they don't reproduce themselves.

When dealing with network security, one trend is certain: Attacks are becoming more complex. Blaster and SoBig.F, which we explain in the following sidebar, are examples of those complex threats called combo malware. *Malware* is a generic term that describes malicious software such as viruses and Trojan horses. *Combo malware* are hybrid menaces that combine destructive components of different threats. For example, a worm that carries a viral payload would be called combo malware.

Infamous Attacks—A Short List

Code Red

Date: July 2001

Characteristics: Worm that infected Microsoft Internet Information Servers (IISs) and defaced web pages of infected servers with the message "HELLO! Welcome to http://www.worm.com! Hacked By Chinese!" The worm continued spreading and infected more IISs on the Internet. After about 20 days following the infection of a server, the worm launched a denial of service (DoS) attack on several fixed IP addresses, among which was the White House address. We explain DoS in detail in the section "Denial of Service Attacks," later in this chapter.

I Love You

Date: May 2000

Characteristics: Often called a virus, this attack's behavior is more related to being a worm, considering how it spread. When a user opened an infected e-mail attachment, that user's system was infected, and it replicated itself to everyone in the user's address book.

Melissa

Date: 1999

Characteristics: Virus that spread inside Microsoft Word macros.

Nimda

Date: September 2001

Characteristics: Worm that infected Microsoft IISs and any computer on which the e-mail attachment was opened. Nimda's payload is a "traffic slowdown," but it doesn't destroy or cause harm other than creating delays.

Slammer

Date: January 2003

Characteristics: Sent traffic to randomly generated IP addresses, hoping to find a host that runs the Microsoft SQL Server Resolution Service so that the target can propagate more copies of the worm.

Blaster

Date: August 2003

Characteristics: The worm was programmed to start a SYN flood attack on August 15 against port 80 of http://www.windowsupdate.com, thereby creating a DoS attack against the site. SYN floods and DoS are explained in the section "Denial of Service Attacks," later in the chapter.

SoBig.F

Date: August 2003

Characteristics: A worm that set a record for the sheer volume of e-mails it generated. It was also a Trojan horse because it masqueraded as an innocuous e-mail with a subject line such as "RE: Details" and with an attachment with a filename such as details.pif.

Hacking

Most of us equate hacking with malicious activities. In fact, *hacking* is defined as working diligently on a computer system until it performs optimally. The popular use of the term *hacking* is more related to *cracking,* which is defined as the act of unlawfully accessing a network infrastructure to perform unethical activities. But for the purposes of this book, the widely accepted term *hacking* denotes malicious activities directed at networks and systems.

Types of Hackers

There are as many motivating factors for hacking as there are hacker types. From the script-kiddy who downloads hacking shareware and follows on-screen instructions to the cyber-terrorist, one thing is certain: They want to inflict pain on your organization.

Also, although they are not necessarily qualifying as hackers, careless employees can also be dangerous to your organization.

Even a CEO Can Be Dangerous to His Company

Following a slideshow presentation, the CEO of a publicly traded company briefly stepped aside from the podium. Upon his return, he discovered that his laptop, with all its precious corporate information, was gone. A security policy that forces employees to use a locking system for their laptop might have prevented this theft.

White-Hat Hackers

Not all hackers spell trouble. *White-hat hackers* are either reformed hackers or network professionals who have achieved mastery of the art and science of hacking. White-hat hackers are paid to provide penetration testing of the corporate network and to produce a detailed report of their findings. White-hat hackers are sometimes hired inconspicuously by senior management to test the ability of the IT department to detect and deal with attacks.

White-Box and Black-Box Hacking

White-box hackers are provided with some design and knowledge of an organization's network infrastructure prior to attempting their hacks of the system. *Black-box hackers* have no prior knowledge of the network before attempting to hack it.

Regardless of whether the hacking motivation is benevolence, carelessness, or maliciousness, hackers wouldn't exist if vulnerabilities weren't available to exploit. The next section delves into network vulnerabilities.

Vulnerabilities

Regardless of the hackers' motivation, they intrude networks by exploiting vulnerabilities, and the consequences can range from embarrassment to significant downtime and revenue losses.

KEY POINT | *Vulnerability* is defined as the characteristics of a system that allow someone to use it in a suboptimal manner or allow unauthorized users to take control of the system in part or entirely.

Vulnerabilities usually fall into one of the following categories:

- Design issues

- Human issues

- Implementation issues

Design Issues

Design issues refer to inherent problems with functionality because of operating system, application, or protocol flaws.

Human Issues

The human issues category of vulnerabilities refers to administrator and user errors, such as unsecured user accounts, unsecured devices, or *open devices* (devices that have not been hardened).

Hardening a Box

When they ship, many servers' operating systems and network appliances are, by default, *open*. It is the system administrator's responsibility to harden a device. *Hardening* a device refers to the process of closing unused ports and limiting the functionality of some features. An example of *hardening a box* would be to close ports that are not being used on a UNIX web server that, by default, might have its ports 21, 23, and 25 open. In this case, only port 80 should be active.

Implementation Issues

Implementation issues deal with creation, configuration, and enforcement of security policies, such as password policies, remote-access policies, Internet usage policies, e-mail policies, and so on.

Because technological advancement usually precedes policy formulation, the organization must promote a secure culture where users know how to extrapolate from current policies to judge actions to be taken when faced with a new networking situation.

For example, an organization might not have had a wireless policy when the first low-cost wireless access point (WAP) became available. Even if it was not specifically detailed in a policy that an employee can't connect his own WAP to the network, he should be able to draw that inference.

Threats

As mentioned earlier, regardless of their motivation, hackers capitalize on vulnerabilities. Hackers exploiting vulnerabilities are real threats to network security.

The following is a generic list of attack categories:

- Reconnaissance attacks

- Access attacks

- Information disclosure attacks

- Denial of service attacks

Reconnaissance Attacks

Reconnaissance attacks consist of intelligence gathering, often using tools like network scanners or packet analyzers. The information collected can then be used to compromise networks.

Some of the proverbial reconnaissance attacks, conducted with specialized tools, are as follows:

- **Ping sweeping**—To discover network addresses of live hosts

- **Network and port scanning**—To discover active ports on target hosts

- **Stack fingerprinting**—To determine the target operating system (OS) and the applications running on targeted hosts

- **Enumeration**—To infer network topology

Access Attacks

During an access attack, the hacker exploits the vulnerabilities he has discovered during the reconnaissance attack. Some common access attacks are as follows:

- **Entry**—Unlawful entry to an e-mail account or database.

- **Collect**—The hacker gathers information or passwords.

- **Plant**—The hacker might create a back door so that he can return at a later time.

- **Occupy**—The hacker might elect to control as many hosts as he wants.

- **Cover**—The hacker might cover his tracks by attempting to change the system logs.

Access Subterfuges

Hackers continuously come up with crafty access attacks. Consider the case of a user who receives an e-mail tantalizing him to play a virtual game of Spinning Wheel for a cash prize by simply opening the attachment. In the short time it takes the user to open the attachment, wait for the spinning wheel to stop turning, and hope the needle points to WINNER, an inconspicuous application meticulously collects all the entries in the user's e-mail address book and sends them back to the originator of the attack. The originator could be a spammer who plans to use this information for future spamming.

Proper dissemination and enforcement of an e-mail security policy would have taught the user not to open an attachment from an unknown source. Alternatively, the organization might have considered installing an e-mail filtering service to purge the message of executable attachments. E-mail filtering is discussed in the section "Content Filtering," later in this chapter.

Information Disclosure Attacks

Information disclosure attacks are different from an access attack in the sense that the information is provided voluntarily through a sophisticated subterfuge. The following attacks, though considered information disclosure attacks, could fall into the category of white-collar crimes:

- Social engineering

- Phishing

Social Engineering

Social engineering, a form of low-tech hacking, is defined as someone, claiming to be someone he is not, who approaches a user either through e-mail or through a phone call for the purpose of infiltrating the organization. Great technical ability is not necessary to perform social engineering.

Phishing

Internet scammers who cast about for people's financial information have a new way to lure unsuspecting victims: they go phishing. *Phishing* is a high-tech scam that uses spam or pop-up messages to deceive readers into disclosing credit card numbers, bank account information, Social Security numbers, passwords, or other sensitive information. Figure 4-1 is an example of an e-mail that looked legitimate but was actually a scam.

Figure 4-1 *Phishing E-mail*

Unfortunately, no security systems can protect against information disclosure. Only the dissemination and enforcement of sound security policies can help users learn to be suspicious and to confirm the origin of these e-mails prior to taking actions.

Denial of Service Attacks

With a DoS attack, a hacker attempts to render a network or an Internet resource, such as a web server, worthless to users. A DoS attack typically achieves its goal by sending large amounts of repeated requests that paralyze the network or a server.

A common form of a DoS attack is a SYN flood, where the server is overwhelmed by embryonic connections. A hacker sends to a server countless Transmission Control Protocol (TCP) synchronization attempts known as SYN requests. The server answers each of those requests with a SYN ACK reply and allocates some of its computing resources to servicing this connection when it becomes a "full connection." Connections are said to be *embryonic* or *half-opened* until the originator completes the three-way handshake with an ACK for each request originated. A server that is inundated with half-opened connections soon runs out of resources to allocate to upcoming connection requests, thus the expression "denial of service attack."

The following sidebars provide the anatomy of DoS attacks and distributed DoS (DDoS) attacks.

Anatomy of a Simple DoS Attack

A proverbial DoS attack called Land.c sends a TCP SYN request, giving the target host's address as both source and destination, and using the same port on the target host as both source and destination (for example, source address 10.0.0.1:139 to destination address 10.0.0.1:139).

Anatomy of a Complex Distributed DoS Attack

A common form of DoS attack is a DDoS attack. In the case of DDoS, an attacker finds hosts that he can compromise in different organizations and turns them into handlers by remotely installing DDoS handler software on them, as shown in Figure 4-2.

Figure 4-2   *DDoS — Creating an Army of Agents[1]*

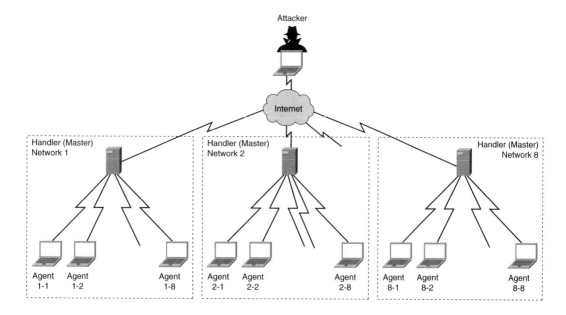

Those *handlers* in turn scan their own corporate network, hunting for workstations to compromise and turn into DDoS *agents*. Those agents are also referred to as *bots,* thus the expression of *botnets.*

When his army of agents is strategically in place, the hacker launches the attack. He transmits his orders for the mission to the handlers and agents; these orders usually cause each of these hosts to send large quantities of packets to the same specific destination, at a precise time, thus overwhelming the victim and the path to it. It also creates significant congestion on corporate networks that are infected with handlers and agents when they all simultaneously launch their attack on the ultimate victim.

As an added twist, the crafty hacker might have requested that the agents use a spoofed source IP address when sending the large quantities of packets to the destination. The target would reply to the best of its ability to the source, which happens to be an innocent bystander, as shown in Figure 4-3.

Figure 4-3   *DDoS—Launching an Attack Using a Spoofed Source IP Address*[2]

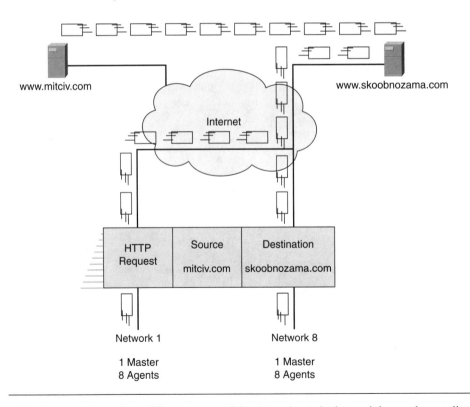

A basic knowledge of the different types of threats and attacks is crucial to understanding the purpose of mitigation equipment and proper network security design. These topics are covered in the following sections.

Mitigating Technologies

Known threats can usually be mitigated by security equipment and sound security policies.

The following sections cover the most pervasive mitigation techniques, which are grouped in these four major categories:

- Threat defense

    — Virus protection

    — Traffic filtering

    — Intrusion detection and prevention

    — Content filtering

- Secure communication

    — Encrypted Virtual Private Network (VPN)

    — Secure Socket Layer (SSL)

    — File encryption

- Trust and identity

    — Authentication, authorization, and accounting (AAA)

    — Network Admission Control (NAC)

    — Public key infrastructure (PKI)

- Network security best practices

    — Network management

    — Assessment and audits

    — Policies

Threat Defense

Threat defense refers to the activities that are necessary to guard against known and unknown attacks, specifically by doing the following:

- Defending the edge

- Protecting the interior

- Guarding the end points

To do so, the campus design should include the following:

- Virus protection

- Traffic filtering

- Intrusion detection and prevention

- Content filtering

Virus protection

Probably the easiest and most cost-effective way to start protecting an organization is through up-to-date virus protection.

Virus scanning can be performed at the following levels on a network:

- **Hosts**—Workstations and servers.

- **E-mail servers**—Incoming messages are scanned prior to being passed to the recipient.

- **Network**—An intrusion detection system (IDS) or intrusion prevention system (IPS), covered in the section "Intrusion Detection and Prevention," later in this chapter, can report to the IT manager that a virus signature was detected.

Practitioners recommend that IT departments implement different brands of virus protection at different junctions and functions of the network, thus benefiting from multiple comprehensive virus-signature databases and hopefully enlarging the spectrum of the virus dragnet.

Traffic Filtering

Traffic filtering can be achieved at many layers of the OSI model. It can be done at the data link layer using the Media Access Control (MAC) address but is most commonly done at the network layer through packet filtering. Packet filtering is further divided into the following areas:

- Static packet filtering

- Dynamic packet filtering

Static Packet Filtering

Static packet filtering is also referred to as *stateless packet filtering* or *stateless firewalling.* It is often performed at the perimeter router, which acts as the logical point of demarcation between the ISP and the corporate network. With stateless firewalling, the router does not track the state of packets and does not know whether a packet is part of the SYN process, the actual transmission, or the FIN process. A stateless firewall typically tracks only IP addresses and therefore can be tricked by a hacker who spoofs IP addresses.

Dynamic Packet Filtering

Dynamic packet filtering is also referred to as *stateful firewalling.* It is usually done by a firewall, which is a dedicated appliance that performs packet scans. Stateful firewalling capabilities are also built into some routers.

The default behavior of a firewall is that outgoing traffic—traffic that flows from the inside network to the outside network—is allowed to leave and its reply traffic is allowed back in. However, traffic that originates from the outside network and attempts to come to the inside network is automatically denied. This is possible because the firewall meticulously tracks connections and records the following connection-state information in a table:

- Source IP address

- Destination IP address

- Source port

- Destination port

- Connection TCP flags

- Randomized TCP sequence number

This default behavior of a firewall is sometimes changed to accommodate the presence of a corporate server to which outside users need access. This "public" server is usually located in the demilitarized zone (DMZ) of a corporate network. A rule can be configured in the firewall to stipulate which outside traffic is permitted to enter for the purpose of visiting the web server, as shown in Figure 4-4.

Figure 4-4 *DMZ and Firewall[3]*

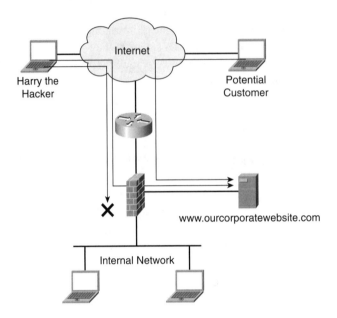

Firewalling is evolving. For example, Cisco offers, on some switch models, a stateful firewall at the port level, thus providing tighter security inside the network, not just at the perimeter. The Cisco Catalyst 6500 Firewall Services Module provides a real-time, hardened and embedded security system.

Intrusion Detection and Prevention

IDSs and IPSs are part of the design solution for protecting primarily the perimeter, extranet, and increasingly internal network. The purpose of IDSs and IPSs is to monitor network traffic by analyzing each packet that enters the network.

Intrusion Detection Systems

As previously explained, an IDS scans network traffic for malicious activity. A management server, located on the inside network, logs the alerts of suspicious activities that are sent by the IDS.

An IDS watches for the following:

■ Attack signatures, such as DoS and virus patterns

■ Traffic anomalies, such as the same source sending countless requests to SYN on a specific target

■ Protocol anomalies, such as a malformed packet

An IDS can be one of the following:

■ **Network-based IDS (NIDS)**—A dedicated appliance installed on the network

■ **Host-based IDS (HIDS)**—Integrated software on a mission-critical system, such as a web server

Network-Based IDSs

NIDSs are efficient and don't introduce latency in a network because they perform their analysis on "copies" of the data, not on the packets themselves, as shown in Figure 4-5. When designing a campus network, set up the NIDS to have its reporting interface on the inside network and its stealth interface on the outside network. A *stealth interface* is physically present on a network but has no IP address. Without an IP address, the hacker cannot address and therefore hack through that stealth interface.

Figure 4-5 *Stealth Operation of an IDS[4]*

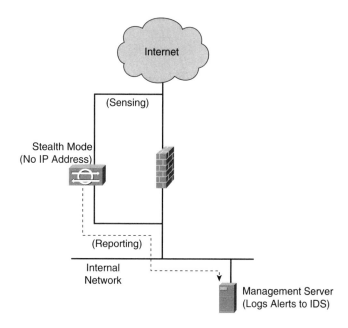

As an alternative to buying a dedicated IDS appliance, your network design might harness the basic IDS capabilities that are built into Cisco PIX Firewalls and specific Cisco router IOS versions.

Host-Based IDSs

HIDSs are typically installed on mission-critical devices, such as web servers and e-mail servers, but can also be installed on desktop and laptop PCs. Cisco offers an HIDS solution called the Cisco Secure Agent (CSA).

CSA closely monitors the behavior of codes that are coming to the end point and prevents attacks while reporting the incident to the management server.

Intrusion Prevention Systems

IPSs have naturally evolved from IDSs. An IPS has the extra capabilities of taking remedial actions when it confirms suspicious activities. Upon discovering malicious activity, the IPS can take at least one of the following actions:

- Alert the management console server

- Send a TCP reset (RST) to the source

- Shun the source of the attack by sending a command to the firewall requesting it to temporarily block the suspect IP address

Currently, only subtle differences exist between IDSs and IPSs; therefore, many vendors interchange the terms.

Target-Based Intrusion Detection Systems

A significant issue with IDSs is the number of alarms that they generate. The number of alarms generated by the sensor can be reduced by locating the monitoring interface on the inside link of a firewall, instead of the outside link. If you put your IDS monitoring connection before the firewall (the outside interface), you will get alarms for traffic that would be stopped by the firewall anyway; however, if you put the IDS monitoring interface on the inside interface, it will only catch, and therefore generate alarms about, malicious traffic that has passed through the firewall. Another significant issue with IDSs/IPSs are false positives. False positives are alerts triggered by legitimate activities, in which case no alarm should have been raised.

A target-based IDS, such as Cisco Threat Response, tries to address this problem by investigating in-depth and relative to the target an alert received by the network management console. The target-based IDS does the following:

- Compares the kind of attack reported to the device targeted

- Evaluates whether the target is truly at risk by comparing the threats to the vulnerabilities of the operating system of the target

- Compares the threat with the patch history of the targeted system

Content Filtering

In addition to controlling outbound traffic through filtering configured in the perimeter router or Internet firewall, the network design might also include the following:

- Uniform resource locator (URL) filtering

- E-mail filtering

URL Filtering

Corporations use content filtering to enforce their Internet usage policies, hoping to protect themselves from possible legal implications should their employees visit objectionable websites.

With content filtering, outbound user traffic that is looking for a specific URL is checked by the firewall against the content-filtering server that is installed on the corporate network. The firewall is provided by the content-filtering server with a *permit* or *deny* for the website requested by the user. The sophisticated content-filtering software installed on a corporate server can have over 5 million websites in its database. The network administrator sets the policies to allow or deny access to groups and individual websites. The permissions can also be based on daily usage or time of day. As an example, a system administrator could set a rule that allows users to visit online banking sites only during the lunch hour.

E-mail Filtering

When designing your corporate e-mail services, consider including an e-mail filtering service. That service, installed on the same network segment as your mail server (usually in a DMZ), sanitizes the e-mail from malware and some executable attachments prior to delivery of the messages to the end user.

Secure Communication

Encryption addresses the need for data confidentiality, which often finds itself in the forefront of network design. Confidentiality of data refers to the inability for wandering eyes to see and/or decipher a message sent from one party to another.

Encryption is a significant topic and can easily fill books by itself. Therefore, this section provides only enough information to assist you in network design. Should you be interested in a detailed book on encryption, read *The Code Book: The Science of Secrecy from Ancient Egypt to Quantum Cryptography,* by Simon Singh (ISBN 0-385-49532-3, Anchor, 2000). Some basic principles of encryption are presented in this section.

As shown in Figure 4-6, the following two components are essential to encryption:

■ Encryption algorithm

■ Encryption keys

Figure 4-6 *Encryption Operation*[5]

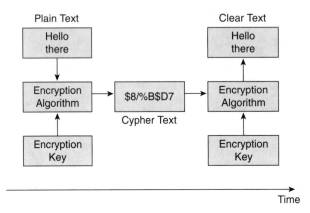

Data Encryption Standard (DES), Triple Data Encryption Standard (3DES), and Advanced Encryption Standard (AES) are all common encryption algorithms used in IP security (IPsec). IPsec is discussed in the next section of this chapter. The algorithm can be seen as the engine of encryption—the morphing device through which the data goes. The "pattern" of morphing is provided by the "key." An encryption key is a code that enciphers and deciphers a stream of data. Encryption keys must be well guarded and shared only between the two parties requiring securing communications. The following are the two types of encryption keys:

■ **Symmetrical keys**—The same key encrypts and decrypts a message.

■ **Asymmetrical keys**—A different key decrypts a message from the key that encrypted the message. This is the case with public and private keys.

A key becomes vulnerable when it has been in service for a long period because the hacker has had time to attempt to break it. A key is also vulnerable if a large quantity of data is encrypted with it: The hacker would then have a large sample of cipher text to try deciphering. Therefore, when designing a network, you should consider having keys that expire frequently and when large amounts of data have been encrypted through that key.

As part of network design activities, you might consider using one of the following common encryption scenarios:

- Encrypted VPN

- SSL

- File encryption

Encrypted VPN

An encrypted VPN consists of a tunnel in which data transiting through it is encrypted, as shown in Figure 4-7. The tunnel can originate from a VPN-enabled device or from a remote user running VPN software on his computer.

Figure 4-7   *Encrypted Tunnels*[6]

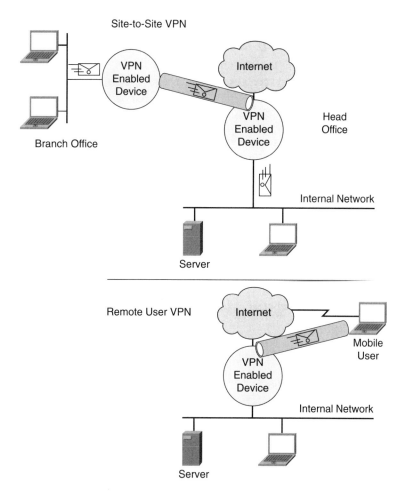

The most common standard for encrypted VPN is IPsec. IPsec provides three optional mechanisms, as explained in Table 4-1.

Table 4-1   *IPsec Mechanisms*

IPsec Option	Description
Authenticity	Only a legitimate sender and receiver would successfully encrypt and decrypt a message, thus providing proof of authenticity of the message.
Confidentiality	The message is encrypted and therefore illegible to onlookers. Only those in possession of the legitimate key can decipher the message.
Integrity	A hash is appended to the message, confirming its integrity. See the following sidebar for more about hashing.

Hashing

Hashing is a process that uses an algorithm to convert data into a fixed-length result, called a *message digest.* (Regardless of whether the data is a short e-mail or thousands of pages of text, a hash is always the same length.) The message digest is then usually appended to the transmission and is checked by the receiver to ensure the integrity of the message. Both the sender and the receiver share a predetermined special key, or shared secret, that they include in the hashing process in addition to the clear text itself. This ensures that only the sender and the receiver can replicate the exact message digest.

The process of hashing can be thought of as a butcher grinding a solid piece of meat. When the butcher has turned the solid meat into ground beef, which would be the equivalent of a message digest, any attempt to reverse-engineer the grinding proves fruitless—it is a one-way function. There is no secret key available for reversal of the hashing process; a message digest cannot be deciphered; it can only be replicated.

VPN-enabled devices that might be included in the design of a network are as follows:

- **VPN concentrator**—Dedicated appliance that is optimized to manage multiple encrypted tunnels and profiles.

- **Router**—IPsec technology is available on specific versions of Cisco IOS.

- **Firewall**—IPsec technology is available on PIX Firewalls.

- **IPsec client**—Mobile workers can harness the potential of IPsec by installing VPN connectivity software, thus creating a tunnel from their laptop up to the VPN-enabled device such as a VPN concentrator, router, or firewall.

SSL

SSL provides encryption of data to and from a web browser and could be included in a network design if a point-to-point encryption is needed for a service. It is commonly seen for online banking or shopping transactions and web mail operations. It is also popular for organizations that do not want to install VPN-client software on remote hosts.

File Encryption

In the case where a document requires confidentiality but the communication might be in clear text, a person can use file-encryption software such as Pretty Good Privacy (PGP) to encrypt the file. The encrypted file must be unencrypted by the reader after it is received.

Trust and Identity

Trust and identity management includes the following:

- Authentication, authorization, and accounting capabilities

- Network Admission Control

Authentication, Authorization, and Accounting

AAA is a crucial aspect of network security and should be considered during the network design. This can be accomplished through a AAA server, which handles the following:

- **Authentication**—*Who?* Checks the identity of the user, typically through a username and password combination.

- **Authorization**—*What?* After the user is validated, the AAA server dictates what activity the user is allowed to perform on the network.

- **Accounting**—*When?* The AAA server can record the length of the session, the services accessed during the session, and so forth.

AAA can be managed by a Cisco Secure Access Control Server (ACS).

The principles of strong authentication should be included in the user authentication.

Strong authentication refers to the two-factor authentication method. The users are authenticated using two of the following factors:

- **Something you know**—Such as a password or personal identification number (PIN)
- **Something you have**—Such as an access card, bank card, or token*
- **Something you are**—For example, some biometrics, such as a retina print or a fingerprint
- **Something you do**—Such as your handwriting, including the style, pressure applied, and so forth

As an example, when accessing an automated teller machine, strong authentication is enforced because a bank card (something you have) and a PIN (something you know) are used.

*Tokens are key-chain-size devices that show, one at a time, in a predefined order, a one-time password (OTP). The OTP is displayed on the token's small LCD, typically for 1 minute, before the next password in the sequence appears. The token is synchronized with a token server, which has the same predefined list of passcodes for that one user. Therefore, at any given time, only one valid password exists between the server and a token.

Network Admission Control

NAC, the latest feature in Cisco's security portfolio, should be considered in the design of your network. NAC ensures that users and their computers comply with corporate network policies.

On a corporate network with NAC, a network access device (NAD)—for example, a router—intercepts attempts to connect from local or remote users. As shown in Figure 4-8, the Cisco trust agent, residing on the end point (for example, a user's laptop), provides the NAD with pertinent information, such as the version of antivirus software and the patch level of the connecting laptop. The NAD passes the end-point security credentials to a policy server, which decides whether access will be granted to the end point. Noncompliant end points are quarantined until they meet NAC standards.

Figure 4-8 *Network Admission Control*

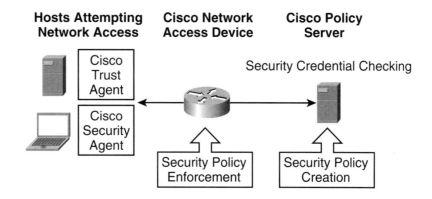

Public Key Infrastructure

PKI is a set of technologies and procedures that authenticate users. It addresses the issue of key distribution by using private keys and public keys. These are asymmetrical keys, and the public keys usually reside on a central repository called a *certification authority (CA)*. The private keys are usually stored locally on devices. PKI operations are shown in Figure 4-9.

Figure 4-9 *Private and Public Key Operations*[7]

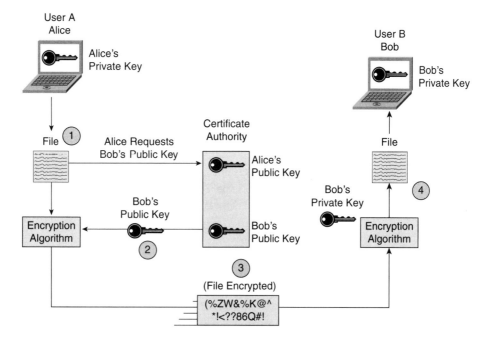

Each unique pair of public and private keys is related, but not identical. Data encrypted with a public key can be deciphered only with the corresponding private key, while data encrypted with a private key can be deciphered only with its corresponding public key.

PKI is usually considered in the design of complex enterprise networks where it is too cumbersome for each party to locally keep the public key of every other party that he or she wants to communicate with using encryption. In a PKI environment, the public keys are kept centrally, thus simplifying the distribution and management of those keys.

Network Security Best Practices

As in any field, network security also possesses a set of best practices. Best practices are the recommendation of due care that subject-matter experts have agreed upon for a particular field.

Network security includes many well-known practices presented in the following sections.

Network Management

Most security appliances, such as firewalls, routers, and IDSs, can send syslog security triggers to a central repository such as a syslog server. There is a saying in network security: "If you log it, read it." This is to say that it's futile to just log information if you never analyze the logs. To help the network administrator sort and extract meaningful information from the large quantity of syslog data received, security event management software should be used. Should a significant anomaly be discovered, the software can notify the network administrator through e-mail, pager, or text messaging. In addition, correlation tool modules can be added to assist the network administrator in seeing security anomaly patterns from what would otherwise appear to be random activity taking place.

Assessment and Audits

Prior to designing your network, you should conduct a security assessment to uncover potential vulnerabilities and therefore target your security efforts where they are the most effective.

Subsequently, when your network security systems are in full production, it can be beneficial to hire a security audit company that can perform penetration testing and report on the corporate network security position.

Policies

Sophisticated security equipment is no match for sloppy user behavior. Organizations must develop basic network policies, disseminate them, and enforce them. Examples of network security policies are as follows:

- Internet usage policy

- E-mail usage policy

- Remote-access policy

- Password-handling policy

- Software and hardware installation policy

- Physical security policy

- Business continuity policy

SAFE Campus Design

Cisco has developed a guide, called the Cisco SAFE Blueprint, of best practices for designing and securing networks. The Cisco SAFE Blueprint addresses design issues by dividing a large network into layers of modularity. This modular approach helps to ensure that proper consideration is provided to each critical part of the network at the time of design, and it provides scalability.

As introduced in Chapter 1, "Network Design," the Cisco Enterprise Composite Network Model is the name given to the architecture used by the SAFE blueprint. At the highest layer, this model divides an enterprise network into the following three main functional areas:

- Enterprise Campus

- Enterprise Edge

- Service Provider Edge

At the second layer of modularity, shown in Figure 4-10, the Enterprise Campus functional area is subdivided into multiple modules, which are listed in Table 4-2. Some of the key devices in each of those modules are listed in Table 4-2, as are some security design considerations.

Figure 4-10 *Enterprise Campus Module Details*

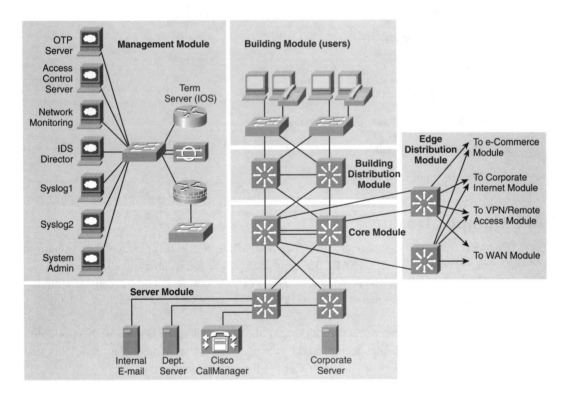

Table 4-2 *Enterprise Campus Detail*

Enterprise Campus Module	Key Devices	Special Security Design Considerations
Network Management Module	HIDS Virus scanning OTP server Access Control Server Network log server Layer 2 switch	Out-of-band management should be preferred over in-band management. If in-band management must be used, employ IPsec, SSL, or SSH.

Table 4-2   *Enterprise Campus Detail (Continued)*

Enterprise Campus Module	Key Devices	Special Security Design Considerations
Core Module	Layer 3 switch	No special consideration, other than the fact that switches are a target and should be protected. We explain this in Chapter 2, "Switching Design."
Building Distribution Module	Layer 3 switch	VLANs can be used to further segment the different departments within a campus.
Building Module (corporate user access)	Layer 2 switch Host virus scanning Network Admission Control	A switched environment is recommended to reduce the risk of packet sniffing.
Server Module	Layer 3 switch HIDS	Often the target of internal attacks, servers should not only be physically secured and running an IDS but should also be kept up to date with the latest patches.
Edge Distribution Module	Layer 3 switch	Depending on the size of the infrastructure, the Edge Distribution Module can be folded into the Core Module. In this case, an IDS should be included in the Core Module. This could be done with the insertion of an IDS card in the Layer 3 switch.

Removing some of the complexity of the redundancy presented in Figure 4-10 and integrating as many elements of security discussed in this chapter, a campus network design might look like what is shown in Figure 4-11.

Figure 4-11 *Enterprise Campus Network Design*

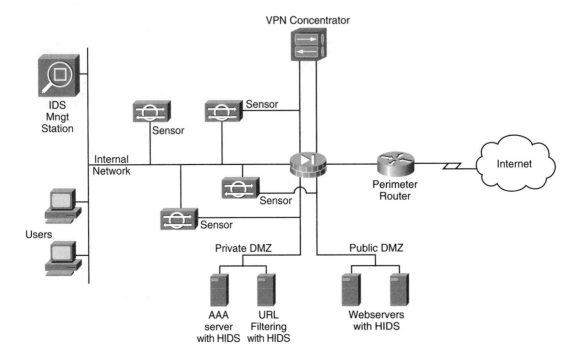

For more information on the Cisco *Secure Blueprint for Enterprise Networks (SAFE)* white paper, visit the http://www.cisco.com/go/safe.

In addition to SAFE, Cisco has been promoting the self-defending network concept. The philosophy for a self-defending network is to have security present in every aspect of an organization. In a self-defending network, every device, from the desktop PC through the LAN infrastructure and across the WAN, plays a role in securing the network. For more on self-defending networks, visit the Cisco website.

This chapter explores the following critical elements of campus security that make up the Self-Defending Network philosophy of Cisco:

■ Firewalls

■ Routers

■ VPN Concentrators

- IDSs and IPSs

- Encryption, VPN, and IPsec

- End-point antivirus software and Cisco Secure Agent

- Access Control Server

- Network Admission Control

- Public key infrastructure

Summary

This chapter summarizes the threats and vulnerabilities that hacking presents as well as the business case for considering security in campus design.

It covers the crucial devices and technologies for mitigating threats and follows this up by discussing the design implications within the framework of the Cisco SAFE Blueprint and the Cisco philosophy to have security present in every aspect of an organization.

Chapter 2 covers security in switches, and in the chapters to come, we further discuss network security as it relates to IP telephony, wireless connectivity, and network management.

Endnotes

[1] Paquet and Saxe, *The Business Case for Network Security: Advocacy, Governance, and ROI,* Indianapolis, Cisco Press, 2005.

[2] Ibid.

[3] Ibid.

[4] Ibid.

[5] Ibid.

[6] Ibid.

[7] Ibid.

This chapter discusses how to design a wireless network, and includes the following sections:

- Making the Business Case
- Wireless Technology Overview
- Wireless Security
- Wireless Management
- Wireless Design Considerations

CHAPTER 5

Wireless LAN Design

This chapter discusses wireless LAN (WLAN) technology and describes how it improves mobility. After introducing WLANs as strategic assets to corporate networks, we discuss WLAN standards and components. The security and management of WLANs are explored, followed by design considerations for WLANs.

NOTE Appendix B, "Network Fundamentals," includes material that we assume you understand before reading the rest of the book. Thus, we encourage you to review any of the material in Appendix B that you are not familiar with before reading the rest of this chapter.

Making the Business Case

The popularity of WLANs is undeniable. The following three main driving forces play in favor of WLANs:

- Flexibility

- Increased productivity

- Cost savings compared to wired deployment

WLANs let users access servers, printers, and other network resources regardless of their location, within the wireless reach. This flexibility means that, for example, a user's laptop stays connected working from a colleague's cubicle, from a small meeting room, or from the cafeteria. Recognizing the benefits brought about by WLAN flexibility, businesses are now deploying WLANs in record numbers.

According to a 2003 NOP World research study,[1] WLAN users stayed connected to their corporate network 3.64 hours per day longer than their wired peers, thus increasing their productivity by 27 percent. Through the flexibility of WLANs, not only does the productivity go up, but the response times are also significantly improved.

The benefits of wireless mobility don't stop at laptops and personal digital assistants (PDAs). IP telephony and videoconferencing are also supported over WLANs, integrating quality of service (QoS) to ensure that the interactive traffic has priority over the less-time-sensitive data transfers.

Another significant benefit of WLANs is their low-cost deployment in locations where the costs of running LAN wire would be prohibitive. The total cost of ownership (TCO) of a WLAN is very low compared to the benefits they bring to an organization, providing that a WLAN is secured and managed properly.

Companies that are not deploying WLANs quickly enough find that employees take the matter in their own hands and install their own WLANs, potentially creating significant breaches in the corporate network security infrastructure. Therefore, wireless security is an important topic to discuss in conjunction with wireless design.

WLANs, seen just a few years ago as a novelty, are now seen as critical to corporate productivity.

Wireless Technology Overview

In its most simplistic form, a WLAN is an LAN that uses radio frequency (RF) to communicate instead of using a wire. As shown in Figure 5-1, wireless clients connect to wireless access points (WAPs).

Figure 5-1 *Wired and Wireless Networks*

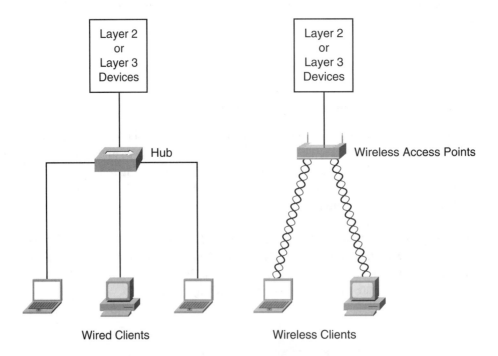

Because WLANs use RF, the throughput (speed) is inversely proportional to the distance between the transmitter and the receiver.[2] Therefore, everything being equal (notwithstanding interferences), the closer a wireless client is to a transmitter, the greater is the throughput, as shown in Figure 5-2.

Figure 5-2   *Throughput (Coverage) Is Related to the Distance from the RF Transmitter*

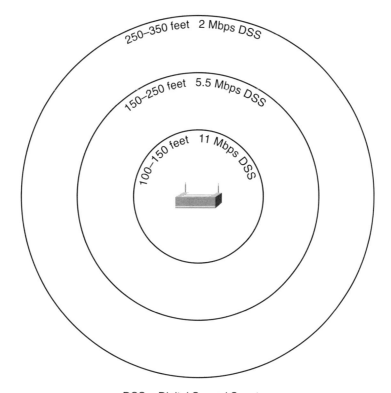

250–350 feet   2 Mbps DSS

150–250 feet   5.5 Mbps DSS

100–150 feet   11 Mbps DSS

DSS = Digital Spread Spectrum

However, wireless communication brings a trade-off between flexibility and mobility versus battery life and usable bandwidth.

Wireless Standards

WLAN standards that are currently supported by major vendors were developed by the working group 11 of the Institute of Electrical and Electronics Engineers (IEEE) 802 committee. The most common standards are shown in Table 5-1.

Table 5-1   *Wireless Standards*

Standard	Maximum Throughput (Mbps)	Frequency (GHz)	Compatibility	Ratified
802.11b	11	2.4	—	1999
802.11a	54	5	—	1999; Product availability 2001
802.11g	54	2.4	Backward-compatible with 802.11b	2003

The 802.11a standard operates in the unlicensed 5-GHz band, which makes the transmission vulnerable to interference from microwave ovens and cordless phones. The strength of 802.11b and 802.11g signals, which operate in the 2.4-GHz band, is affected negatively by water, metal, and thick walls.

The 802.11b and 802.11g standards divide the 2.4 GHz into 14 overlapping individual channels. Channels 1, 6, and 11 do not overlap and therefore can be used to set up multiple networks. The 802.11a standard is an amendment to the original standard. The advantage of using 802.11a is that it suffers less from interference, but its use is restricted to almost line of sight, thus requiring the installation of more access points than 802.11b to cover the same area.

The medium access method of the 802.11 standards, called the Distribution Coordination Method, is similar to the carrier sense multiple access collision detect (CSMA/CD) mechanism of Ethernet.

The following types of frames are transferred over the airwaves:

■ **Data frame**—Network traffic.

■ **Control frame**—Frame controlling access to the medium, similar to a modem's analog connection control mechanism, with its Request To Send (RTS), Clear To Send (CTS), and acknowledgment (ACK) signals.

■ **Manager frame**—Frames similar to data frames, pertaining to the control of the current wireless transmission.

Other Wireless Standards

Other wireless standards include the following:

HomeRF—In 1998, a consortium was formed to promote the idea of HomeRF to be used with products in the home market. The participants were, among others, Siemens, Motorola, and Compaq.

Bluetooth—This is a specification for short-range radio links between mobile computers, mobile phones, digital cameras, and other portable devices, such as headsets. Bluetooth could be considered a standard for *personal area networks.*

Wireless Components

The main components of wireless networks are as follows:

- Wireless access points

- Wireless client devices

Wireless Access Points

WAPs provide connectivity between wireless client devices and the wired network, as shown earlier in Figure 5-1.

Integrated Access Point

The WAP does not need to be a stand-alone device. Cisco offers integrated access point functionality[3] for some small- to medium-business (SMB) routers, as shown in Figure 5-3. By installing a high-speed wireless interface card (HWIC) in Cisco 1800, 2800, or 3800 routers, customers can run concurrent routing, switching, and security services and include IEEE 802.11 wireless LAN functionality in a single platform.

Figure 5-3 *Integrating Routing and Wireless Functionality*

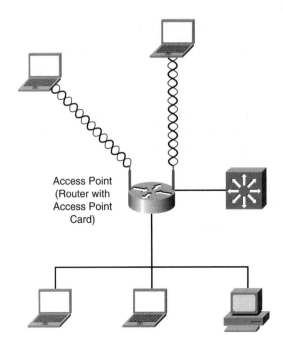

Wireless Client Devices

A wireless client device is equipped with a wireless interface card (WIC), which the device uses to communicate over RF with WAPs. Wireless clients can be the following items, among other things:

■ User workstations and laptops

■ PDAs

■ Wireless IP phones

User Workstations and Laptops: Ad-Hoc Network

In addition to connecting to a WLAN access point, two wireless end stations can form an exclusive, point-to-point, wireless network without the intervention of an access point. This type of independent network is known as an *ad-hoc network*.

PDAs

Wireless PDAs—PDAs that connect directly on the corporate network—play a significant role in an organization where time is extremely sensitive. An example of where 802.11b-compatible devices (wireless PDAs) are put to benefit is triage nurses who are faster at inputting their assessment and sharing their findings on the spot rather than walking back to the nurses' station to do so.

Wireless IP Phones

Absolute campus mobility is probably best demonstrated by Cisco wireless IP phones.[4] These 802.11b phones have built-in security, QoS, and management features. Wireless IP phones leverage existing IP telephony deployments, as shown in Figure 5-4.

Figure 5-4   *Deploying Wireless IP Phones*

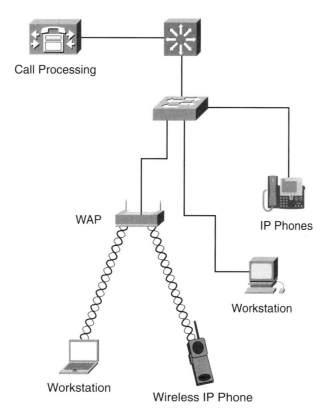

Wireless Security

Although security was originally included with 802.11 standards, it soon became obvious that it wasn't enough. Wireless security — or the lack of it — has been a major contributor to IT managers' reluctance to adapt wireless LANs.

Recently, wireless security has improved dramatically, providing IT managers with an acceptable level of comfort to proceed with the installation of WLANs. IEEE 802.11i, released in June 2004, addresses current security concerns.

In addition to the 802.11 suite of standards, the 802.1x standard can be used for wireless security. More precisely, 802.1x addresses port-based access control.

Wireless Security Issues

A main issue with wireless communication is unauthorized access to network traffic or, more precisely, the watching, displaying, and logging of network traffic, also known as *sniffing*. Contrary to a wired network, where a hacker would need to be physically located at the corporate premises to gain access through a network drop, with a wireless network, the intruder can access the network from a location outside the corporate building. WLANs use radio frequencies, and their signals propagate through ceilings and walls. Therefore, wireless eavesdropping, known as *war driving* or *walk-by hacking,* and rogue WAPs—unauthorized WAPs that allow a hacker access to a network—are two significant security issues with wireless networks.

Moreover, wireless equipment tends to ship with open access. Not only is traffic propagated in clear text, but WAPs also voluntarily broadcast their identity, known as Service Set Identifiers (SSIDs).

Wireless Threat Mitigation

Thanks to the wireless open-access default mode, we can join a wireless network from our favorite coffee shop or hotel room; however, this unrestricted access is not advisable for corporate networks. Wireless network security can be classified into the following three categories:

- Basic wireless security

- Enhanced wireless security

- Wireless intrusion detection

Basic Wireless Security

Basic wireless security is provided by the following built-in functions:

- SSIDs

- Wired Equivalent Privacy (WEP)

- Media Access Control (MAC) address verification

SSIDs

An SSID is a code that identifies membership with a WAP. All wireless devices that want to communicate on a network must have their SSID set to the same value as the WAP SSID to establish connectivity with the WAP.

By default, a WAP broadcasts its SSID every few seconds. This broadcast can be stopped so that a drive-by hacker can't automatically discover the SSID and hence the WAP. However, because the SSID is included in the beacon of every wireless frame, it is easy for a hacker equipped with sniffing equipment to discover the value and fraudulently join the network.

Beacon Frame

The WAP periodically advertises SSID and other network information using a special 802.11 management frame known as a *beacon.*

Being able to join a wireless network by the mere fact of knowing the SSID is referred to as *open authentication.*

Wired Equivalent Privacy

WEP can be used to alleviate the problem of SSID broadcasts by encrypting the traffic between the wireless clients and WAPs. Joining a wireless network using WEP is referred to as *shared-key authentication,* where the WAP sends a challenge to the wireless client who must return it encrypted. If the WAP can decipher the client's response, the WAP has the proof that the client possesses valid keys and therefore has the right to join the wireless network. WEP comes in two encryption strengths: 64-bit and 128-bit.

NOTE   Even if a user manages to proceed with open authentication—for example, he guesses the SSID—if WEP is activated, he could not communicate with the WAP until he obtains the keys.

However, WEP is not considered secure: A hacker sniffing first the challenge and then the encrypted response could reverse-engineer the process and deduce the keys used by the client and WAP.

MAC Address Verification

To further wireless security, a network administrator could use MAC address filtering, in which the WAP is configured with the MAC addresses of the wireless clients that are to be permitted access.

Unfortunately, this method is also not secure because frames could be sniffed to discover a valid MAC address, which the hacker could then spoof.

Enhanced Wireless Security

Stronger security standards, shown in Table 5-2, were created to replace the weaknesses in WEP.

Table 5-2   *Wireless Security Standards*

Security Component	802.11 Original Standards	Security Enhancement
Authentication	Open authentication or shared-key	802.1x
Encryption	WEP	Wireless Fidelity (Wi-Fi) Protected Access (WPA), then 802.11i

802.1x

IEEE 802.1x is a port-based network access control standard. It provides per-user, per-session, mutual strong authentication, not only for wireless networks but also for wired networks, if need be.

Depending on the authentication method used, 802.1x can also provide encryption. Based on the IEEE Extensible Authorization Protocol (EAP), 802.1x allows WAPs and clients to share and exchange WEP encryption keys automatically. The access point acts as a proxy, doing the heavier computational load of encryption. The 802.1x standard also supports a centralized key management for WLANs.

Wi-Fi Protected Access

WPA was introduced as an intermediate solution to WEP encryption and data integrity insecurities while the IEEE 802.11i standard was being ratified.

When WPA is implemented, access to the WAP is provided only to clients that have the right passphrase. Although WPA is more secure than WEP, if the preshared key is stored on the wireless client and the client is stolen, a hacker could get access to the wireless network.

WPA supports both authentication and encryption. Authentication done through preshared keys is known as WPA Personal; when done through 802.1x, it is known as WPA Enterprise.

WPA offers Temporal Key Integrity Protocol (TKIP) as an encryption algorithm and a new integrity algorithm known as Michael. WPA is a subset of the 802.11i specification.

802.11i
In June 2004, the IEEE ratified the draft for the 802.11i standard, also known as WPA2. The 802.11i standard formally replaces WEP and other security features of the original IEEE 802.11 standard.

WPA2 is the *product certification* attributed to wireless equipment that is compatible with the 802.11i standard. WPA2 certification provides support for the additional mandatory 802.11i security features that are not included in WPA. WPA2, like WPA, supports both Enterprise and Personal modes for authentication.

In addition to stricter encryption requirements, WPA2 also adds enhancements to support fast roaming of wireless clients by allowing a client to preauthenticate with the access point toward which it is moving, while maintaining a connection to the access point that it is moving away from.

Wireless Intrusion Detection
Many products provide rogue access point detection. However, some third-party products integrate better than others with Cisco Aironet WAPs and the CiscoWorks Wireless LAN Solution Engine (WLSE), discussed in the next section. One such third-party product is from AirDefense.[5] This product provides wireless intrusion detection that uses the access points to scan the airwaves and report wireless activity.

Wireless Management
Wireless LANs require the same level of security, dependability, and management that wired networks do.

Network management tasks related to WLANs are as follows:

- RF management services
- Interference detection
- Assisted site survey
- RF scanning and monitoring

Cisco Integrated Wireless Network[6] is an evolution of the Cisco Structured Wireless-Aware Network (SWAN), which has been available from Cisco since 2003. The main components of Structured Wireless-Aware Networks[7] are as follows:

- Cisco Aironet WAP

- Management and security servers, specifically CiscoWorks WLSEs

- Wireless clients

- SWAN-aware Cisco Catalyst switches and Cisco routers

Cisco Integrated Wireless Network addresses wireless security, deployment, management, and control issues. It seeks to provide the same level of security, scalability, reliability, ease of deployment, and management for wireless LANs as is expected from wired LANs.

Cisco Integrated Wireless Network requires wireless clients to send RF management (RM) data to a Cisco Aironet WAP, Cisco IOS router, or Cisco Catalyst switch running Wireless Domain Services (WDS), as shown in Figure 5-5.

Figure 5-5 *Campus Infrastructure and Cisco Integrated Wireless Network*

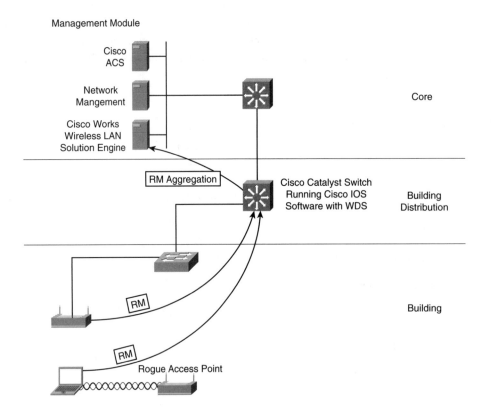

The WDS devices aggregate all the RM data. All access points and clients register with WDS using 802.1x. The WDS devices forward the authentication information to a CiscoWorks WLSE.

One of the many benefits of WDS is Fast Secure Roaming, which assists a wireless client when migrating from one WAP to another. Another significant benefit of Cisco Integrated Wireless Network is the alert generated should a rogue WAP or rogue wireless client connect to the network, because all connecting devices are reported to the WDS device for further authentication.

Although they should be concerned with wireless security, organizations shouldn't forget the basics of physical security, as demonstrated by the following story. In 2005, a Middle Eastern bank was broken into. The thief didn't take anything, but rather left something—a WAP in the wiring closet connecting to the bank's LAN. The hacker was already *inside* the bank network and therefore effortlessly proceeded to transfer money until his stratagem was discovered.

Wireless Design Considerations

The following sections discuss some items that should be considered when designing and provisioning a wireless network.

Site Survey

Site surveys, originally introduced to make the most of scarce resources, are sometimes seen as unnecessary in this age of inexpensive WAPs, where wireless saturation seems so economical. Maybe the days of serious physical surveying, where one would look under the ceiling tiles, are long gone, but you should still perform surveying to determine the optimal locations for WAPs to minimize channel interference while maximizing the range.

Whether you are performing an in-depth site survey or a rudimentary one, you should ask the following questions:

- Which wireless system is best suited for the application?

- Does a line-of-sight requirement exist between antennas?

- Where should the WAP be located so that it is as close as possible to clients?

- What potential sources of interference are in this building? Example sources are cordless phones, microwave ovens, natural interference, or other access points using the same channel.

- Should any federal, provincial, or local regulations and legislation be considered in this deployment?

Site Surveys Have Their Purpose

Some WAPs have an autoconfiguration option with which, after listening on the network, they can autoconfigure themselves for the least-used wireless channel. This is not always desirable, though. For example, if a WAP is installed on the sixth floor of a multi-WAP, multistory building, it might select a channel that it perceived to be available. If that channel is already used by a WAP on the first floor, a client on the third floor could have difficulty staying connected because the channels overlap there.

Overlapping channels in a wireless network perform similarly to an overcrowded wired network plagued by continuous collisions. Undoubtedly, performance will suffer and clients might not be able to establish consistent connectivity to the wireless network.

This problem could be more easily solved with rudimentary planning and by using nonoverlapping channels. Channels 1, 6, and 11 do not overlap, as mentioned in the "Wireless Standards" section, earlier in this chapter.

WLAN Roaming

WLANs are relatively inexpensive to deploy compared to wired networks, and because, as shown earlier in Figure 5-2, throughput is directly related to the proximity of WAPs, network managers often install WAPs to provide overlapping signals, as shown in Figure 5-6. Using this overlapping design, coverage (radius) area is traded for improved throughput.

Figure 5-6 *Overlapping Signals Eliminate Dead Spots*

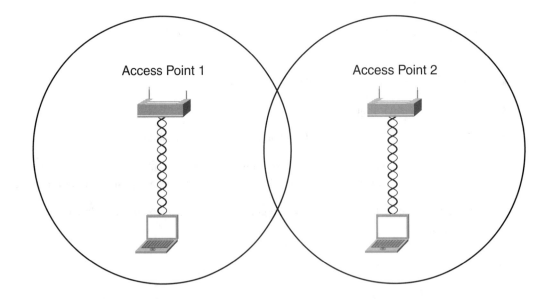

Note that these overlapping signals must be in nonoverlapping channels. This scenario, however, requires WLAN roaming. WLAN roaming plans consider that as a user moves away from a WAP and is therefore losing signal strength, his connection should seamlessly jump to a WAP that provides a stronger signal.

Point-to-Point Bridging

It is not always feasible to run a network cable between two buildings to join their respective LANs into a single Layer 3 broadcast domain. If the two buildings are a reasonable distance apart and preferably in direct line of sight with each other, wireless bridges can be configured, as shown in Figure 5-7. It takes two WAPs to create one logical two-port bridge. In this mode, WAPs are operating in a dedicated point-to-point bridge mode and therefore are no longer operating as wireless access points for clients.

Figure 5-7   *Point-to-Point Bridging*

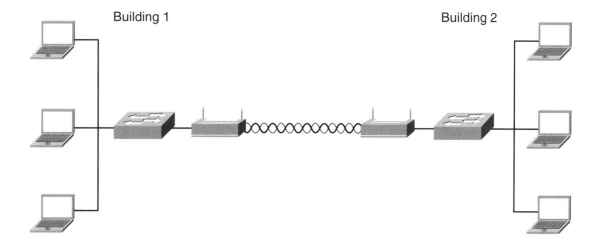

Design Considerations for Wireless IP Phones

Because wireless IP phones have different coverage and wireless characteristics than common wireless clients, a system administrator should conduct another site survey.

Another consideration for wireless IP phones is roaming. The roaming described in the "WLAN Roaming" section, earlier in this chapter, is Layer 2 roaming. With Layer 2 roaming, devices keep their IP address and therefore the changing to another switch would not be noticeable by users. Layer 3 roaming would mean that a device would have to change its IP address; this would mean an interruption in the user's connection. If the connection was to a wireless IP phone, the call would be disconnected; this scenario would likely be unacceptable to users. When wireless IP phones are used, the network needs to be equipped with a Cisco Catalyst 6500 Series Wireless LAN Services Module (WLSM). WLSM, an integral component of SWAN, provides aggregation of access point radio management information, thus enabling Layer 2 and Layer 3 roaming and client mobility management.

Layer 2 roaming refers to an IP phone switching WAP within its subnet of origin. Layer 3 roaming refers to an IP phone switching connectivity from a WAP in its subnet to a WAP located in another subnet. Prior to WLSM, Layer 3 roaming was an issue because the phone would end up in a subnet to which its IP address and default gateway wouldn't belong.

Summary

In this chapter, you learned about wireless technology and implementation. The following topics were covered:

- The prevalence and rapid growth of wireless networks

- Industry standards pertaining to wireless LANs

- Equipment comprising wireless LANs

- Wireless security and threat mitigation such as the following:

  — WEP

  — WPA and 802.11i

  — 802.1x

  — Wireless intrusion detection

- Wireless management using Cisco Integrated Wireless Networks

- Design considerations for wireless networks such as site surveys and roaming capabilities

Endnotes

[1]"Cisco Business Ready Campus Solutions" http:// www.cisco.com/application/pdf/en/us/ guest/ netsol/ns431/c654/cdccont_0900aecd800d8124.pdf.

[2]"Wireless LANs At-A-Glance," Cisco 2004, http://www.cisco.com/application/pdf/en/us/guest/ netsol/ns24/c643/cdccont_0900aecd800dc92e.pdf.

[3]"Cisco HWIC-AP WLAN Module for Cisco 1800 (Modular), 2800 and 3800." http://www.cisco.com/en/US/products/ps5949/products_data_sheet0900aecd8028cc7b.html.

[4]"Cisco Wireless IP Phone 7920," http://www.cisco.com/en/US/partner/products/hw/phones/ps379/ps5056/index.html.

[5]http://www.airdefense.net/cisco.

[6]"Cisco Integrated Wireless Network," http://www.cisco.com/en/US/netsol/ns340/ns394/ns348/ns337/networking_solutions_package.html.

[7]"Cisco Structured Wireless-Aware Network (SWAN) Multimedia Presentation." http://www.cisco.com/en/US/netsol/ns340/ns394/ns348/ns337/networking_solutions_presentation0900aecd8022d512.shtml.

This chapter discusses how to design quality of service into a network, and includes the following sections:

- Making the Business Case

- QoS Requirements for Voice, Data, Video, and Other Traffic

- QoS Models

- QoS Tools

- QoS Design Guidelines

Quality of Service Design

This chapter introduces quality of service (QoS) models, tools, and design guidelines.

We first introduce what QoS is and why it is an important service in today's networks. The QoS-related requirements for various types of traffic are described next. Two models for deploying end-to-end QoS in a network are then examined: Integrated Services (IntServ) and Differentiated Services (DiffServ). QoS tools, including classification and marking, policing and shaping, congestion avoidance, congestion management, and link-specific tools are explained. The Cisco Automatic QoS (AutoQoS) feature on routers and switches is introduced; this tool provides a simple, automatic way to enable QoS configurations in conformance with Cisco's best-practice recommendations. We conclude with some QoS design considerations.

> **NOTE** Appendix B, "Network Fundamentals," includes material that we assume you understand before reading the rest of the book. Thus, we encourage you to review any of the material in Appendix B that you are not familiar with before reading the rest of this chapter.

Making the Business Case

QoS can be defined as the "measure of transmission quality and service availability of a network (or internetworks)."[1] Another definition of QoS is that it "refers to the ability of a network to provide improved service to selected network traffic over various underlying technologies."[2] The common theme here is that QoS ensures quality service to network traffic.

Recall from Chapter 1, "Network Design," that QoS is an intelligent network service—a supporting, but necessary, service provided by the network. QoS is not an ultimate goal of a network; rather, it is a necessary service that enables network applications. In contrast, voice communication is an example of an intelligent network solution—a network-based application that requires the support of network services, including QoS.

A network within which no QoS strategy, tools, or techniques have been implemented treats all traffic the same way and is said to be offering a *best-effort service*—it does its best to send all packets and treats all packets equally. So, if a company's CEO is on a voice call with an important client and someone starts to download a movie to watch over the weekend, the network treats both types of traffic equally and does not consider voice traffic any differently if contention for network resources exists. This is probably not the way the CEO imagined the network should work. The QoS strategies presented in this chapter can be used to ensure, for example, that voice traffic takes priority over movie downloads.

A *converged network* is one in which data, voice, and video traffic coexist on a single network. These diverse traffic types have different characteristics and hence different quality requirements. The QoS tools introduced in this chapter are designed to improve the QoS in networks with a variety of traffic types. Specifically, the QoS parameters affected are the factors that affect the quality of the service provided to the transmission of traffic: packet loss, delay, and jitter.

Packets are typically lost because of network congestion. The effect of the loss depends on the application being used. For example, loss of a single voice packet is not detrimental to the quality of the voice signal at the receiving end because it can be interpolated from other voice samples; loss of multiple voice packets, though, can cause the received message to be unintelligible. On the other hand, a packet sent through the Transmission Control Protocol (TCP) (for example, a file sent with a File Transfer Protocol [FTP] application) that is lost would amplify the congestion problem because it would have to be resent and would therefore consume more bandwidth.

Delay, also called *latency,* is the time it takes packets to travel through the network. Delay has two components: fixed and variable. These terms are described as follows:

■   *Fixed delays* are the predictable delays associated with preparing and encapsulating the data, transmitting it onto the wire, and having it travel to the receiver. Fixed delays can be further categorized as follows:

— **Processing or packetization delay**—The time it takes to create the data that is to be sent. For example, for voice traffic, the analog voice must be sampled, converted to digital data, and then encapsulated in packets.

— **Serialization delay**—The time it takes to transmit the data onto the wire. This delay is related to the speed of the physical link.

— **Propagation delay**—The time it takes the data to travel on the network. In most cases, propagation delay is small enough that it can be ignored.

■   *Variable delays* are the unpredictable delays that result from a packet waiting for other traffic that is queued on the interface to be sent. As more and larger packets are being sent, these delays increase.

Jitter is the variation in the delay experienced by packets in the network. In the example of jitter illustrated in Figure 6-1, the sender sends the data out at consistent time intervals, Δt. The receiver is seeing a variation in the delay of received packets—some are greater than Δt while others are less than Δt. Jitter is usually not noticeable for applications such as file transfers. However, applications such as voice are sensitive to differences in packet delays—for example, a listener might hear silent pauses where none should exist.

> **NOTE**   Special dejitter buffers are incorporated into voice-enabled routers to smooth out the differences in packet delays by converting the variable delay to a fixed delay. However, these dejitter buffers increase the overall delay in the network.

Figure 6-1   *Jitter Is the Variation in the Delay of Received Packets*

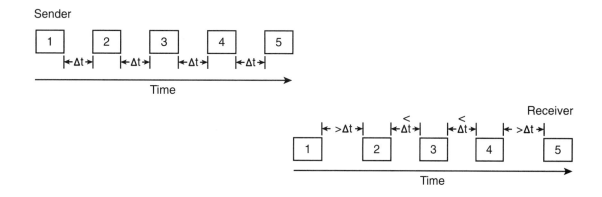

QoS allows you to control and predict the service provided by your network for a variety of applications. Implementing QoS has many advantages, including the following:[3]

■ Controlling which network resources (bandwidth, equipment, wide-area facilities, and so on) are being used

■ Ensuring that your resources are used efficiently by the mission-critical applications—those that are most important to your business—and that other applications get fair service without interfering with this mission-critical traffic

■ Creating a solid foundation for a fully integrated converged network in the future

QoS Requirements for Voice, Data, Video, and Other Traffic

Later in this chapter (in the "Classification and Marking" section), the Cisco QoS Baseline is presented, representing best-practice recommendations for how QoS should be implemented for various types of traffic. These recommendations are based on the requirements for that traffic, as described in this section.

Voice traffic (discussed in more detail in Chapter 7, "Voice Transport Design") is sensitive to delays, variation in delays (jitter), and packet loss. The guidelines for ensuring acceptable voice quality are as follows:

■   The one-way delay should be no more than 150 milliseconds (ms).

■   The jitter should be no more than 30 ms.

■   No more than 1 percent of packets should be lost.

NOTE   While 150 ms is the standard for acceptable voice delay, tests have shown that a negligible quality difference is found with a 200-ms delay.

The bandwidth required for voice traffic varies with the algorithm that compresses the traffic and the specific Layer 2 frame type it is encapsulated in, as described further in Chapter 7. Call-signaling traffic requires at least 150 bps (not including Layer 2 overhead), depending on the protocols used.

Interactive video, or video conferencing, has the same delay, jitter, and packet loss requirements as voice traffic. The difference is the bandwidth requirements—voice packets are small while video conferencing packet sizes can vary, as can the data rate. A general guideline for overhead is to provide an additional 20 percent of bandwidth over that required by the data.

Streaming video has different requirements than interactive video. An example of the use of streaming video is when an employee views an online video during an e-learning session. As such, this video stream is not nearly as sensitive to delay or loss as interactive video is—requirements for streaming video include a loss of no more than 5 percent and a delay of no more than 4 to 5 seconds. Depending on the importance to the organization, this traffic can be given precedence over other traffic.

NOTE   When you start watching a video stream (a recording) on the Internet, you might see messages such as "Buffering x%" before the video starts in the application that you are running. This buffering is to compensate for any transmission delays that might occur.

Many other types of application data exist within an organization. For example, some are relatively noninteractive and therefore not delay sensitive (such as e-mail), while others involve users entering data and waiting for responses (such as database applications) and are therefore very delay sensitive. Data can also be classified by its importance to the overall corporate business objectives. For example, a company that provides interactive, live e-learning sessions to its customers would consider that traffic to be mission-critical, while a manufacturing company that is one of the e-learning company's customers might consider that same traffic important, but not critical to its operations.

Traffic related to the operation of the network itself must also be considered. One example of this type of traffic is routing protocol messages—the size and frequency of these messages vary, depending on the specific protocol used and the stability of the network. Network management data is another example, including Simple Network Management Protocol (SNMP) traffic between network devices and the network management station.

QoS Models

Two models exist for deploying end-to-end QoS in a network for traffic that is not suitable for best-effort service: IntServ and DiffServ. *End-to-end QoS* means that the network provides the level of service required by traffic throughout the entire network, from one end to the other.

KEY POINT

With IntServ, an application requests services from the network, and the network devices confirm that they can meet the request, before any data is sent. The data from the application is considered to be a flow of packets.

In contrast, with DiffServ, each packet is marked as it enters the network based on the type of traffic that it contains. The network devices then use this marking to determine how to handle the packet as it travels through the network.

IntServ

IntServ uses an explicit signaling mechanism from applications to network devices. The application requests a specific service level, including, for example, its bandwidth and delay requirements. After the network devices have confirmed that they can meet these requirements, the application is assumed to only send data that requires this level of service.

Applications in an IntServ environment use the Resource Reservation Protocol (RSVP) to indicate their requirements to the network devices. The network devices keep information about the flow of packets, and ensure that the flow gets the resources it needs by using appropriate queuing (prioritizing traffic) and policing (selectively dropping other packets) methods. Two types of services provided in an IntServ environment are as follows:

- **Guaranteed Rate Service**—This service allows applications to reserve bandwidth to meet their requirements. The network uses weighted fair queuing (WFQ) with RSVP to provide this service. (WFQ is described in the "Congestion Management" section, later in this chapter.)

- **Controlled Load Service**—This service allows applications to request low delay and high throughput, even during times of congestion. The network uses RSVP with weighted random early detection (WRED) to provide this kind of service. (WRED is described in the "Congestion Avoidance" section, later in this chapter.)

Because IntServ requires RSVP on all network devices, it is currently not used as much as DiffServ.

DiffServ

An application in a DiffServ environment does not explicitly signal the network before sending data. Instead, the network tries to deliver a specific level of service based on the QoS specified in the header of each packet. Network devices, typically on the edge of the network, are configured to classify and mark packets according to their source, the destination, or the type of traffic in them. Devices within the network then provide appropriate resources based on this marking. For example, packets that contain voice traffic are usually given higher priority than file transfer data because of the unique requirements of voice.

The Cisco Internet Operating System (IOS) incorporates QoS features that support DiffServ, as described in the following section.

QoS Tools

Some of the various tools that implement QoS are described in this section and illustrated in Figure 6-2.

Figure 6-2 *QoS Tools Manage Network Traffic*

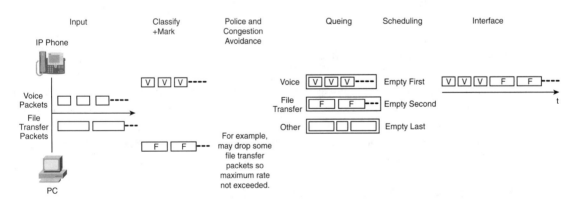

Many devices send data into a network. In the example shown in Figure 6-2, an IP phone produces packets that contain voice traffic, and a PC sends file transfer data. As the data enters the network, it is analyzed and classified according to how it should be dealt with in the network. After it is classified, the data is marked accordingly.

KEY POINT | Classification and marking form the basis for the rest of the QoS tools; it is here that business policies, priorities, and so forth are first implemented.

The markings can then be used by other tools. For example, packets can be dropped by policing tools so that the maximum rate on an interface is not exceeded. Or packets can be dropped by congestion-avoidance tools to avoid anticipated interface congestion. Remaining packets are then queued, again according to their markings, and scheduled for output on the interface. Other tools, such as compression, can be implemented on the interface to reduce the bandwidth consumed by the traffic.

The following sections explore these QoS tools:

- Classification and Marking

- Policing and Shaping

- Congestion Avoidance

- Congestion Management

- Link-Specific Tools

- AutoQoS

Classification and Marking

Before any traffic can be given priority over or treated differently than other traffic, it must first be identified.

KEY POINT | *Classification* is the process of analyzing packets and sorting them into different categories so that they can then be suitably marked; after they are marked, the packets can be treated appropriately.

Marking is the process of putting an indication of the classification of the packet within the packet itself so that it can be used by other tools.

The point within the network where markings are accepted is known as the *trust boundary;* any markings made by devices outside the trust boundary can be overwritten at the trust boundary. Establishing a trust boundary means that the classification and marking processes can be done once, at the boundary; the rest of the network then does not have to repeat the analysis. Ideally, the trust boundary is as close to end devices as possible—or even within the end devices. For example, a Cisco IP phone could be considered to be a trusted device because it marks voice traffic appropriately. However, a user's PC would not usually be trusted because users could change markings (which they might be tempted to do in an attempt to increase the priority of their traffic).

Classification

Classification can be done based on data at any of the OSI layers. For example, traffic can be differentiated based on the Layer 1 physical interface that it came in on or the Layer 2 source Media Access Control (MAC) address in the Ethernet frame. For Transmission Control Protocol/Internet Protocol (TCP/IP) traffic, differentiators include the source and destination IP addresses (Layer 3), the transport (Layer 4) protocol—TCP or User Datagram Protocol (UDP), and the application port number (indicating Layer 7).

Some applications require more analysis to correctly identify and classify them. For these cases, the Cisco Network-Based Application Recognition (NBAR) classification software feature, running within the IOS on Cisco routers, can be used. NBAR allows classification (and therefore marking) of a variety of applications, including web-based and other difficult-to-classify protocols that use dynamic TCP/UDP port assignments. For example, Hypertext Transfer Protocol (HTTP) traffic can be classified and marked by specifying uniform resource locators (URLs) so that a customer who is accessing an online ordering page could be given priority over someone accessing a general information page. Support for new protocols can be easily and quickly added through downloadable packet description language modules (PDLMs).

> **NOTE**   You must enable Cisco Express Forwarding before you configure NBAR.[4] (See Chapter 2, "Switching Design," for information about Cisco Express Forwarding.) NBAR examines only the first packet of a flow; the rest of the packets belonging to the flow are switched by Cisco Express Forwarding.

Marking

Marking can be done either in the Layer 2 frame or in the Layer 3 packet.

For Ethernet frames, Layer 2 marking can be done using the following methods:[5]

■   For an Institute of Electrical and Electronics Engineers (IEEE) 802.1q frame, the three 802.1p user priority bits in the Tag field are used as class of service (CoS) bits. (Recall from Chapter 2 that 802.1q is a standard trunking protocol in which the trunking information is encoded within a Tag field that is inserted inside of the frame header itself.)

■   For an Inter-Switch Link (ISL) frame, three of the bits in the user field in the ISL header are used as CoS bits. (Recall from Chapter 2 that ISL is a Cisco-proprietary trunking protocol that encapsulates the data frame between a 26-byte header and a 4-byte trailer.)

■   No CoS representation exists for non-802.1q/non-ISL frames.

Because the CoS is represented by 3 bits, it can take on one of eight values, 0 through 7.

Layer 2 markings are not useful as end-to-end QoS indicators because the media often changes throughout a network (for example, from Ethernet to a Frame Relay wide-area network [WAN]). Thus, Layer 3 markings are required to support end-to-end QoS.

For IP version 4 (IPv4), Layer 3 marking can be done using the type of service (ToS) field in the packet header. Recall (from Appendix B) that this 8-bit field is the second byte in the IP packet header. (Figure B-11 illustrates all the fields in the IP packet header.) Originally, only the first 3 bits were used; these bits, called the *IP Precedence bits,* are illustrated in the middle of Figure 6-3. Packets with higher precedence values should get higher priority within the network. Because 3 bits again can only specify eight marking values, IP precedence does not allow a granular classification of traffic.

Figure 6-3 *The ToS Field in an IPv4 Header Supports IP Precedence or DSCP*

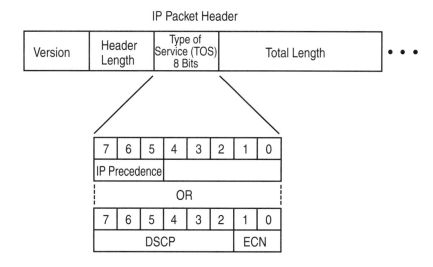

Thus, more bits are now used: The first 6 bits in the ToS field are now known as the *DiffServ Code Point (DSCP) bits,* and are illustrated in the lower portion of Figure 6-3. (The lower 2 bits in the ToS field are used for explicit congestion notification [ECN], which is described in the "Congestion Avoidance" section, later in this chapter.) With 6 bits, DSCP allows 64 marking values.

DSCP values can be expressed numerically (with binary values from 000000 through 111111 or decimal values from 0 through 63) or by using Per-Hop Behavior (PHB) values; PHBs are just keywords that represent some numeric DSCP values. (The name *per-hop behavior* indicates that each device, or hop, should behave consistently when determining how to treat a packet.)

Four PHB classes exist; they are described as follows:

- **Default or Best Effort (BE) PHB**—This PHB has a DSCP binary value of 000000 and represents the best-effort service.

- **Class Selector (CS) PHB**—This PHB has the lower three DSCP bits set to 000. Because this PHB uses only the upper 3 bits, it is compatible with the IP precedence values and is in fact written as CS*x*, where *x* is the decimal IP precedence value. For example, the CS PHB with the value 011000 represents IP precedence binary 011 or decimal 3; it is written as CS3.

- **Expedited Forwarding (EF) PHB**—This PHB represents a DSCP value of binary 101110 (decimal 46) and provides a low-loss, low-latency, low-jitter, and guaranteed bandwidth service. The EF PHB should be reserved for only the most critical applications, such as voice traffic, so that if the network becomes congested, the critical traffic can get the service it requires.

- **Assured Forwarding (AF) PHBs**—Four classes of AF PHBs exist, each with three drop preferences. These classes are represented as AF*xy*, where *x* is the class (a value from 1 to 4) and *y* is the drop preference (a value from 1 to 3). The AF class is determined by the upper 3 bits of the DSCP, while the drop preference is determined by the next 2 bits. (The lowest bit is always set to 0.) A drop preference of 1 is the lowest and 3 is the highest; this field determines which traffic should be dropped in times of congestion. For example, AF21 traffic would be dropped less often than AF22 traffic. Figure 6-4 illustrates the AF PHBs.

Figure 6-4 *AF PHB and DSCP Values*

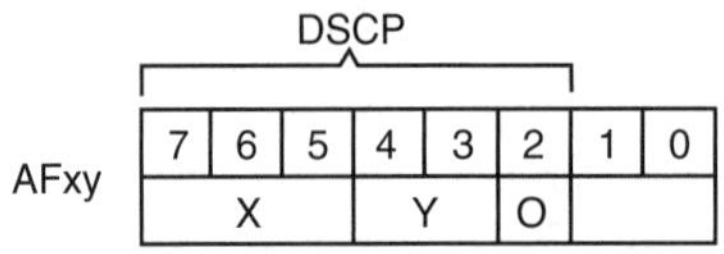

AF Class 1		DSCP Binary x	DSCP Binary y		DSCP Decimal
low drop pref	AF11	001	01	0	10
med drop pref	AF12	001	10	0	12
high drop pref	AF13	001	11	0	14
AF Class 2					
low drop pref	AF21	010	01	0	18
med drop pref	AF22	010	10	0	20
high drop pref	AF23	010	11	0	22
AF Class 3					
low drop pref	AF31	011	01	0	26
med drop pref	AF32	011	10	0	28
high drop pref	AF33	011	11	0	30
AF Class 4					
low drop pref	AF41	100	01	0	34
med drop pref	AF42	100	10	0	36
high drop pref	AF43	100	11	0	38

KEY POINT

We found that it is easy to get lost in the details of QoS markings, especially when the different PHBs, AF classes, and so forth are introduced.

To hopefully avoid this confusion, remember these key points about QoS DSCP markings:

- The ToS field within an IPv4 packet header marks, or indicates, the kind of traffic that is in the packet. This marking can then be used by other tools within the network to provide the packet the service that it needs.

- The first 6 bits in the ToS field are known as the DSCP bits.

DSCP values can be represented numerically (in binary or decimal) or with keywords, known as PHBs. Each PHB (BE, CSx, EF, and AFxy) represents a specific numeric DSCP value and therefore a specific way that traffic should be handled.

Cisco has created a QoS Baseline that provides recommendations to ensure that both its products, and the designs and deployments that use them, are consistent in terms of QoS. Although the QoS Baseline document itself is internal to Cisco, it includes an 11-class classification scheme that can be used for enterprises; this QoS Baseline suggestion for enterprise traffic classes is provided in Figure 6-5. This figure identifies the 11 types of traffic and the QoS marking that each type should be assigned. As described earlier, the QoS marking is either a Layer 2 CoS (specified within the 802.1q Tag field or ISL header) or a Layer 3 value marked in the IP packet header. The Layer 3 markings can either be done with a 3-bit IP precedence value (shown in the IPP column in Figure 6-5) or with a 6-bit DSCP value; both the numeric DSCP value and the PHB keyword representation of that value are shown in the figure.

Figure 6-5 *Cisco QoS Baseline Provides Guidelines for Classification and Marking*[6]

Application	L3 Classification			L2 COS
	IPP	PHB	DSCP	
IP Routing	6	CS6	48	6
Voice	5	EF	46	5
Interactive Video	4	AF41	34	4
Streaming Video	4	CS4	32	4
Mission-Critical Data	3	AF31	26	3
Call Signaling	3	CS3	24	3
Transactional Data	2	AF21	18	2
Network Management	2	CS2	16	2
Bulk Data	1	AF11	10	1
Scavenger	1	CS1	8	1
Best Effort	0	0	0	0

The classes of traffic in the QoS Baseline are defined as followed:

- **IP Routing class**—This class is for IP routing protocol traffic such as Border Gateway Protocol (BGP), Enhanced Interior Gateway Routing Protocol (EIGRP), Open Shortest Path First (OSPF), and so forth.

- **Voice class**—This class is for Voice over IP (VoIP) bearer traffic (the conversation traffic), not for the associated signaling traffic, which would go in the Call Signaling class.

- **Interactive Video class**—This class is for IP videoconferencing traffic.

- **Streaming Video class**—This class is either unicast or multicast unidirectional video.

- **Mission-Critical Data class**—This class is intended for a subset of the Transactional Data applications that are most significant to the business. The applications in this class are different for every organization.

- **Call Signaling class**—This class is intended for voice and video-signaling traffic.

- **Transactional Data class**—This class is intended for user-interactive applications such as database access, transactions, and interactive messaging.

- **Network Management class**—This class is intended for traffic from network management protocols, such as SNMP.

- **Bulk Data class**—This class is intended for background, noninteractive traffic, such as large file transfers, content distribution, database synchronization, backup operations, and e-mail.

- **Scavenger class**—This class is based on an Internet 2 draft that defines a "less-than-Best Effort" service. If a link becomes congested, this class will be dropped the most aggressively. Any nonbusiness-related traffic (for example, downloading music in most organizations) could be put into this class.

- **Best Effort class**—This class is the default class. Unless an application has been assigned to another class, it remains in this default class. Most enterprises have hundreds, if not thousands, of applications on their networks; the majority of these applications remain in the Best Effort class.

KEY POINT

The QoS Baseline does not mandate that these 11 classes be used; rather this classification scheme is an example of well-designed traffic classes. Enterprises can have fewer classes, depending on their specific requirements, and can evolve to using more classes as they grow. For example, at one point, Cisco was using a 5-class model (the minimum recommended in a network with voice, video, and data) on its internal network.[7]

Figure 6-6 illustrates an example strategy for expanding the number of classes over time—from a 5-class, to an 8-class, and eventually to the 11-class model—as needs arise.

Figure 6-6   *The Number of Classes of Service Can Evolve as Requirements Change[8]*

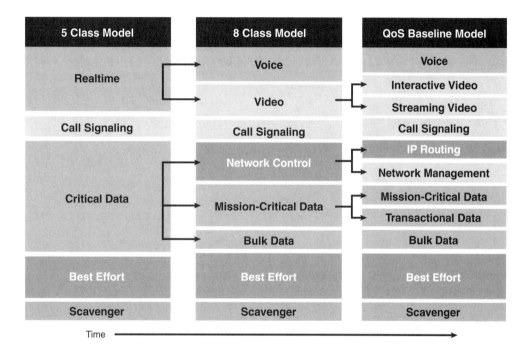

After traffic has been classified and marked and sent on its way through the network, other devices can then read the markings and act accordingly. The following sections examine the QoS tools that these devices can use.

Policing and Shaping

Policing and shaping tools identify traffic that violates some threshold or service-level agreement (SLA). The two tools differ in the way that they respond to this violation.

KEY POINT

Policing tools drop the excess traffic or modify its marking.

Shaping tools buffer the extra data until it can be sent, thus delaying but not dropping it.

The difference between these tools is illustrated in Figure 6-7.

Figure 6-7 *Policing Drops Excess Traffic While Shaping Delays It*

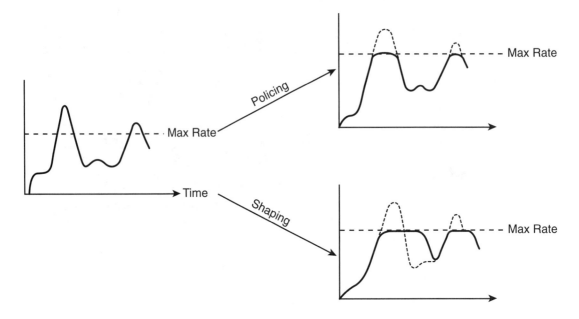

The diagram on the left in Figure 6-7 illustrates traffic that is being presented to an interface; note that some of the traffic exceeds the maximum rate allowed on the interface. If policing tools were configured on the interface, the excess traffic would simply be dropped, as indicated in the upper-right diagram. In contrast, the lower-right diagram shows that shaping tools would send all the data by delaying some of it until bandwidth is available.

Policing Tools

The Cisco IOS traffic policing feature allows control of the maximum rate of traffic sent or received on an interface. It is often configured on interfaces at the edge of a network to limit traffic into or out of the network. Traffic that does not exceed the specified rate parameters is sent, while traffic that exceeds the parameters is either dropped or is sent with a lower priority.

NOTE Committed access rate (CAR) is an older IOS policing tool that can be configured to rate-limit (drop) certain traffic if it exceeds a specified speed. It can also be configured to set or change the markings within the packet header for traffic, depending on whether it meets or exceeds the acceptable rate.

Shaping Tools

Traffic shaping allows you to control the traffic going out of an interface to match its flow to the speed of the destination interface or to ensure that the traffic conforms to particular policies. The IOS software supports the following QoS traffic-shaping features:

■ **Generic Traffic Shaping (GTS)**—GTS provides a mechanism to reduce the flow of outbound traffic on an interface to a specific bit rate. You can use access lists to define particular traffic to be shaped. GTS is useful when the receiving device has a lower access rate into the network than the transmitting device.

■ **Class-based shaping**—This type of shaping provides the means for configuring traffic shaping on a class of traffic, based on the marking in the packet header, rather than only on an access list basis. Class-based shaping also allows you to specify average rate or peak rate traffic shaping.

■ **Distributed Traffic Shaping (DTS)**—DTS is similar to class-based shaping; however, DTS is used on devices that have distributed processing (such as the Cisco 7500 Versatile Interface Processor [VIP]) and don't support class-based shaping.

■ **Frame Relay Traffic Shaping (FRTS)**—Although GTS works for Frame Relay, FRTS offers the following capabilities that are more specific to Frame Relay networks:

— **Rate enforcement on a per–virtual circuit (VC) basis**—A peak rate can be configured to limit outbound traffic to either the committed information rate (CIR) or to some other defined value.

— **Generalized backward explicit congestion notification (BECN) support on a per-VC basis**—The router can monitor the BECN field in frames and throttle traffic if necessary.

— **Priority and custom queuing support on a per-VC basis**—This allows finer granularity in the queuing of traffic on individual VCs.

> **NOTE**   Priority and custom queuing are described in the "Congestion Management" section, later in this chapter.

Congestion Avoidance

KEY POINT | Congestion-avoidance techniques monitor network traffic loads so that congestion can be anticipated and then avoided, before it becomes problematic.

If congestion-avoidance techniques are not used and interface queues get full, packets trying to enter the queue will be discarded, regardless of what traffic they hold. This is known as *tail drop*— the packets arriving after the tail of the queue are dropped.

In contrast, congestion-avoidance techniques allow packets from streams identified as being eligible for early discard (those with lower priority) to be dropped when the queue is getting full.

Congestion avoidance works well with TCP-based traffic; TCP has a built-in flow control mechanism so that when a source detects a dropped packet, the source slows its transmission.

Weighted random early detection (WRED) is the Cisco implementation of the random early detection (RED) mechanism. RED randomly drops packets when the queue gets to a specified level (in other words, when it is nearing full). RED is designed to work with TCP traffic: When TCP packets are dropped, TCP's flow-control mechanism slows the transmission rate and then progressively begins to increase it again. RED therefore results in sources slowing down and hopefully avoiding congestion.

WRED extends RED by using the IP precedence in the IP packet header to determine which traffic should be dropped; the drop-selection process is weighted by the IP precedence. Similarly, DSCP-based WRED uses the DSCP value in the IP packet header in the drop-selection process. WRED selectively discards lower-priority (and higher-drop preference for DSCP) traffic when the interface begins to get congested.

Starting in IOS Release 12.2(8)T, Cisco has implemented an extension to WRED called explicit congestion notification (ECN), which is defined in RFC 3168, *The Addition of Explicit Congestion Notification (ECN) to IP*, and uses the lower 2 bits in the ToS byte (as shown earlier in Figure 6-3). Devices use these two ECN bits to communicate that they are experiencing congestion. When ECN is in use, it marks packets as experiencing congestion (rather than dropping them) if the senders are ECN-capable and the queue has not yet reached its maximum threshold. If the queue does reach the maximum, packets are dropped as they would be without ECN.

Congestion Management

While congestion avoidance manages the tail, or back, of queues, congestion management takes care of the front of queues.

KEY POINT

As the name implies, congestion management controls congestion after it has occurred. Thus, if no congestion exists, these tools are not triggered, and packets are sent out as soon as they arrive on the interface.

Congestion management can be thought of as two separate processes: queuing, which separates traffic into various queues or buffers, and scheduling, which decides from which queue traffic is to be sent next.

Queuing algorithms sort the traffic destined for an interface. Cisco IOS Software includes many queuing mechanisms. Priority queuing (PQ), custom queuing (CQ), and weighted fair queuing (WFQ) are the three oldest. IP Real-Time Transport Protocol (RTP) priority queuing was developed to provide priority for voice traffic, but it has been replaced by class-based weighted fair queuing (CBWFQ) and low latency queuing (LLQ). These queuing mechanisms are described as follows:

- **PQ**—A series of filters based on packet characteristics (for example, source IP address and destination port) are configured to place traffic in one of four queues—high, medium, normal, and low priority. For example, voice traffic could be put in the high queue and other traffic in the lower three queues. The high-priority queue is serviced first until it is empty. The lower-priority queues are only serviced when no higher-priority traffic exists; these lower-priority queues run the risk of never being serviced.

- **CQ**—Traffic is placed into one of up to 16 queues, and bandwidth can be allocated proportionally for each queue by specifying the maximum number of bytes to be taken from each queue. CQ services queues by cycling through them in a round-robin fashion, sending the specified amount of traffic (if any exists) for each queue before moving on to the next queue. If one queue is empty, the router sends packets from the next queue that has packets ready to send.

- **WFQ**—WFQ classifies traffic into *conversations* and applies weights, or priorities, to determine the relative amount of bandwidth each conversation is allowed. WFQ recognizes IP precedence values marked in IP packet headers. For example, WFQ schedules voice traffic first and then fairly shares the remaining bandwidth among high-volume flows.

- **IP RTP priority queuing**—This type of queuing provides a strict priority-queuing scheme for delay-sensitive traffic. This traffic can be identified by its RTP port numbers and classified into a priority queue. As a result, delay-sensitive traffic such as voice can be given strict priority over other nonvoice traffic.

NOTE   RTP is a protocol designed to be used for real-time traffic such as voice. RTP runs on top of UDP (to avoid the additional overhead and delay of TCP). RTP adds another header that includes some sequencing information and time-stamping information to ensure that the received data is processed in the correct order and that the variation in the delay is within acceptable limits.

- **CBWFQ**—CBWFQ provides WFQ based on defined classes but does not have a strict priority queue available for real-time traffic such as voice. All packets are serviced fairly based on weight; no class of packets can be granted strict priority.

- **LLQ**—LLQ is a combination of CBWFQ and PQ, adding strict priority queuing to CBWFQ. This allows delay-sensitive data, such as voice data, to be sent first, giving it preferential treatment over other traffic.

KEY POINT | LLQ is the recommended mechanism for networks with voice traffic.

Link-Specific Tools

KEY POINT | Link-specific tools are those that are enabled on both ends of a point-to-point WAN connection to reduce the bandwidth required or delay experienced on that link. The QoS tools available include header compression (to reduce the bandwidth utilization) and link fragmentation and interleaving (LFI) (to reduce the delay encountered).

Voice packets typically have a small payload (the voice data) relative to the packet headers—the RTP, UTP, and IP headers add up to 40 bytes. So, compressing the header of such packets can have a dramatic effect on the bandwidth they require. RTP header compression, called cRTP, compresses this 40-byte header to 2 or 4 bytes.

> **NOTE**   Voice compression, which reduces the size of the voice payload while still maintaining the quality at an acceptable level, is described in Chapter 7.

Even with queuing and compression in place, a delay-sensitive packet (such as a voice packet) could be ready to go out of a WAN interface just after a large packet (for example, part of a file transfer) has been sent on that interface. After forwarding of a packet out of an interface has begun, queuing has no effect and cannot recall the large packet. Therefore, a voice packet that gets stuck behind a large data packet on a WAN link can experience a relatively long delay and, as a result, the quality of the voice conversation can suffer. To counteract this, LFI can be configured on WAN links to fragment large packets (split them into smaller packets) and interleave those fragments with other packets waiting to go out on the interface. The smaller, delay-sensitive packets can travel with minimal delay. The fragments of the larger packets need to be reassembled at the receiving end, so the larger packets will experience some delay. However, because the applications sending these packets are not delay-sensitive, they should not be adversely affected by this delay. Figure 6-8 illustrates the LFI concept.

Figure 6-8   *LFI Ensures That Smaller Packets Do Not Get Stuck Behind Larger Packets*

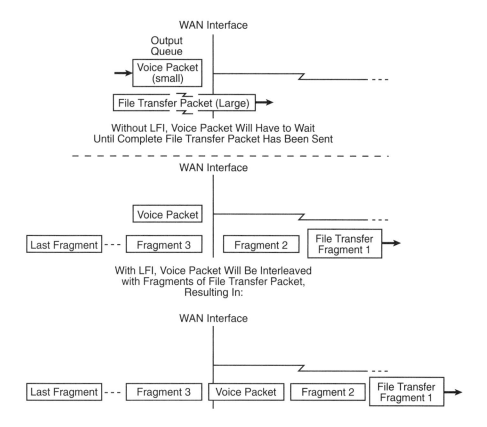

> **NOTE**   Recall from Appendix B that the IPv4 packet header includes a 16-bit identification field consisting of 3 bits of flags and 13 bits of fragment offset. This field indicates whether the packet is a fragment and, if so, the offset of the fragment in the original packet. The receiving end can then reassemble the fragments to create the original packet.

AutoQoS

The Cisco AutoQoS feature on routers and switches provides a simple, automatic way to enable QoS configurations in conformance with Cisco's best-practice recommendations. Only one command is required. The router or switch then creates configuration commands to perform such things as classifying and marking VoIP traffic and then applying an LLQ queuing strategy on WAN links for that traffic. The configuration created by AutoQoS becomes part of the normal configuration file and can, therefore, be edited if required.

The first phase of AutoQoS, available in various versions of router IOS Release 12.3, only creates configurations related to VoIP traffic.

> **NOTE** The Cisco Feature Navigator tool, available at http://www.cisco.com/go/fn, allows you to quickly find the Cisco IOS and switch Catalyst Operating System (CatOS) Software release required for the features that you want to run on your network. For example, you can use this tool to determine the IOS release required to run AutoQoS on the routers in your network.

The second phase of AutoQoS is called AutoQoS Enterprise and includes support for all types of data. It configures the router with commands to classify, mark, and handle packets in up to 10 of the 11 QoS Baseline traffic classes. The Mission-Critical traffic class is the only one not defined, because it is specific to each organization. As with the earlier release, the commands created by AutoQoS Enterprise can be edited if required.

> **NOTE** Further information on AutoQoS can be found at http://www.cisco.com/en/US/products/ps6656/products_ios_protocol_opt and at http://www.cisco.com/en/US/tech/tk543/tk759/tk879/tsd_technology_support_protocol_home.html.

QoS Design Guidelines

As discussed in Chapter 1, the first step in any design process is to determine the requirements that you are trying to meet. Only then should you attempt to design the network features to meet those requirements. Recall that this process is called a top-down approach. Compare this to a bottom-up approach, in which features (queuing, for example) are deployed on some interfaces without considering why they are being deployed.

Thus, when designing QoS features into your network, the QoS-related requirements of the network must be clearly defined. For example, if the network includes VoIP, video, or other delay-sensitive traffic, you need to determine whether that traffic is considered important enough to warrant providing it strict priority.

The number of classes of traffic that are to be used in the network and which applications are to be considered mission-critical need to be determined. In general, the number of applications in the Mission-Critical class should be minimized. If too many are considered critical, each one becomes just part of a large group and does not necessarily get the services it truly needs.

QoS can be considered "a system of managed unfairness"[9] in that some traffic is given less priority than other traffic, which might be seen by some users to be unfair. Thus, it is important to get agreements and buy-ins from high-level management about which data is considered critical to and within the organization, and to flow the QoS requirements from these agreements. Any complaints of unfairness can then be rebuked by referring to the agreements.

QoS tools can be used in all areas of the Enterprise Composite Network Model. As discussed earlier, the ideal trust boundary—where classification and marking of traffic are performed and trusted by the rest of the network—is as close to the end devices as possible. While the network administrator might not want to trust end users or their applications to set markings consistent with the network's policy, the access switches to which the users' PCs are connected could perform this task.

Using Layer 3 DSCP QoS markings allows QoS to be provided end to end throughout the network. If some access switches support only Layer 2 (CoS) markings, these markings must be mapped to the appropriate DSCP values; this would be a function performed by the distribution switches. These switches must also apply DSCP values to any traffic that has not been marked elsewhere. The campus core should not be involved in classifying and marking traffic; its role is to process the traffic quickly, based on previous markings.

Policing (dropping) traffic is best performed as close to the source of the traffic as possible, to avoid having the traffic travel through the network (and therefore consume resources such as bandwidth) unnecessarily. Again, within the campus infrastructure, policing should be performed on the access or distribution devices.

QoS tools can be enabled on either switches or routers. When performed in software however, QoS operations can consume considerable CPU resources, so ideally they should be enabled on devices that execute the necessary computations in hardware to achieve higher performance.

Although we typically think of applying queuing only to slow WAN links, LAN links can also be congested. For example, uplinks between switches that aggregate traffic from many other links are potential locations of congestion. Although this is less likely to occur than on WAN links, queuing should be deployed on any link that could potentially experience congestion, to provide the needed services to the network traffic. Queuing policies—in other words, how each traffic class is handled—should be consistent across the enterprise.

Summary

In this chapter, you learned about QoS models, tools, and design guidelines, including the following topics:

- Why QoS is important in a converged network—one in which data, voice, and video traffic flows

- The QoS-related requirements of various types of traffic

- The two models for deploying end-to-end QoS: IntServ and DiffServ

- The QoS tools available to implement QoS policies, including the following:

  - **Classification and marking**—Analyzing packets and sorting them into different categories, and then putting an indication of the classification of the packet within the packet header itself

  - **Policing**—Tools that drop the excess traffic or modify its marking

  - **Shaping**—Tools that buffer extra data until it can be sent, thus delaying but not dropping it

  - **Congestion avoidance**—Monitoring traffic loads so that congestion can be anticipated and then avoided, before it becomes problematic

  - **Congestion management**—Controlling congestion after it has occurred

  - **Link-specific tools**—Compression (to reduce the bandwidth utilization) and LFI (to reduce the delay experienced)

  - **AutoQoS**—A simple, automatic way to enable QoS configurations in conformance with the Cisco best-practice recommendations

- The Cisco QoS Baseline guidelines for classifying traffic

- QoS design guidelines

Endnotes

[1]"Enterprise QoS Solution Reference Network Design Guide, Version 3.1," June 2005, http://www.cisco.com/univercd/cc/td/doc/solution/esm/qossrnd.pdf.

[2]"Cisco IOS Quality of Service Solutions Configuration Guide, Release 12.2." http://www.cisco.com/en/US/products/sw/iosswrel/ps1835/products_configuration_guide_book09186a00800c5e31.html.

[3]Ibid.

[4]"Network-Based Application Recognition and Distributed Network-Based Application Recognition." http://www.cisco.com/en/US/products/ps6350/
products_configuration_guide_chapter09186a0080455985.html.

[5]"QoS Classification and Marking on Catalyst 6500/6000 Series Switches Running CatOS Software." http://www.cisco.com/en/US/products/hw/switches/ps700/
products_tech_note09186a008014f8a8.shtml.

[6]Adapted from "QoS Best Practices" session at Cisco Technical Symposium 2004, Tom Szigeti, October 5, 2004, Toronto, and Szigeti and Hattingh, *End-to-End QoS Network Design: Quality of Service in LANs, WANs, and VPNs,* Indianapolis, Cisco Press, 2004.

[7]"QoS Best Practices" session at Cisco Technical Symposium 2004, Tom Szigeti, October 5, 2004, Toronto.

[8]Ibid.

[9]Szigeti and Hattingh, *End-to-End QoS Network Design: Quality of Service in LANs, WANs, and VPNs,* Indianapolis, Cisco Press, 2004.

This chapter discusses how to design the transport of voice within a network, and includes the following sections:

- Making the Business Case

- What Is Voice Transport?

- Quality of Service

- VoIP Components

- IP Telephony Components

- Voice Coding and Compression Techniques

- Bandwidth Requirements

- IP Telephony Design

- Voice Security

Voice Transport Design

This chapter describes how voice can be transported along with other data within a network.

We first introduce why it would be advantageous to include voice in your network design. The mechanics of voice transport, including digitization, packetization, and call processing are explained. Quality of service (QoS) for voice is reviewed. The components required in a Voice over IP (VoIP) network and those in an IP telephony network are described. The standards for how voice calls are coded and compressed are introduced, and the bandwidth requirements for voice traffic are explored. IP telephony design scenarios are examined. We conclude with an introduction to security considerations for voice.

> **NOTE** Appendix B, "Network Fundamentals," includes material that we assume you understand before reading the rest of the book. Thus, we encourage you to review any of the material in Appendix B that you are not familiar with before reading the rest of this chapter.

While those in the networking world have been hearing about Voice over IP for quite a while now, over the past couple of years (at least within North America), the mainstream press has been introducing the term *VoIP* to the ordinary consumer. Although the residential market is currently small, it is growing quickly, as prices are slashed for VoIP packages that include such features as unlimited calls within the continent, low-cost international calling, voice mail, selection of your own area code, call forwarding, and call display.

An enterprise might also want to implement VoIP, in other words, to use its data network to also carry its voice traffic. Referring to the discussion in Chapter 1, "Network Design," a new technology shouldn't be implemented just because it can be, but rather because it meets the network's requirements. The goal for converging an organization's voice and data networks is to positively "impact key initiatives, business processes and business results."[1] This can be accomplished in many ways, including the following:

- Direct cost savings, which is typically the initial reason that a company considers converging its voice and data networks. These savings include the following items:

— **Toll bypass**—Long-distance voice calls go over the data network instead of the public switched telephone network (PSTN), thus saving the associated charges. For example, calls between branch offices and headquarters can go on the same network as data. Calls to customers can go as far as possible over the converged network, and then onto the PSTN for the last segment.

— **Having only one network to implement, maintain, manage, and operate**—Cost reductions can include those for equipment purchases, equipment space, maintenance contracts, and so forth.

— **Reduced add/move/change costs**—Employees can take their extension number with them when they move offices, and new employees can be added easily.

— **Reduced cabling costs**—Because voice travels over the data network, no additional cabling is required.

— **Possible reduced capital expenditures costs**—For example, the company might not have to buy a new private branch exchange (PBX) switch to manage the corporate phone system.

■ Increased end-user productivity, because more applications are available through the Internet or from an IP phone. Two examples are a video telephony application that allows video conference calls between any locations, and unified messaging that allows employees to pick up voice-mail messages on the Internet, thus avoiding costly long-distance charges when they are traveling.

■ Revenue-generation opportunities, which can also be a competitive advantage. For example, a call center could be set up to take sales orders and provide customer service.

■ Improved customer service and response, because more information can be made available to customers themselves or to the customer-service agents.

■ Improved employee empowerment and satisfaction, for example, by providing employees that do not currently have a workstation access to the Internet and applicable applications through an IP phone.

What Is Voice Transport?

A *converged network* is one in which data, voice, and video traffic coexist on a single network. Transporting voice and video across the network means that they become applications, just like file transfers, to the network. It also means that the capabilities of the network can be used to provide even more functionality and features than were previously available.

To transport voice across the network, it must first be digitized—converted from analog to digital signals—and then packetized, that is, put into IP packets. These voice IP packets can then be sent over the data network, just like any other IP packets.

Digitization

Figure 7-1 illustrates the digitization process for analog speech, as described in this section.

Figure 7-1   *Converting Analog Speech into Digital Signals*

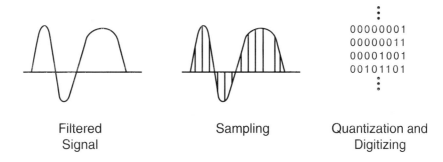

Analog speech contains components at many different frequencies, representing the range of sounds that we hear. Most analog speech components are in the frequency range of 300 hertz (Hz) to 3400 Hz. The first step in the digitization process is to filter out anything higher than 4000 Hz, thus isolating the speech component.

This filtered signal is then sampled by a process called pulse amplitude modulation (PAM), which uses the original analog signal to change the amplitude of a pulse signal. The rate at which the sampling is done is driven by the Nyquist theorem, which states that the sampling rate must be at least twice the highest frequency, so it is possible to reconstruct the analog signal from the digital signal. If too few samples are taken, not enough information would be available to re-create the original speech. Thus, for speech filtered at 4000 Hz, sampling must be done at 8000 Hz, or 8000 times per second.

Using a pulse code modulation (PCM) process, each of these samples is then quantized, which means that it is assigned a discrete binary value and then digitized. Eight bits are used for each sample, resulting in $2^8 = 256$ possible values.

Because the original analog signal is sampled at 8000 times per second and each sample is represented by 8 bits, voice digitized using PCM is sent at a rate of 8000 * 8 = 64,000 bits per second (bps), or 64 kilobits per second (kbps).

Packetization and Call Processing

The packetization of voice is implemented in the following two ways, as illustrated in Figure 7-2:

■ Using traditional phones and a PBX (or digital phones attached to a PBX) to digitize the voice, and then connecting the PBX to a voice-enabled router to perform the packetization. The result is voice encapsulated inside IP packets, or VoIP. These packets are carried across the converged network, therefore replacing the traditional tie trunks between PBXs. This scenario is illustrated at the top of Figure 7-2, and the devices required are detailed in the "VoIP Components" section, later in this chapter.

> **NOTE**   A PBX is a telephone switch used within an organization to provide features such as call holding, call forwarding, conference calling, and voice mail.

■ Using IP phones to digitize and packetize the voice. The call-processing function previously performed by the PBX is now handled by a call-processing manager—for example, Cisco CallManager (CCM) is a software-based system that provides functions such as setting up and terminating calls, routing to voice mail, and so forth. Similar to the previous scenario, this results in VoIP packets traversing the network. VoIP, together with the enhanced features provided by CCM and other applications that are now possible, are collectively known as *IP telephony*. This scenario is illustrated in the lower portion of Figure 7-2. IP telephony also supports devices other than IP phones, to provide even more flexibility and functionality within the converged network. The devices used in IP telephony are described in the "IP Telephony Components" section, later in this chapter.

Figure 7-2   *VoIP and IP Telephony*

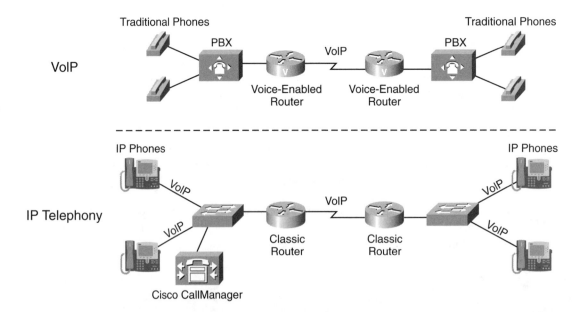

NOTE   Figure 7-2 does not show connectivity to the PSTN. IP telephony scenarios with PSTN connections are described in the "IP Telephony Design" section, later in this chapter.

Conversation and Control Traffic

Two categories of voice traffic exist: conversation traffic (the audio, also called *bearer traffic*) and control (or signaling) traffic.

KEY POINT | Within VoIP, conversation packets are sent using the User Datagram Protocol (UDP), which provides connectionless transmission.

Because it does not have the overhead that the sequencing, acknowledging, and error-checking features of the Transmission Control Protocol (TCP) require, UDP provides a more efficient, lower-delay service. Voice conversation is susceptible to delay—if a voice packet is delayed too much, it could lose its relevance. On the other hand, the loss of a single voice packet is not detrimental to the quality of voice at the receiving end because it can be interpolated from other voice samples.

Conversation packets are sent using the Real-Time Transport Protocol (RTP), which runs on top of UDP. RTP was designed to be used for real-time traffic such as voice. RTP adds another header to the UDP segment that includes some sequencing information and time-stamping information to ensure that the received data is processed in the correct order and that the variation in the delay is within acceptable limits.

Call control traffic is sent using TCP, because the signals must be received in the order in which they were sent, and loss of these packets cannot be tolerated.

Quality of Service

Earlier we described how residential VoIP is becoming popular. These calls are being sent over the Internet, not over a private corporate wide-area network (WAN). You saw in Chapter 6, "Quality of Service Design," how important QoS is to voice calls, to ensure that the delay and variation in delay (jitter) remain within acceptable levels. However, the Internet is known as a *best-effort service:* in general it has no QoS support. Thus, the quality of these voice calls over the Internet is not guaranteed. For residential and small-business needs, the quality might be acceptable, especially when weighed against the cost savings. For organizations that require enterprise-class voice-enabled network services and quality, though, Cisco does not recommend using best-effort WAN connections such as the Internet. For these networks, dedicated WAN connections with QoS support should be used for voice traffic between sites.[2]

> **NOTE**   It is interesting to consider the quality of service provided by the best-effort Internet. For example, when we send an e-mail to someone, it usually arrives almost immediately. While we have probably all experienced a few instances of e-mails never arriving at their destination, in general, we think of the Internet as providing good service.

Voice traffic is sensitive to delays, jitter, and extensive packet loss. Recall from Chapter 6 that the guidelines for ensuring acceptable voice quality are as follows:

- The one-way delay should be no more than 150 milliseconds (ms).

- The jitter should be no more than 30 ms.

- No more than 1 percent of the packets should be lost.

> **NOTE**   While 150 ms is the standard for acceptable voice delay, tests have shown that a negligible quality difference exists with a 200-ms delay.

Chapter 6 also identifies the tools that are available to implement the QoS required by voice traffic, including classification and marking, policing and shaping, congestion avoidance, congestion management, and link-specific tools.

VoIP Components

KEY POINT | When implementing VoIP using traditional phones, components include the phones, a PBX, and a voice-enabled router, as illustrated earlier in the VoIP portion of Figure 7-2.

Traditional phones and PBXs have been installed in businesses for many years. The addition of a voice-enabled router, also called a *voice gateway,* can be the first step toward a fully converged voice and data network. The voice-enabled router contains digital signal processors (DSPs) to perform its functions in hardware, which is much faster than doing it in software.

To support VoIP, an underlying IP infrastructure must be functioning and robust—in other words, don't even think of adding voice to a network that is experiencing other problems, such as congestion or network failures.

Voice-specific recommendations for the IP infrastructure are as follows:

■ QoS, as described earlier and detailed in Chapter 6, should be implemented within the network. Queuing should be deployed on any link (WAN or LAN) that could potentially experience congestion, to meet delay and jitter requirements for the voice traffic.

■ WANs for voice networks should use a hub-and-spoke topology, with a central hub site and multiple remote spoke sites connected to the central hub site.[3] Each remote site is then one WAN link hop away from the central site and two WAN link hops away from all other spoke sites. This ensures that call admission control—limiting the number of calls allowed over the network so that the quality of all calls is within acceptable limits—at the central site can keep track of the bandwidth available between any two sites.

■ Redundancy should be implemented within the network. For example, WAN links should be redundant to ensure the availability of the voice traffic between sites, and redundant devices and links should be deployed within the campus where necessary to ensure the availability within each site.

■ Compression of voice traffic over WANs should be implemented to reduce the required bandwidth. The various compression techniques are described later in the "Voice Coding and Compression Techniques" section—G.729 compression is recommended for WAN links.

IP Telephony Components

KEY POINT | IP telephony components include a robust IP infrastructure, IP phones, a video telephony option, a call-processing engine, applications, and optionally a voice gateway to the PSTN.

NOTE   More information on Cisco IP telephony is available at http://www.cisco.com/go/ipc.

IP Infrastructure

The IP infrastructure requirements noted in the previous section apply equally to an IP telephony implementation. However, additional items must be considered in this environment because of the other components, including the following:

■ The LAN access switches to which IP phones and users' PCs are connected should define two separate virtual LANs (VLANs) each, one for data and one for voice, allowing easier implementation of QoS tools. (VLANs are described in Chapter 2, "Switching Design.") Recall from Chapter 1 that the LAN access switches are interconnected by distribution Layer 3 switches (routers) to provide communication between the workgroups.

■ As discussed in Chapter 6, while the network administrator might not want to trust end users to classify and set QoS markings consistent with the organization's policy, the access switches to which they are connected could perform this task.

■ Access switches can provide in-line power for the IP phones.

■ Consideration should be given to deploying resources over WANs in a distributed design, rather than a centralized design. For example, the CCM application should be distributed when possible so that the voice network remains available if the WAN fails.

IP Phones

KEY POINT | IP phones digitize and packetize voice. They connect to the network through an Ethernet cable (or through a wireless network), just as a PC does. Many different types of IP phones are available, including both hardware- and software-based.

The following are some of the features available on Cisco IP phones:

■ Support for power over Ethernet (PoE), to allow the phone to be powered from the switch to which it is connected (if it supports in-line power) rather than from a power outlet.

■ Extensible markup language (XML) support enables access to applications; new features and applications can be added easily. The IP phone contains a micro-browser that enables limited web-browsing capability. Higher-end phones have web-client capabilities, while lower-end phones support text-based XML applications.

■ Display and audio features include liquid crystal displays (LCDs), speakerphones, and audible and visual alerts.

■ Some models have integrated Ethernet switches, with speeds up to 1 gigabit per second (Gbps).

■ Some models support multiple phone lines.

The Cisco portfolio also includes IP Communicator, a software-based IP phone, and a wireless IP phone (which is discussed in Chapter 5, "Wireless LAN Design"). IP Communicator runs on a PC to give users the flexibility of having their IP phone wherever they can access the network.

Cisco also has analog telephone adapters and gateways, allowing analog phones to be connected to a network as though they were IP phones.

NOTE   More information about Cisco IP phones is available at http://www.cisco.com/en/US/products/hw/phones/ps379/index.html.

Video Telephony

The Cisco VT Advantage product provides Cisco IP phone users with the ability to add video telephony to their phone calls. VT Advantage includes the Cisco VT Advantage software application and a video telephony Universal Serial Bus (USB) camera. With the camera attached to a PC that is colocated with a Cisco IP phone, a user can place and receive video calls on his enterprise IP telephony network using the phone interface.

Call Processing

CCM is a software-based call-processing system that provides enterprise telephony features to an IP network. CCM can be installed on a Cisco Media Convergence Server (MCS) and selected third-party servers. The software also provides a suite of integrated voice applications and utilities, including a software-only manual attendant console and an auto-attendant; a software-only conferencing application; tools for detailed reporting and analysis of calls, adding and deleting users, and configuring phones; and tools for monitoring the CCM components. Multiple CCM servers can be clustered to support up to 30,000 IP phones per cluster; multiple clusters can also be integrated to support up to 1 million users. In networks with up to 2500 phones, two servers are typically deployed: One acts as a publisher (to store the master copy of the configuration database), and the other acts as a subscriber (the device with which phones register).[4] The subscriber also acts as a backup to the publisher in this scenario.

CCM can be configured to route calls in various ways, using a dial plan. For example, some phones might be allowed to only reach certain destinations within a building and local PSTN calls, while others might have unlimited access. As another example, different paths, such as the PSTN or the WAN, can be selected to reach the same destination, depending on which device is placing the call.

Applications

Voice applications are independent from the call-processing and voice-processing infrastructure, and can reside anywhere within the network. The main applications available from Cisco include the following:

- **Cisco IP Contact Center (IPCC) (available in Enterprise and Express editions)**—For managing customer voice contacts and deploying a distributed contact center infrastructure. For example, IPCC Enterprise provides intelligent contact routing, call treatment, network-to-desktop computer telephony integration (CTI), and multichannel automatic call distributor (ACD) functionality.

- **Cisco MeetingPlace**—A rich-media conferencing solution that integrates voice, video, and web-conferencing capabilities. This application uses existing corporate voice (IP and circuit-switched) and data networks to reduce or eliminate toll charges and conferencing charges.

- **Cisco Unity**—This unified messaging solution delivers e-mail, voice mail, and fax messages to a single inbox so that users can, for example, listen to their e-mail over the telephone, check voice messages from the Internet, and forward faxes to wherever they might be.

- **Cisco Personal Assistant**—A personal productivity application that helps users manage how and where they want to be reached. For example, it provides speech-enabled access to Cisco Unity voice messages, a corporate directory, and personal contact lists, from any telephone. The web-based and telephone user administration interfaces help prevent missed calls or interruptions by allowing calls to be forwarded or screened, in advance or in real time.

Voice Gateway

A voice gateway to the PSTN can be implemented with a variety of devices. For example, the Cisco 3700 Series multiservice access routers communicate directly with CCM and support a range of interfaces and signaling protocols. Voice gateway modules can also be installed in Cisco switches, including the Catalyst 4000 and 6000 Series.

These gateways could communicate with CCM using the H.323 protocol, the Session Initiation Protocol (SIP), or the Media Gateway Control Protocol (MGCP). H.323 is a standard protocol for packet-based audio, video, and data communications over IP. SIP is a standard application layer protocol for multimedia conferencing over IP. MGCP is a standard protocol that allows call agents, such as CCM, to control specific ports on a gateway.

Voice Coding and Compression Techniques

Recall that voice digitized with PCM is sent at 64 kbps. You can reduce the bandwidth required by voice in many ways, as detailed in the following sections.

Voice Compression

Voice compression reduces the size of the voice payload while still maintaining the quality at an acceptable level. As a result of technology advances, a variety of International Telecommunications Union (ITU) standards exist for voice coding/decoding and compression; these standards are known as *codecs*. Some of these standards and the bandwidth they use for one voice channel are summarized in Table 7-1. The quality of the resulting voice is represented by the average of the results of a wide variety of listeners' opinions, on a scale of 1 (bad) to 5 (excellent), known as the mean opinion score (MOS), which is also shown in Table 7-1. Notice the variety of bandwidth and MOSs; both should be considered when choosing a codec.

Table 7-1   *Voice Coding and Compression Standards[5]*

ITU Standard Codec	Bandwidth (kbps)	MOS
G.711	64	4.1
G.723	6.3/5.3	3.9/3.65
G.726	16/24/32	3.85
G.728	16	3.61
G.729	8	3.92

KEY POINT   In general, G.729 is the recommended voice compression technique over most WAN networks because of its combination of low bandwidth and high MOS.

NOTE   Using a single codec in WANs is recommended; this can also simplify the bandwidth-requirement calculations.

A DSP is a hardware component within a voice-enabled router that digitizes, compresses, and packetizes voice. Some of the codecs require more processing resources than others, so the number of voice calls that can be supported by one DSP depends on the codec implemented. The codecs are divided into two categories, known as medium complexity and high complexity, for this purpose. A single DSP can process up to four voice calls for medium-complexity codecs or up to two calls for high-complexity codecs. The two categories are summarized in Table 7-2.

Table 7-2   *Medium- and High-Complexity Codecs[6]*

Medium-Complexity Codecs	High-Complexity Codecs
G.711	G.723
G.726	G.728
G.729a	G.729
G.729ab	G.729b

> **NOTE** G.729a (also known as G.729 Annex-A) is a medium-complexity variant of G.729 with slightly lower voice quality. G.729b has more features than G.729. G.729ab is a medium-complexity variant of G.729b with slightly lower voice quality.

Voice Activity Detection

Another way to reduce the bandwidth required by voice calls is to use voice activity detection (VAD). On average, about 35 percent of a call is in fact silence; when VoIP is used, this silence is packetized along with the conversation. VAD suppresses the silence, so instead of sending IP packets of silence, only IP packets of conversation are sent. The network bandwidth is therefore being used more efficiently and effectively.

> **NOTE** In some cases, Cisco recommends disabling VAD, for example, when faxes are to be sent through the network. VAD can also degrade the perceived quality of the call, because when VAD is enabled, the silence is replaced by comfort noise played to the listener (by the device at the listener's end of the network). If this is causing problems, VAD can be disabled.

Compressed Real-Time Transport Protocol

Recall that voice conversation packets are sent using RTP, which runs on top of UDP. Thus, VoIP packets consist of two parts: the voice and the headers (IP/UDP/RTP). The voice samples can be compressed, and therefore their size can vary depending on the codec used—for example, a typical G.729 call has 20 bytes of voice samples. The headers, though, are always 40 bytes, which can be a significant amount of overhead.

RTP header compression, called cRTP, compresses this 40-byte header to 2–4 bytes. The cRTP compression can be configured on an interface and is recommended on low-bandwidth WANs (up to 2 megabits per second [Mbps]). The cRTP compression is not recommended on higher-speed interfaces, though, because it is CPU intensive; the use of CPU resources outweighs the benefits on these faster links.

> **NOTE** The cRTP compression is configured on an interface and therefore must be configured on both ends of a WAN if it is used.

Bandwidth Requirements

The bandwidth requirements for voice traffic depend on many factors, including the number of simultaneous voice calls, grade of service required, codec and compression techniques used, signaling protocol used, and network topology.

On a WAN, for example, the bandwidth required for all applications, including voice, should be no more than 75 percent of the available bandwidth on the link;[7] the rest is for overhead, including routing protocol traffic.

The following sections detail how to calculate the WAN bandwidth that is required to support a number of voice calls with a given probability that the call will go through.

Definitions

To determine how much bandwidth is required, you must understand the following terminology:

- Grade of service (GoS)

- Erlangs

- Centum call seconds (CCSs)

- Busy-hour traffic (BHT)

KEY POINT The *grade of service* is the probability that a call will be blocked —the caller will get a busy signal because of insufficient capacity—during the busiest hour.

The GoS is written as P*xx,* where *xx* is the percentage of calls that are blocked. For example, a GoS of P05 means that a 5 percent probability exists that callers will be blocked when they call during the busiest hour.

Erlangs and CCSs are common methods of measuring voice traffic.

KEY POINT One Erlang equals 1 hour, or 3600 seconds, of a telephone conversation.

A CCS is 1/36 of an Erlang. One Erlang therefore equals 36 CCSs.

The BHT, in Erlangs or CCSs, is the number of hours of traffic during the busiest hour of operation. BHTs are calculated as follows:

- To calculate the BHT in CCSs, multiply the number of calls in the busiest hour by their average duration in seconds, and divide the result by 100.

To calculate the BHT in Erlangs, multiply the number of calls in the busiest hour by their average duration in seconds, and divide the result by 3600.

For example, 1 hour of conversation—one Erlang—can be one 60-minute call, three 20-minute calls, or fifteen 4-minute calls. Receiving 200 calls with an average length of 3 minutes in the busiest hour is 600 minutes or 36,000 seconds of traffic; this would be 10 Erlangs, or 360 centum call seconds of traffic.

Erlang tables show the potential traffic for a specified number of circuits at a given probability of receiving a busy signal. The potential traffic in the Erlang tables is the BHT—the number of hours of traffic during the busiest hour of the telephone system's operation.

One place that Erlang tables and calculators can be found is at http://www.erlang.com; other sites can also be found by using your favorite search engine. An Erlang B table is the most common traffic model that determines the number of circuits required for a given amount of busy-hour traffic and a required grade of service. For example, according to the Erlang B calculator, a BHT of 4.46 Erlangs at a GoS of P01 requires ten circuits.

After the number of circuits required is determined, the bandwidth required on the WAN for voice calls can be determined. This required bandwidth is also known as the *trunk capacity*.

Calculating Trunk Capacity or Bandwidth

KEY POINT

The trunk capacity for voice calls can be calculated by the following formula:

Trunk capacity = Number of simultaneous calls to be supported * Bandwidth required per call

The first component of this formula, the number of simultaneous calls to be supported, is simply the number of circuits required for the known amount of traffic, as calculated from the Erlang tables.

NOTE   If 100 percent of calls must go through, Erlang tables are not required; instead, the maximum number of simultaneous calls required should be used.

The bandwidth required for one call depends on the codec used and whether cRTP and VAD are used.

Using IP/UDP/RTP headers of 40 bytes and assuming that the Point-to-Point Protocol (PPP) is used at Layer 2 (so the Layer 2 header is 6 bytes), the following calculations can be made:[8]

Voice packet size = Layer 2 header size + IP/UDP/RTP header size + Voice payload size
Voice packets per second (pps) = Codec bit rate / Voice payload size
Bandwidth per call = Voice packet size (bits) * Voice pps

For example, the bandwidth required for a G.729 call (8-kbps codec bit rate) with a default 20-byte voice payload is calculated as follows:

Voice packet size (bytes) = Layer 2 header (6 bytes) + IP/UDP/RTP header (40 bytes) + Voice payload (20 bytes) = 66 bytes
Voice packet size (bits) = 66 bytes * 8 bits per byte = 528 bits
Voice pps = 8-kbps codec bit rate / (8 bits per byte * 20-byte voice payload size) = 8-kbps codec bit rate / 160 bits = 50 pps
Bandwidth per call = Voice packet size (528 bits) * 50 pps = 26.4 kbps

Table 7-3 summarizes the required bandwidth for G.711 and G.729 codec calls.

Table 7-3   *Voice Bandwidth Requirements*

Codec	Payload Size (bytes)	Bandwidth Required per Call (kbps)
G.711 (64-kbps)	160	82.4
G.729 (8-kbps)	20	26.4

VAD and cRTP reduces the bandwidth required per call. The results of the calculations for G.711 and G.729 at 50 pps are illustrated in Table 7-4.

Table 7-4   *Per-Call Voice Bandwidth Requirements*

Codec	Payload Size (bytes)	Bandwidth Required per Call Without cRTP or VAD (kbps)	Bandwidth Required per Call with cRTP (kbps)	Bandwidth Required per Call with cRTP and VAD (kbps)
G.711	160	82.4	67.2	33.6
G.729 (8-kbps)	20	26.4	11.2	5.6

CAUTION   Including VAD in bandwidth calculations can result in insufficient bandwidth being provisioned if the calls do not include as much silence as assumed and when features such as music on hold are used.

Recall that the trunk capacity for voice calls can be calculated by the following formula:

Trunk capacity = Number of simultaneous calls to be supported * Bandwidth required per call

As an example of calculating the trunk capacity, assume that G.729 compression is used over a PPP connection at 50 pps and cRTP is used. From Table 7-4, 11.2 kbps are used by each call. If five simultaneous calls are to be supported, 5 * 11.2 = 56 kbps are required for the voice calls. (The bandwidth for other traffic that is to be on the link must also be accounted for so that no more than 75 percent of the available bandwidth on the link is used.)

Signaling Traffic Bandwidth

Assuming that call control traffic must be sent to the CCM at a central site, the signaling traffic bandwidth requirements between the central site and remote sites depend on the number of IP phones and gateway devices.

In the case of a remote branch where no Telephony Application Programming Interface (TAPI) applications (such as Cisco IP Communicator software phone) are deployed, the recommended bandwidth needed for call control traffic can be determined from the following formula:[9]

Bandwidth (bps) = 150 * Number of IP phones and gateways in the remote site

In the case where a TAPI application is deployed at the remote site, the recommended bandwidth is higher because the TAPI protocol requires more messages to be exchanged between CCM and the endpoints. The formula then becomes as follows:[10]

Bandwidth with TAPI (bps) = 225 * Number of IP phones and gateways in the remote site

---

NOTE The previous two formulas assume that an average of ten calls per hour is made on each phone. The referenced document provides more advanced formulas that should be used if this assumption is not true.

IP Telephony Design

IP telephony can be designed in a network in many scenarios, including single-site and multisite deployments.

Single-Site IP Telephony Design

A single-site design has all the IP telephony components at one site, as illustrated in Figure 7-3.

Figure 7-3   *IP Telephony Single-Site Design*

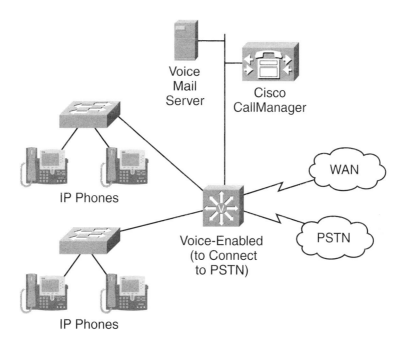

In this scenario, the IP phones (connected to switches that can provide them in-line power), a call-processing engine (CCM), application servers, and optionally a voice gateway to the PSTN are at the same physical location. Each site is self-contained, and all calls between sites are through the PSTN. This means that the IP WAN is not involved in voice calls and is therefore not a voice bottleneck.

Multisite Centralized IP Telephony Design

A multisite design has many sites, interconnected through a WAN. A centralized design means that the call-processing engine and application servers are at one of the sites, and the other sites connect to those devices for all call-processing and application requirements, as illustrated in Figure 7-4.

Figure 7-4   *IP Telephony Multisite Centralized Design*

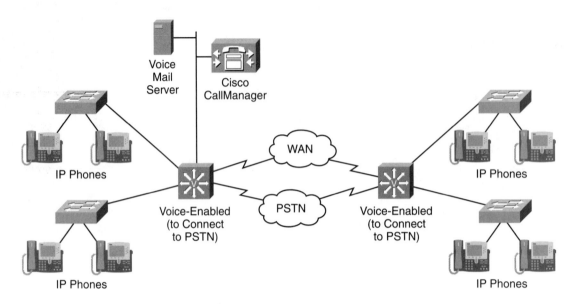

Because the remote sites must send call-processing information to the main site, they must have IP connectivity with the main site. Therefore, if the WAN is down, calls cannot be processed. To prevent a total breakdown of the IP telephony system, the Survivable Remote Site Telephony (SRST) feature on remote routers can be used to provide basic call processing to the remote sites if the WAN fails.

If PSTN access is not required, a voice-enabled router is not necessary in this scenario, because only IP packets are sent across the WAN. However, if PSTN access is required (which is the usual case), a voice gateway is required.

Multisite Distributed IP Telephony Design

Similar to the centralized design, a distributed multisite network has many sites, interconnected through a WAN. In this case, though, each site has call-processing resources. Calls between sites can be through the IP WAN or through the PSTN.

Voice Security

As with most emerging technologies, in its infancy, IP telephony deployments were more concerned with features and quality than with security. Because IP telephony is offered through convergence with data on one network, it can be thought of as simply another application running over the data network. As such, IP telephony can be made secure if its transmissions are treated like any other application that requires security, including authenticity, integrity, and confidentiality. With this perspective, it is easy to integrate IP telephony security into the design and security framework of a corporate network.

The security issues associated with IP telephony can be categorized as follows:

- Network security concerns

- Platform security issues

IP Telephony Network Security Concerns

Network attack risks associated with IP telephony typically belong to two of the four categories of attacks seen in Chapter 4, "Network Security Design":

- Access attacks

- Denial-of-service attacks

Access Attacks

Nonauthorized and even fraudulent use of the IP telephony network could be the outcome of an access attack. During an access attack, communications could be intercepted and even replayed. Another concern would be a replay attack or even an impersonation attack.

Denial of Service Attacks

In the case of a denial of service (DoS) attack, the quality of the communication could be severely impaired by a large quantity of bandwidth wasted to parasite traffic.

Platform Security Issues

Many IP telephony control applications run on servers. Those servers can themselves be running a commonly available operating system (OS) such as UNIX or Microsoft Windows XP. Those platforms are themselves vulnerable to attacks. It is therefore fundamental that best practices associated with servers be strictly implemented. Some of those practices, as described in Chapter 4, are as follows:

- Closing all unused TCP and UDP ports

- Timely patching of OS software

- Using antivirus software and ensuring that it is up to date

- Installing the servers in a secure location

Mitigating to Protect IP Telephony

A properly protected data network is by the same token a safe network for IP telephony. Best-practices-level protection can be accomplished by implementing the mitigation technologies that we explain in Chapter 4. This is a multipronged approach, where the perimeter and inside traffic, as well as the outbound traffic, are protected.

The following recommendations, beneficial to a converged network, can protect both data and voice traffic:

- **Threat defense:**

    — **Virus protection**—Protect the CCM server against viruses.

    — **Hardened servers and workstations**—Close all unused ports and perform timely patch management.

    — **Traffic filtering**—This is done by a stateful firewall that has the capability to ensure that only legitimate interactive traffic is crossing into and out of the corporate network.

    — **Intrusion detection and prevention**—Detect and possibly remediate an incoming attack.

- **Secure communication:**

    — **Encrypted Virtual Private Networks (VPNs)**—Used between VoIP-enabled networks to communicate over nonsecure links to ensure the authenticity, confidentiality, and integrity of the communication.

    — **Switched networks**—Prevent incidences of eavesdropping.

- **Trust and identity:**

    — **Authentication**—Forcing IP phones to authenticate prior to being provided with transmission capabilities.

Security must be natively incorporated in your network design for the benefit of data and consequently VoIP traffic. But as with any good thing, too much can prove to be detrimental. For example, incorporating too much security could lead to noticeable transmission delays, or worse, effectively creating your own DoS attack. Furthermore, at some point in your quest for pervasive security, you will reach a point of diminishing returns, where additional security equipment only provides your network with a marginal rate of security return.[11] So stay vigilant and keep up with the technology and the hackers, but don't try to be overzealous.

Summary

In this chapter, you learned how voice can be transported along with other data within your network; the following topics were presented:

- The benefits of including voice within your data network.

- How voice is transported across the network, including how it is digitized and then packetized.

- The two ways that the packetization of voice is implemented:

    — Using traditional phones and a PBX (or digital phones attached to a PBX) to digitize the voice, and then connecting the PBX to a voice-enabled router to perform the packetization.

    — Using IP phones to digitize and packetize the voice. The call-processing function previously performed by the PBX is now handled by a call-processing manager such as CCM.

- The two categories of voice traffic: conversation traffic (the audio, also called bearer traffic) and control (or signaling) traffic.

- The components of an IP telephony system, including an underlying functioning and robust IP infrastructure and QoS support.

- The hardware and software IP phones available from Cisco, the features of CCM, and the voice applications that can be supported.

- The voice compression and coding techniques, including the recommended G.729 codec that compresses a call to 8 kbps while still maintaining voice quality.

- Calculating the bandwidth requirements for voice traffic and understanding the associated terminology.

- Examples of single-site and multisite IP telephony designs.

- Security issues associated with IP telephony.

Endnotes

[1]"IP Telephony & Business Applications Productivity Session," Cisco Technical Symposium 2004, Brantz Myers, October 5, 2004, Toronto.

[2]"Cisco IP Telephony Solution Reference Network Design (SRND)," Cisco CallManager Release 4.0, November 2004, http://www.cisco.com/go/srnd.

[3]Ibid.

[4]Hutton and Ranjbar, *CCDP Self Study: Designing Cisco Network Architectures (ARCH)*, Indianapolis, Cisco Press, 2005.

[5] Teare, *CCDA Self Study: Designing for Cisco Internetwork Solutions (DESGN)*, Indianapolis, Cisco Press, 2004.

[6]Ibid.

[7]"Cisco IP Telephony Solution Reference Network Design (SRND)," Cisco CallManager Release 4.0, November 2004, http://www.cisco.com/go/srnd.

[8]Teare, *CCDA Self Study: Designing for Cisco Internetwork Solutions (DESGN)*, Indianapolis, Cisco Press, 2004.

[9]"Cisco IP Telephony Solution Reference Network Design (SRND)," Cisco CallManager Release 4.0, November 2004, http://www.cisco.com/go/srnd.

[10]Ibid.

[11]Paquet and Saxe, *The Business Case for Network Security: Advocacy, Governance, and ROI*, Indianapolis, Cisco Press, 2004, Chapter 8.

This chapter discusses the components and design of content networking, and includes the following sections:

- Making the Business Case

- Content Networking

- Content Caches and Content Engines

- Content Routing

- Content Distribution and Management

- Content Switching

- Designing Content Networking

CHAPTER **8**

Content Networking Design

This chapter describes how content networking (CN) can be implemented to provide content to users as quickly and efficiently as possible.

We first introduce the advantages that CN can provide to your network. The services provided under CN and the components that provide those services are introduced. The use of these components—the content engine, content router, content distribution and management device, and content switch—is then described in more detail. We conclude by examining two content network design scenarios.

> **NOTE** Appendix B, "Network Fundamentals," includes material that we assume you understand before reading the rest of the book. Thus, we encourage you to review any of the material in Appendix B that you are not familiar with before reading the rest of this chapter.

Making the Business Case

We have all come to expect that the data we are trying to access will be available almost instantaneously, whether it be from the hard drive on our PC or from a website on the other side of the world. When we try to access a website and we have to wait for more than a few seconds, for example, many of us tend to give up or try another site, because we assume that the first site is either no longer available or is temporarily down.

This behavior has implications for enterprises that provide e-commerce, e-learning, or any other information that is needed by customers, employees, investors, or any other stakeholder: The data and services requested must be available as fast as possible, regardless of the location of the user relative to the data. CN aids in this quest.

CN is an intelligent network solution. In other words, it adds intelligence to the network so that the network devices are aware of the content that users are accessing. CN implements a content delivery network (CDN) that provides efficient distribution of content across the network, selection of the best site for a user to obtain the content, and load balancing of content stored on multiple devices.

Some example applications that could benefit from CN services are e-learning, video on demand (VoD), and IP television (IP/TV). IP/TV uses one-way streaming live video, while VoD transfers prerecorded video files to users upon request.

CN provides many benefits, including the following:

- **Increased loyalty**—If data is available when customers request it, they might not be as enticed to go elsewhere to get it.

- **Maximizing internal productivity**—Employees can access data when they need it, allowing them to be more productive and to service customers more quickly.

- **Reduced bandwidth use**—CN places data closer to users, thus reducing the WAN bandwidth they require.

- **Enabling new applications**—As the data bottleneck is reduced, new applications become possible, including e-learning, video communication, e-commerce, customer self-help, and so forth.

- **Scalability**—As demand grows in specific areas, data can be distributed where required, without impacting existing users.

Content Networking

The following services fall under the CN umbrella:

- Efficient distribution of content across the network

- Selection of the best site for a user to obtain the content

- Load balancing of content stored on multiple devices

The components of a CDN can include the following:

- **Content cache or content engine**—A content engine is a device that caches, or stores, selected content from origin servers (servers from which the content originates) and sends it upon request to users. Content engines can be located, for example, at each branch office to reduce the WAN bandwidth required by the branch-office users.

- **Content router**—Content routers direct users' requests for content to the closest content engine.

- **Content distribution and management device**—This is a device, such as the Cisco Content Distribution Manager, that is responsible for distributing content to the content engines and ensuring that the material is kept up to date.

- **Content switch**—Content switches load-balance requests to servers or content engines. For example, a content switch can be deployed in front of a group of web servers; when a user requests data from the server, the content switch can forward the request to the least-loaded server.

A CDN does not have to include all of these components. For example, content engines can be deployed as stand-alone devices. Alternatively, a Cisco Content Distribution Manager can be deployed to manage the content engines, and content routers can be added to redirect content requests. Content switches can also be deployed with or without any of the other components.

Because CN is considered a network *solution,* it requires a robust network infrastructure and appropriate network services to be in place. The network services required by CN include quality of service (QoS), security, and IP multicast.

NOTE   IP multicast reduces the bandwidth used on a network by delivering a single stream of traffic to multiple recipients (defined in a multicast group), rather than sending the same traffic to each recipient individually. IP multicast is explained further in Chapter 10, "Other Enabling Technologies."

The CDN components are further described in the following sections.

Content Caches and Content Engines

A content cache transparently caches, or stores, content that is frequently accessed so that it can be retrieved from the cache rather than from a distant server. A content engine can extend this caching functionality by interacting with a content distribution and management device, and optionally content routers, to store selected content and retrieve it on request, as part of a CDN.

NOTE   The type of software running on Cisco content engines can determine the features supported by the device. For example, the Cisco 7320 content engine is available with a choice of cache software (providing only transparent caching), CDN software, or Application and Content Networking System (ACNS) software.[1] The ACNS software combines the caching and CDN functionality.

Content engine functionality is also available on modules that fit into the Cisco modular routers.

Some content-engine hardware that runs ACNS software can be configured with a choice of personalities: as a content engine, a content router, or a Content Distribution Manager.[2] In fact, Cisco stand-alone Content Distribution Managers have been phased out in favor of the ACNS-enabled content engine.
(Note that a device can have only one personality at a time; it cannot perform multiple functions simultaneously.)

Caching is best suited for data that doesn't change often, such as static application data and web objects, versus entire web pages, which might include frequently changing objects.

KEY POINT | When not used with a content router, a content engine can be deployed in a network in three ways: transparent caching, nontransparent caching (also called proxy caching), and reverse proxy caching.

Transparent caching, nontransparent caching, and reverse proxy caching are described in the following sections. The use of a content engine with a content router is described in the "Content Routing" section, later in this chapter.

Content engines can also be configured to preload specific content from an origin web server that stores the primary content, and to periodically verify that the content is still current, or update any content that has changed. This is described in the "Content Distribution and Management" section, later in this chapter.

Transparent Caching

KEY POINT | A network that uses transparent caching includes a content engine and a Web Cache Communication Protocol (WCCP)–enabled router. WCCP is part of the Cisco Internet Operating System (IOS) router software (available in some IOS feature sets) and is the communication mechanism between the router and the stand-alone content engine.

Transparent caching is illustrated in Figure 8-1.

Figure 8-1 *With Transparent Caching, a WCCP-Enabled Router Passes Users' Requests to the Content Engine*

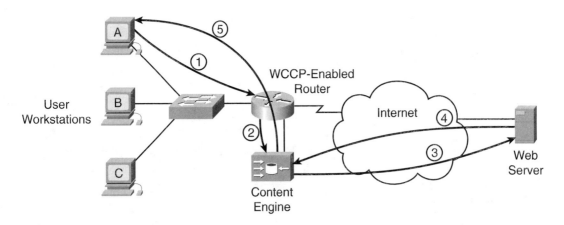

> **NOTE** The WCCP-enabled router in this scenario is not a content router; it is simply an IOS routerwith WCCP functionality. Refer to the Feature Navigator tool at http://www.cisco.com/go/fn to determine the feature set required to support WCCP for various IOS platforms.

Transparent caching operates as follows:

Step 1   In Figure 8-1, the user at workstation A requests a web page that resides on the web server. This request is received first by the WCCP-enabled router.

Step 2   The router analyzes the request and, if it meets configured criteria, forwards it to the content engine. For example, the router can be configured to send specific Transmission Control Protocol (TCP) port requests to the content engine, while not redirecting other requests.

Step 3   If the content engine does not have the requested page, it sends the request to the server.

Step 4   The server responds to the content engine with the requested data.

Step 5   The content engine forwards the web page to the user and then caches it for future use.

At Step 3, if the content engine did have the requested web page cached, it would send the page to the user. After the content engine has the content, any subsequent requests for the same web page are satisfied by the content engine, and the web server itself is not involved.

Transparent caching can also be deployed using a Layer 4 switch instead of a WCCP-enabled router. In this case, a content switch transparently intercepts and redirects content requests to the content engine.

The benefits of transparent caching include a faster response time for user requests and reduced bandwidth requirements and usage. User workstations are not aware of the caching and therefore do not have to be configured with information about the content engine. Content engines in transparent mode are typically positioned on the user side of an Internet or WAN connection.

Nontransparent Caching

KEY POINT   Nontransparent caching, as its name implies, is visible to end users. As such, workstations must be configured to know the address of the content engine; the content engine acts as a proxy.

NOTE A *proxy* is an action performed on behalf of something else (for example, a proxy vote is one that you give to someone else so that she can vote on your behalf). In networking, a proxy server (also sometimes referred to as simply a proxy) is a server that accepts clients' requests on behalf of other servers. If the proxy has the desired content, it sends it to the client; otherwise, the proxy forwards the request to the appropriate server. Thus, a proxy server acts as both a client (to the servers to which it connects) and a server (to the client that is requesting the content).

Nontransparent caching is illustrated in Figure 8-2.

Figure 8-2 *With Nontransparent Caching, the Content Engine Acts as a Proxy Server*

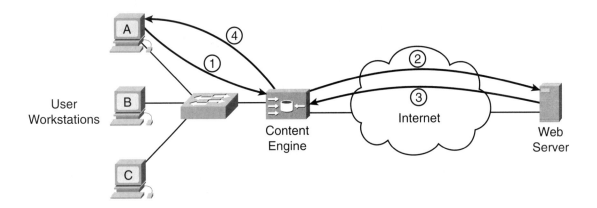

This scenario operates as follows:

Step 1   In Figure 8-2, the browser on workstation A is configured with the content engine as its proxy. The user at this workstation requests a web page that resides on the web server. This request is therefore sent to the content engine.

Step 2   Assuming that the content engine has been configured to handle the protocol and port number in the received request, the content engine checks to see whether it has the requested page. If the content engine does not have the requested page, it sends the request to the server.

Step 3   The server responds to the content engine with the requested data.

Step 4   The content engine forwards the web page to the user and then caches it for future use.

At Step 2, if the content engine had the requested web page cached, it would send the page directly to the user. Similar to transparent caching, after the content engine has the content, any subsequent requests for the same web page are satisfied by the content engine; the web server is not involved.

This nontransparent caching shares the benefits of faster response time and reduced bandwidth usage with transparent caching. An additional benefit of nontransparent caching is that it does not require WCCP-enabled routers; however, a drawback is the requirement to configure workstation browsers with the address of the content engine.

Content engines in nontransparent mode are also typically positioned on the user side of an Internet or WAN connection.

Reverse Proxy Caching

Reverse proxy caches are positioned on the server side of an Internet or WAN connection to help alleviate the load on the server, as illustrated in Figure 8-3.

Figure 8-3 *Reverse Proxy Caches Help Alleviate Server Load*

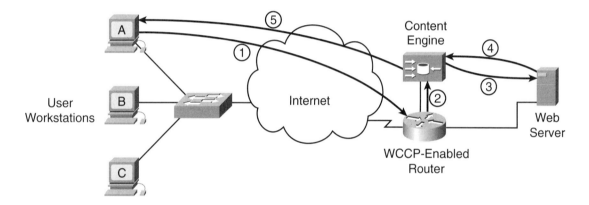

<table>
<tr><td>**KEY POINT**</td><td>Reverse proxy mode is different from the previous two modes discussed because its goal is not to reduce bandwidth requirements but rather to reduce load on the server.</td></tr>
</table>

The steps involved in reverse proxy caching are as follows:

Step 1   In Figure 8-3, the user at workstation A requests a web page that resides on the web server. This request is received by the WCCP-enabled router on the server side of the Internet.

Step 2   The router analyzes the request and, if it meets configured criteria, forwards it to the content engine. For example, the router can be configured to send specific TCP port requests to the content engine while not redirecting other requests.

Step 3   If the content engine does not have the requested page, it sends the request to the server.

Step 4   The server responds to the content engine with the requested data.

Step 5   The content engine forwards the web page to the user and then caches it for future use.

At Step 3, if the content engine had the requested web page cached, it would send the page to the user. After the content engine has the content, any subsequent requests for the same web page are satisfied by the content engine, and the web server itself is not involved, thus reducing the load on the server.

> **KEY POINT**
>
> A variety of content caches can be deployed throughout a network, in any combination of these three modes.
>
> Clusters of caches can also be deployed to provide redundancy and increased caching capacity.

Content Routing

A content router can be added to a CDN to redirect users' requests to the closest content engine that contains the desired content.

The closest content engine is the one that has the shortest delay to the user. To determine this, the list of candidate content engines is configured on the content router, and a *boomerang* protocol is used between the content router and each content engine to determine the delay between the two devices.

This delay is then used in a *Domain Name System (DNS) race* process. When a content router receives a request for content that is serviced by multiple content engines, the content router forwards that request to a selection of the appropriate content engines, delaying each request by the delay determined by the boomerang protocol. Thus, each content engine should receive the request at the same time. The content engines then all respond to the request; the first response that is received by the client or the client's local DNS server is the winner of the race and is therefore the best content engine from which that particular client should receive the desired content. The client then requests the desired content from the winning content engine.

The content router can be used in either of two modes[3]—direct mode or WCCP mode—as described in the following sections.

Direct Mode

> **KEY POINT**
>
> When used in direct mode, the content router acts as the authoritative DNS server for all domains for which it is configured. DNS address requests are sent directly from a DNS server that is local to the client to the content router.

As an example of a content router operating in direct mode, assume that the content router is to handle requests to http://www.cisco.com. The DNS server is thus configured to point to the content router as the name server for http://www.cisco.com, and all requests for content from this site are sent to the content router.

Figure 8-4 illustrates how a direct-mode content router interacts with other devices in the network.

Figure 8-4   *A Content Router in Direct Mode Acts as a DNS Server*

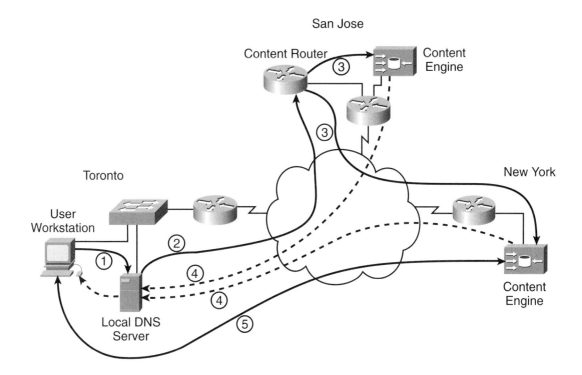

The steps involved when a content router is operating in direct mode are as follows:

Step 1   In Figure 8-4, the user at the workstation in Toronto requests a web page from a server. The user's workstation (the client) sends a DNS query for the IP address of the content that it is looking for. This request goes to the client's local DNS server.

Step 2   The local DNS server sends the query to the content router (which is in San Jose, in this example).

Step 3   The content router forwards the request to a selection of the appropriate content engines (assuming that multiple content engines service the requested content). In this example, the request is forwarded to the content engines in San Jose and New York.

Step 4   The content engines receive the request and then reply to the local DNS server. The first response is from the best content engine for this client, and this response is passed to the client.

Step 5   The client communicates with the best content engine (which is in New York, in this example) and retrieves the requested web page for the user.

WCCP Mode

KEY POINT   When a content router is used in WCCP mode, users' requests are intercepted by a WCCP-enabled router and forwarded to the content router. (This is different from when the content router is used in direct mode, in which the user's local DNS server is configured to point directly to the content router.) If the content router cannot handle the user's request, it forwards the request on to the DNS server specified in the request. Otherwise, the content router handles the request in the same way as it does in direct mode, as described in the previous section.

The use of WCCP mode requires that WCCP be enabled both on the content router and on another router in the path between the user and the primary DNS server. This second router must be configured to send DNS address requests to the content router.

Figure 8-5 illustrates how a WCCP-mode content router interacts with other devices in the network.

Figure 8-5   *A Content Router in WCCP Mode Receives Requests Intercepted by a WCCP-Enabled Router*

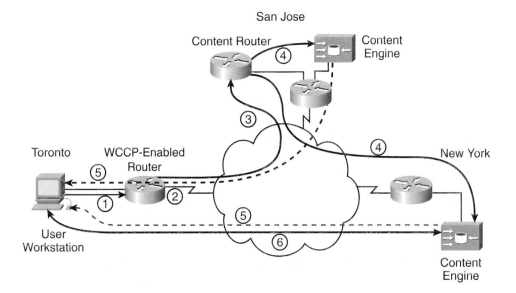

The steps involved when a content router is operating in WCCP mode are as follows:

Step 1   In Figure 8-5, the user at the workstation in Toronto requests a web page from a server. The user's workstation (the client) sends a DNS query for the IP address of the content that it is looking for.

Step 2   This request is destined for a DNS server but is intercepted by the WCCP router.

Step 3   The WCCP router forwards the request to the content router.

Step 4   The content router forwards the request to a selection of the appropriate content engines (assuming that multiple content engines service the requested content). In this example, the request is forwarded to the content engines in San Jose and New York.

Step 5   The content engines receive the request and then reply to the client. The first response is from the best content engine for this client.

Step 6   The client communicates with the best content engine (which is in New York, in this example) and retrieves the requested web page for the user.

Content Distribution and Management

The Cisco Content Distribution Manager can be used to manage how content is distributed to content engines, and to control other content engine settings.

KEY POINT | Cisco defines three types of content: on-demand, pre-positioned, and live.

On-demand content is what the content engines store as a result of users' requests, as described in the "Content Caches and Content Engines" section, earlier in this chapter. Content engines can check with the origin server to see whether on-demand content is up to date. This occurs, for example, when the content expires (as specified by the server), when a user explicitly requests it (such as when the user clicks the **Reload** button in his browser), or when configurable timers set on the content engine expire. If the content has changed, the content engine caches the updated content from the server.

Pre-positioned content is that which has been retrieved and distributed through a network of content engines; the network administrator configures the Content Distribution Manager to pre-position this bandwidth-intensive content (typically during off-peak hours) so that it will be available upon users' requests. Some terminology related to pre-positioned content is as follows:[4]

■ **Channel**—A set of content from a single website and the configuration that defines how the content is to be acquired, distributed, and stored. Content engines are assigned to a channel so that they can handle requests for this content.

- **Root content engine**—The content engine that is designated to download a channel's content from the origin server and forward it to the other content engines that are assigned to the channel.

- **Manifest file**—Specifies the location from which the root content engine should fetch the pre-positioned content objects and the frequency with which the content engine should check for updates.

> **NOTE** Manifest files define content accessed through Hypertext Transfer Protocol (HTTP), Secure HTTP (HTTPS), and File Transfer Protocol (FTP). Thus, only these file types can be pre-positioned.

Live content is a stream of content, such as a CEO's annual message to employees, that is being broadcast and that is to be relayed by the content engines to the users according to specific policies (such as maximum bit rate and bandwidth). Live content is not associated with a manifest file but rather with a *program file*. The program file describes attributes of the program, such as the start and end time and the server to be used.

Content Switching

KEY POINT | A content switch load-balances requests to servers, content engines, or firewalls.

A content switch can be used in a data center environment, for example. Here the content switch can be used in front of a group of application servers to balance the connection requests sent to each, as illustrated in Figure 8-6.

Figure 8-6 *A Content Switch Can Load-Balance Connections to a Server Farm*

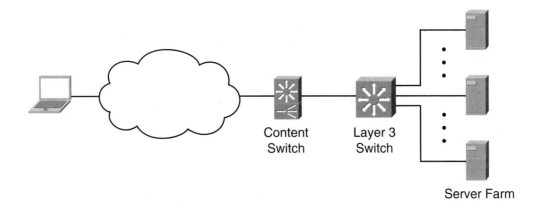

Content switches can be configured with various policies that define how messages are shared among devices. For example, when load-balancing across a set of servers, a policy might specify some of the following:[5]

- That all connections from a single user will go to the same server

- That all connections from a specific type of device (for example, from a cell phone) will go to a subset of the servers that can handle that device type

- That all requests for specific file types (for example, video files) will be directed to a specific server

The load balancing can be based on a variety of algorithms, including distributing requests on a round-robin basis or distributing to the least-loaded device.

A content switch can also monitor the status of the devices and fail over to another if one should become unavailable.

Designing Content Networking

Content networking encompasses a selection of device types that can be deployed in a variety of ways. This section examines the following two scenarios and example designs using CN devices:

- School curriculum

- Live video and video on demand for a corporation

School Curriculum

In this first scenario, a school board wants to provide curriculum and other course information to all its students, who are distributed across a wide geographical area. The content is relatively static and therefore lends itself well to a CN solution, as shown in Figure 8-7.

Figure 8-7 *Performance Can Be Improved Significantly with Content Networking*

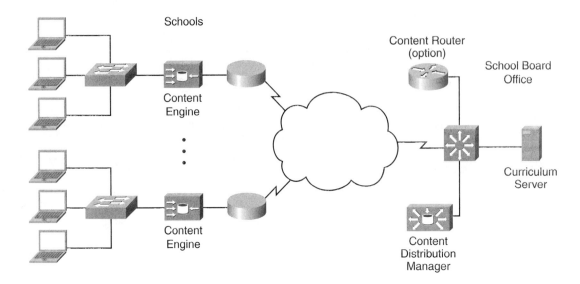

In the network in Figure 8-7, the course content resides on the curriculum server located at the school board office. A Content Distribution Manager is deployed in the same office to handle the distribution of the content to the content engines deployed in each of the schools. An optional content router (in direct mode) can also be deployed at the main office if not all schools are to be equipped with the content engines; in this case, the content router directs users' requests to the closest content engine.

The content engines in this scenario are deployed in nontransparent caching mode. Therefore, the workstations in the schools must be configured with the address of the school's content engine as their proxy address.

Live Video and Video on Demand for a Corporation

In this scenario, a corporation wants to be able to deliver live video, such as company meetings, and VoD, such as training videos, to its employees over the network. The organization uses an IP/TV broadcast server to create and send the live video and stores the VoD files on servers in its head office, as illustrated in Figure 8-8. A content switch is used in the head office to load-share among the servers.

Figure 8-8 *Content Networking Ensures That Video Is Available Throughout the Enterprise*

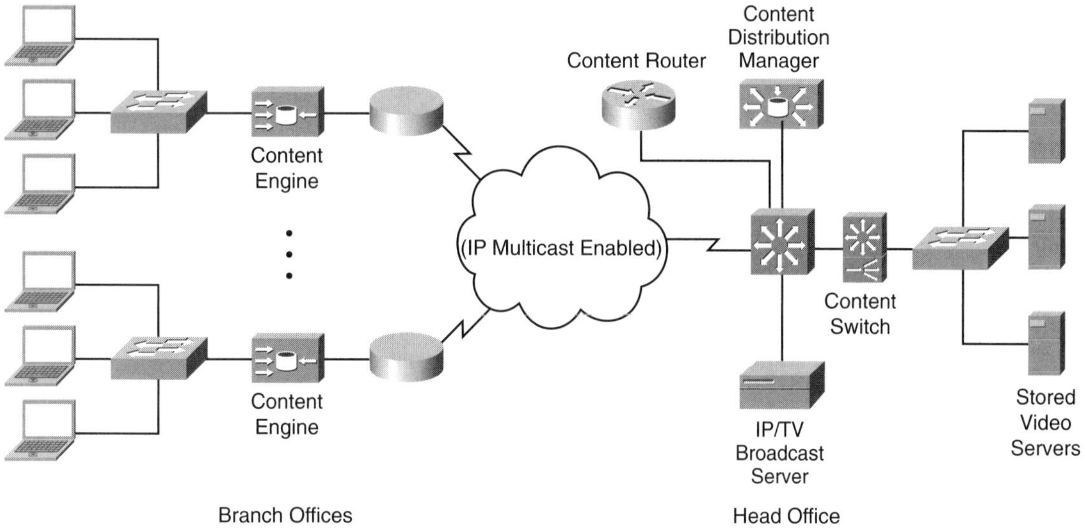

A Content Distribution Manager is also deployed in the head office to handle the distribution of the content to the content engines that are deployed in each of the branch offices. An optional content router can again be deployed at the head office if not all branch offices are to be equipped with the content engines; in this case, the content router directs users' requests to the closest content engine.

The content engines in this scenario are deployed in nontransparent caching mode. Therefore, the workstations in the branch offices must be configured with the address of the office's content engine as their proxy address.

IP multicast must be enabled on this network to ensure efficient distribution of the live video.

NOTE   As an alternative to implementing CN, an enterprise can contract with a provider of CDN services. A CDN service provider implements a CDN so that its clients can access CN services and features from different locations, anywhere in the world. For example, consider a company that provides e-learning—the company has course files (including, for example, videos) on its servers for customers to access worldwide. Those users closer to the servers would tend to experience faster response times than those farther away, who might experience unacceptable response times. The company can therefore contract with a CDN service provider to replicate the e-learning content on the service provider's many worldwide servers. Distant users accessing the courses are then directed to the server closest to them, drastically improving the response times they experience.

Summary

In this chapter, you learned about integrating content networking devices into your network; the following topics were presented:

- The benefits of employing the CN intelligent network solution.

- The following components that are used in CN:

  - **Content engine**—Caches, or stores, selected content from origin servers and sends it upon request to users. When not used with a content router, a content engine can be deployed in a network in three ways: transparent caching, nontransparent caching, and reverse proxy caching.

  - **Content router**—Directs users' requests for content to the closest content engine. A content router can operate in either direct mode or WCCP mode.

  - **Content distribution and management device**—Responsible for distributing content to the content engines and for ensuring that the material is kept up to date.

  - **Content switch**—Load-balances requests to servers, content engines, or firewalls.

- The three types of content: on-demand, live, and pre-positioned.

- Example CN design scenarios.

Endnotes

[1]"Cisco Content Engine 7320," http://www.cisco.com/en/US/products/hw/contnetw/ps766/prod_release_note09186a00800d9f74.html.

[2]"Cisco Content Engine and CDN Hardware Data Sheet," http://www.cisco.com/en/US/products/hw/contnetw/ps761/products_data_sheet09186a008014b5d4.html.

[3]"Introducing the Content Routing Software," http://www.cisco.com/univercd/cc/td/doc/product/webscale/cr/crsw11/77509ov1.pdf.

[4]"Cisco ACNS Software Configuration Guide for Centrally Managed Deployments Release 5.3." http://www.cisco.com/application/pdf/en/us/guest/products/ps6049/c2001/ccmigration_09186a00803b0ca7.pdf.

[5]"White Paper: Scalable Content Switching," http://www.cisco.com/en/US/products/hw/contnetw/ps792/products_white_paper09186a0080136856.shtml.

This chapter discusses how network management is designed and includes the following sections:

- Making the Business Case

- ISO Network Management Standard

- Network Management Protocols and Tools

- Managing a Network

- Network Management Design

CHAPTER 9

Network Management Design

This chapter describes network management design. After introducing the importance of effective network management, we describe the related International Organization for Standardization (ISO) standard and then explore various protocols and tools available. The chapter includes a description of network management strategy and discusses how performance measurements can be made to ensure that requirements are being met. We conclude with a discussion of network management design considerations, including the importance of security.

> **NOTE**   Appendix B, "Network Fundamentals," includes material that we assume you understand before reading the rest of the book. Thus, we encourage you to review any of the material in Appendix B that you are not familiar with before reading the rest of this chapter.

Making the Business Case

As you have seen in previous chapters in this book, many technologies can be involved in today's networks. After the network has been designed and implemented, all of these technologies must then be managed.

Recall from Chapter 1, "Network Design," how important it is to clearly define the requirements of the network. When deciding on the network management strategy, protocols, and tools, it is also critical to go back to those requirements; only then can you determine what is valuable to measure and track.

Being proactive, rather than reactive, is crucial to managing your network. This means that you need to understand both the business's and the end users' perspectives and priorities, and manage the network so that their expectations are met. To do this, you need to understand the network and have baseline measurements so that you can see that something might be going wrong, before it causes a problem. As networks are being used for more applications (for example, Voice over IP [VoIP], e-commerce, and so forth), they are getting more complicated, which in turn complicates the management of the network.

Effective network management is crucial to ensuring the success of today's businesses that rely so heavily on their networks. The key to effective network management is to recognize that a network exists to meet the needs of the business—the requirements. Therefore, network management should not be managing the technology for technology's sake, but as a means to meet these requirements—delivering an appropriate level of service, at an appropriate cost. For example, network management must go beyond traditional measurements (such as effective bandwidth) and instead focus on the availability of critical applications, because those are what the business relies on.

ISO Network Management Standard

As network management became vital to businesses, ISO developed a standardized framework known as fault, configuration, accounting, performance, and security management (FCAPS). These five functional areas of network management are defined as follows:

- **Fault management**—Detects, isolates, notifies users about, and corrects faults that occur in the network

- **Configuration management**—Tracks and maintains network configuration information, including device inventory, configuration files, and software

- **Accounting management**—Tracks device and network resource usage

- **Performance management**—Monitors and collects performance measurements from network devices and analyzes the information so that network performance can be proactively managed to meet requirements

- **Security management**—Controls and logs access to network resources in support of security polices

FCAPS can serve as a reminder of areas of management that need to be included as you design your network. The following sections introduce you to a wide variety of protocols and tools that are available for network management.

Network Management Protocols and Tools

In this section, we first introduce some terminology that is related to network management protocols. This is followed by a discussion of the following protocols and tools:

- Simple Network Management Protocol (SNMP)

- Management Information Base (MIB)

- Remote Monitoring (RMON)

- Cisco NetFlow

- Syslog

- CiscoWorks

We conclude with a discussion of some other network management tools that are available.

Terminology

Figure 9-1 illustrates some terms that are related to network management; the terms are described as follows:

- **Managed device**—A device (for example, a router or a switch) that is to be managed

- **Management information**—Data used for and collected during the management of a device

- **Management agent**—Software on a managed device that collects and stores management information

- **Network management system**—A system that includes the applications that monitor and control managed devices

- **Network management protocol**—A protocol that exchanges management information between the network management system and managed devices

Figure 9-1 *Network Management Terminology*

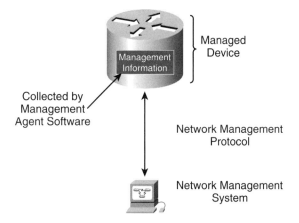

SNMP is the simplest network management protocol. The management information standard is the MIB, a detailed definition of the information on a managed device. MIB data is accessible through a network management protocol, such as SNMP. The RMON standard is an extension to the MIB; while the MIB only provides static information about a managed device, an RMON agent creates specific groups of statistics that can be collected for long-term trend analysis. These standards are described in the following sections.

SNMP

KEY POINT | SNMP is an IP application protocol that runs on top of User Datagram Protocol (UDP) to transport management data. It allows both the configuring and retrieval of management information.

The initial SNMP version 1 (SNMPv1) was extended to SNMP version 2 (SNMPv2) and its variants and then further extended to SNMP version 3 (SNMPv3).

SNMPv1 defines five message types between the management application and management agents, as follows:

- **Get request**—Requests a specific MIB variable from the agent

- **Get next request**—Retrieves the next object from a table or list after the initial *get request*

- **Set request**—Sets a MIB variable on an agent

- **Get response**—A response to a *get request* or *get next request* from a manager

- **Trap message**—Sends an unsolicited alarm to the manager, for example, when a device detects a failure

SNMPv2 includes the following two new message types:

- **GetBulk**—Retrieves large amounts of data (for example, tables) in one request so that multiple *get next request* messages are no longer needed

- **InformRequest**—Similar to the SNMPv1 trap message

SNMPv3 (implemented on Cisco routers in Internetwork Operating System [IOS] Release 12.0 and later) adds security, including the ability to add authentication and privacy to SNMP communication on a per-user or group-of-users basis. This can be used, for example, to define which objects a user can read or write, and which notifications a user can receive.

MIB

A MIB is a standard for collecting management information.

KEY POINT | A MIB stores the information gathered by a management agent locally on a managed device, for later retrieval by a network management protocol.

NOTE The MIB acronym is usually pronounced as a word (that rhymes with *bib*), not as individual letters.

As shown in Figure 9-2, the MIB structure is logically represented as a tree hierarchy. The root of the tree is not named and splits into three main branches: Consultative Committee for International Telegraph and Telephone (CCITT), ISO, and joint ISO/CCITT.

Figure 9-2 *Internet MIB Hierarchy[1]*

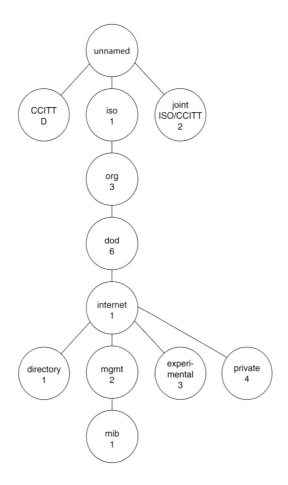

The branches in the MIB tree are identified by short text strings and integers, which form object identifiers. For example, the Internet standard MIB is represented by the object identifier 1.3.6.1.2.1; this can also be written as iso.org.dod.internet.mgmt.mib. Each object in a MIB has a unique object identifier. Network management applications specify this identifier when they want to set or retrieve a specific object.

Along with the standard MIBs, vendors can reserve their own private branch of the MIB, under which they can create custom objects. For example, Cisco devices have objects in the private section of the MIB tree (1.3.6.1.4.1.9, or iso.org.dod.internet.private.enterprise.cisco) for parameters related to Cisco's proprietary protocols and other variables. As an example, the Cisco 3800 Series integrated services router's object identifier is 1.3.6.1.4.1.9.1.544.

Standard MIBs are defined in different Requests For Comments (RFCs). MIB-II, defined by RFC 1213 ("Management Information Base for Network Management of TCP/IP-based Internets: MIB-II"), is an extension of the original MIB (which is now called MIB-I). MIB-II supports some new protocols and provides more detailed and structured information.

RMON

RMON is defined as part of the MIB-II collection of objects. RMON not only collects and stores data, but RMON agents within managed objects (or on separate RMON probe devices) also perform some analysis of the data. For example, RMON data can include statistical information for conversations between two hosts, from the perspective of the managed object. The RMON MIB is 1.3.6.1.2.1.16 (iso.ord.dod.internet.mgmt.mib.rmon). Because RMON agents must look at every frame on the network, they can cause performance problems on a managed device. Thus, separate RMON probes can be used to offload the processing to another device.

RMON1 provides statistics at the data link and physical layers of the Open Systems Interconnection (OSI) model, while RMON2 extends RMON1 through to the application layer, as illustrated in Figure 9-3 and described in the following sections.

Figure 9-3   *RMON1 Provides Visibility at the Lower Two Layers While RMON2 Extends to the Upper Layers*

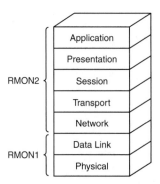

RMON 1

RMON1, defined in RFC 2819, "Remote Network Monitoring Management Information Base," provides statistics and analysis for remote LAN segments.

KEY POINT | RMON1 works at the data link layer and physical layer. It therefore provides information relating to Media Access Control (MAC) addresses and LAN traffic.

RMON1 defines nine groups of statistics (ten, including Token Ring extensions, defined in RFC 1513, "Token Ring Extensions to the Remote Network Monitoring MIB") that can be implemented by RMON1 agents and that can then be requested by the network management system. The RMON1 groups are as follows:

- **Statistics**—Contains real-time statistics for each monitored interface on the device, including, for example, the number of packets and bytes sent, the number of broadcast and multicast packets, and so forth

- **History**—Stores periodic statistical samples

- **Alarm**—Contains specific thresholds for managed objects that, when reached, trigger an event, as specified in an events group

- **Host**—Contains statistics associated with each host that is discovered on the network

- **HostTopN**—Contains statistics for the top *N* hosts on a list ordered by one of their observed variables

- **Matrix**—Contains statistics for conversations between sets of two hosts

- **Filters**—Contains definitions of packet filters that generate events or define what should be stored locally in a packet capture group

- **Packet capture**—Contains data packets that matched filters

- **Events**—Controls the generation and notification of alarms or filters on the device

- **TokenRing**—Contains Token Ring interface statistics

RMON2

RMON2 is defined in RFC 2021, "Remote Network Monitoring Management Information Base Version 2 using SMIv2."

| RMON2 is not a replacement for RMON1, but an extension to it. RMON2 adds nine more groups that provide the visibility into the upper layers.

With RMON2, conversations can be viewed at the network and application layers. For example, statistics can be gathered for traffic generated by a specific application on a specific host, such as a file-transfer program.

The RMON2 groups added are as follows:

- **Protocol directory**—Holds a list of the protocols supported by the device

- **Protocol distribution**—Contains traffic statistics for each of the supported protocols

- **Address mapping**—Provides a mapping of network layer addresses to MAC addresses

- **Network layer host**—Contains statistics for the network layer traffic to or from each host

- **Network layer matrix**—Contains network layer traffic statistics for conversations between sets of two hosts

- **Application layer host**—Contains statistics for the application layer traffic to or from each host

- **Application layer matrix**—Contains application layer traffic statistics for conversations between sets of two hosts

- **User history collection**—Contains periodic samples of user-specified variables

- **Probe configuration**—Provides a standard way to remotely configure probe parameters

RMON Extensions

RFC 3577, "Introduction to the Remote Monitoring (RMON) Family of MIB Modules," describes RMON1 and RMON2; it also has references to various RMON extensions needed to support today's networks, including the following:

- RFC 2613, "Remote Network Monitoring MIB Extensions for Switched Networks Version 1.0," defines objects for managing remote network-monitoring devices in switched network environments.

- RFC 3144, "Remote Monitoring MIB Extensions for Interface Parameters Monitoring," defines a method of sorting the interfaces of a monitored device according to values of parameters specific to the interfaces.

- RFC 3273, "Remote Network Monitoring Management Information Base for High Capacity Networks," defines objects for managing remote network-monitoring devices for use on high-speed networks.

- RFC 3287, "Remote Monitoring MIB Extensions for Differentiated Services," describes managed objects used to monitor Differentiated Services Code Point (DSCP) usage in packets that contain a DSCP field. Recall that DSCP values indicate or mark the type of traffic; this marking can then be used by other tools to provide the appropriate quality of service (QoS) for that traffic.

Cisco NetFlow

Cisco NetFlow technology allows the measurement of flows that pass through devices.

KEY POINT

A *network flow* is a unidirectional stream of packets between a given source and destination. A flow is very granular—it can be defined by the source and destination IP addresses, source and destination port numbers, protocol type, type of service (ToS), and input interface.

NetFlow has two key components:[2] the NetFlow cache, which stores the flow information, and the NetFlow export mechanism, which sends the flow data to a network management collector for data reporting.

NetFlow can benefit the network in the following ways:

- NetFlow can be used to monitor network data, application use, and users. Billing or other accounting can be done based on network flows, allowing intercompany or customer charges to be based on actual usage. Aggregated usage data can also be helpful for other uses, such as marketing efforts (for example, for keeping track of who is using which data) and when planning an upgrade to the network.

- The NetFlow cache switches packets that belong to a flow, resulting in faster processing of those packets.

How does NetFlow compare with RMON? NetFlow provides more detailed information and more types of data on a per-interface basis, and can scale to include more interfaces. NetFlow has less of a performance impact than RMON and does not require external probes.

Syslog

Cisco network devices, such as routers and switches, produce messages with the following format:

```
mm/dd/yy:hh/mm/ss:%FACILITY-SUBFACILITY-SEVERITY-MNEMONIC: Message-text
```

The portions of this code are described as follows:

■ *mm/dd/yy:hh/mm/ss*—The timestamp, if enabled.

■ *FACILITY*—The hardware device, protocol, or module of the system software to which the message pertains. Some examples of the facility are IP, IF (for interface), and LINK (for data link).

■ *SEVERITY*—A number from 0 to 7 that indicates the severity of the condition, as follows:

 — Emergency (level 0, which is the highest level)

 — Alert (level 1)

 — Critical (level 2)

 — Error (level 3)

 — Warning (level 4)

 — Notice (level 5)

 — Informational (level 6)

 — Debugging (level 7)

■ *MNEMONIC*—Uniquely identifies the error message.

■ *Message-text*—A text string that further describes the event, including, for example, addresses, port numbers, and so forth.

These messages are sent to console sessions by default, but devices can be configured to send the messages to a syslog server. A *syslog server* is a server that runs a syslog application, a standard for logging system messages. The messages can then be retrieved and analyzed by the network manager.

> **NOTE** Syslog output generated by network devices is clear text, so for security purposes, it could be sent to the syslog server using an encrypted communication channel, such as a virtual private network (VPN) tunnel. This is most important when the syslog data is traversing a publicly accessible network, such as a demilitarized zone.

CiscoWorks

Cisco has a variety of network management products; the full portfolio is listed on the Network Management Products and Services page on the Cisco website (http://www.cisco.com/en/US/ products/sw/netmgtsw/index.html).

CiscoWorks is the Cisco network management application. CiscoWorks is available either as stand-alone applications or as bundles of tools for specific uses. For example, the CiscoWorks LAN Management Solution (LMS) version 2.5 bundles the following components to allow the configuration, administration, monitoring, and troubleshooting of networks:[3]

- **CiscoWorks Device Fault Manager (DFM)**—Provides real-time, detailed detection, analysis, and reporting of faults that can occur on Cisco devices

- **CiscoWorks Campus Manager (CM)**—Includes tools for configuring, managing, visualizing, and identifying discrepancies in OSI Layer 2 infrastructures

- **CiscoWorks Resource Manager Essentials (RME)**—Provides tools for managing network inventory, device configurations and changes, and software updates

- **CiscoWorks Internetwork Performance Monitor (IPM)**—Performs proactive measurement of network response time and availability, providing both real-time and historical analysis of congestion and latency problems

- **CiscoWorks CiscoView (CV)**—Provides graphical displays of Cisco devices so that users can easily interact with device components to change configuration parameters and monitor statistics

- **CiscoWorks Common Services (CS)**—Is an application infrastructure for all CiscoWorks applications, providing common data storage, login, user role definitions, access privileges, and security protocols

NOTE The components available, and those included in the various CiscoWorks bundles, change with each version; check the Cisco website for the latest information.

Other Tools

In a recent Networkers presentation, Cisco included a simplified network management framework and some of the suggested tools that would help to manage each aspect within the framework, as illustrated in Figure 9-4.

Figure 9-4   *Cisco Network Management Framework[4]*

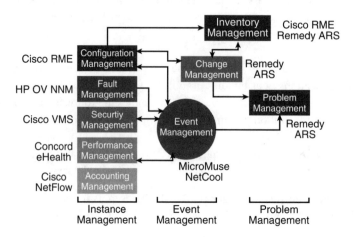

This framework includes the five elements of the FCAPS model, as described in the "ISO Network Management Standard" section, earlier in this chapter. In addition, the following four new elements are introduced:

- **Inventory management**—Procedures and processes for maintaining an up-to-date inventory of all assets

- **Change management**—Procedures, documentation, systems, and metrics for successfully managing change within an organization

- **Event management**—Procedures and processes for managing significant events within the network, including faults, security breaches, and so forth

- **Problem management**—Systems, procedures, and organizational structure for documenting, tracking, reporting, resolving, and analyzing problems

The tools mentioned in Figure 9-4 that we have not already introduced include the following:

- **CiscoWorks VPN/Security Management Solution (VMS)**—Includes Web-based tools for configuring, monitoring, and troubleshooting VPNs, firewalls, network intrusion detection systems (IDSs), and host intrusion prevention systems (IPSs). CiscoWorks VMS also includes network device inventory, change audit, and software distribution features.

- **MicroMuse Netcool**—Tools for collecting and consolidating real-time data from the network, and then analyzing and acting upon the results (http://www.micromuse.com).

- **Remedy's Action Request System (ARS)**—Platform and development environment for automating service management business processes (http://www.remedy.com).

- **Concord eHealth**—For performance management, including measuring and monitoring application performance management (http://www.concord.com).

- **HP OpenView (OV) Network Node Manager (NNM)**—For network discovery, identifying network problems, monitoring, and alarm management (http://www.openview.hp.com/products/nnm/index.html).

A variety of other network management tools are available, many of which are also discussed in this same Networkers presentation (see http://www.cisco.com/warp/public/732/Tech/grip/docs/deploymanage.pdf).

One network analysis tool available for 802.11a/b/g wireless LANs (WLANs) is Fluke's OptiView Series II Integrated Network Analyzer (http://www.flukenetworks.com/) equipped with the wireless option.

NOTE   The tools mentioned in this chapter are examples of available tools and are provided for your information only; their inclusion here does not represent an endorsement or recommendation by the authors.

Another tool that can be useful for network management is the Cisco Network-Based Application Recognition (NBAR) classification software feature, running within the IOS on Cisco routers. As mentioned in Chapter 6, "Quality of Service Design," NBAR allows classification (and marking) of a wide variety of applications, including web-based and other difficult-to-classify protocols that use dynamic Transmission Control Protocol (TCP)/UDP port assignments.

One more tool, specifically for managing networks of small to medium businesses (SMBs)—which Cisco defines as having 250 employees or less—is the Cisco Network Assistant Windows-based management application.[5] Network Assistant can be used to manage Cisco switches, routers, access points, and IP phones, and includes configuration management, inventory reporting, password synchronization, and IOS upgrade capability. This tool also includes the Smartports Advisor, which automatically detects the type of device connected to a switch port (for example, an IP phone, a wireless access point, or a PC) and then applies Cisco's recommended best-practice configuration to the port appropriate for that device.

Managing a Network

Now that we have explored some of the various network management tools and protocols available, we next look at how these can be incorporated into a strategy for successfully managing a network, including service-level contracts (SLCs) and service-level agreements (SLAs).

Network Management Strategy

It is important to develop a network management strategy that details what information is to be collected from each device and how that information is to be analyzed. The appropriate protocols and tools, as described in the previous section, can then be selected.

Thresholds should be set so that alerts or alarms can be raised if parameters start to go out of range. To determine what these threshold levels should be, baseline measurements can be taken to create a snapshot of the "working" network. Instead of waiting for a failure and reacting to it, alerts and alarms relative to baseline measurements help the network manager to be proactive and solve problems before the network is adversely affected.

Cisco recommends the following network management best practices:[6]

- Keep an archived copy of the software images (for example, Cisco IOS) and configurations of all devices.

- Keep an up-to-date inventory and log any configuration and software changes.

- Monitor critical parameters, including any syslog-reported errors, SNMP traps, and RMON statistics that are important for your network.

- Use tools to identify any configuration discrepancies (for example, CiscoWorks Campus Manager can detect inconsistent trunking configurations on switch ports).

SLCs and SLAs

SLCs and SLAs can also be a part of a network management strategy.

KEY POINT

An *SLC* specifies connectivity and performance levels for the service's end user, to be met by the service provider.

SLAs define specific service performance measurements between pairs of devices, for example, between a router and a server.

An SLC typically includes multiple SLAs, so a violation of any particular SLA could result in a violation of the overall SLC.

The service provider could be either within the organization—for example, an IT department providing services to internal users—or an external company, such as an ISP providing hosted application services.

Traditional SLCs and SLAs concentrated on measurements over a specific network; for example, Frame Relay committed information rates. However, today's complex applications, including VoIP, for example, require end-to-end guarantees of service levels. For this type of environment, a new way of measuring and ensuring network performance is required. The Cisco IP SLAs technology, described in the next section, provides this functionality.

IP Service-Level Agreements

Cisco IOS IP SLAs[7] technology is embedded in most IOS devices to allow users to analyze service levels being experienced by IP applications. IP SLAs allows test traffic to be generated and then measures the performance of that traffic through the network, either between Cisco IOS devices or from a Cisco IOS device to a remote device such as a server. Figure 9-5 illustrates IP SLAs operation.

Figure 9-5   *IP SLAs Provides Network Performance Measurements*

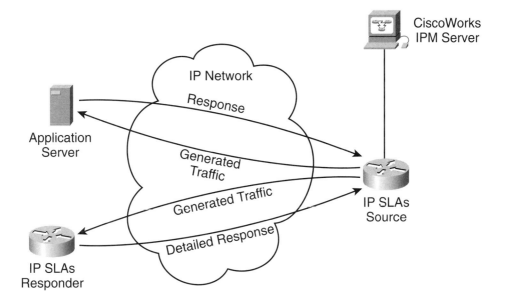

In Figure 9-5, the IP SLAs source generates some traffic destined for the application server, similar to an extended ping. The server's response includes a timestamp, which can then be used by the source to determine the network delay. The IP SLAs source also generates traffic destined for the IP SLAs responder device, which has IP SLAs software enabled. In this case, the response is more detailed, including, for example, the processing delays within the device.

NOTE The Cisco IOS IP SLAs monitoring and management feature set replaced the Cisco IOS Service Assurance Agent (SAA) feature in Cisco IOS Release 12.3(14)T.[8] This feature set incorporates most of the features available in SAA, and SAA commands have been replaced by the IP SLAs monitor's command set and configuration structure.

The traffic generated by IP SLAs simulates real data by allowing many options to be configured, including source and destination IP addresses, UDP/TCP port numbers, ToS (either DSCP or IP precedence bits), VPN routing/forwarding instance (VRF), and Uniform Resource Locator (URL) web address. IP SLAs can be configured end to end over an entire network to best represent the metrics that an end user is likely to experience.

Measurements taken can include response time, latency, jitter, packet loss, voice quality scoring, network resource availability, application performance, and server response time.

IP SLAs is accessible using the command-line interface or SNMP. Performance-monitoring applications such as CiscoWorks IPM and other third-party Cisco partner performance management products can also use SNMP to configure and retrieve information from IP SLAs.

Network Management Design

Recall from Chapter 1 that the Enterprise Composite Network Model Enterprise Campus functional area includes a Management module that encompasses the network management functions. The Management module provides monitoring, logging, security, and other management features to the campus. The Cisco SAFE blueprint (available at http://www.cisco.com/go/safe) provides recommendations for what should be included in this module and how it should be secured. The devices and services provided within this module are illustrated in Figure 9-6.

Figure 9-6 *Management Module Provides Monitoring, Logging, and Security Functions*[9]

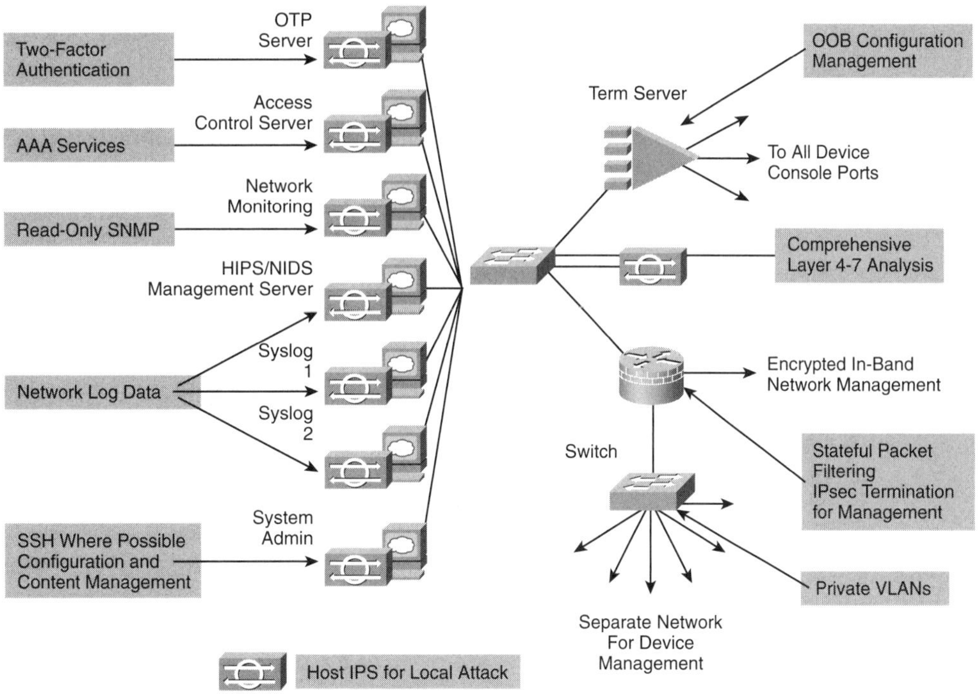

The Management module contains one or more of the following:

■ **Authentication server**—Provides strong authentication services for remote and local users on the network. An example is a two-factor, one-time password (OTP) system based on token cards (as described in Chapter 4, "Network Security Design").

■ **Access control server**—Provides centralized command and control for all user authentication, authorization, and accounting (AAA).

■ **Network-monitoring server**—Is responsible for monitoring the devices in the network.

■ **Host intrusion prevention system (HIPS)/network intrusion detection system (NIDS) management server**—Provides configuration and viewing of alarms on IDS and IPS sensors deployed throughout the campus network.

■ **Syslog server**—Collects network events and traps.

■ **System administration server**—Configures network management and other network devices.

Because the management network provides administrative access to the rest of the network it must be secure. The previously mentioned servers, and the routers that act as terminal servers (to provide a reverse Telnet to the console port of devices throughout the rest of the network), are on the inside segment of a firewall router. An outside segment connects to all the devices that require management, on a separate network, for SNMP and other management traffic. These two segments provide out-of-band (OOB) management—the management data is separate from other traffic, providing a first level of security for this critical data. A third interface connects to the production network for in-band management where it is required; this segment should be encrypted with IPsec so that management traffic cannot be compromised.

Other security features implemented in the management module can include the following:[10]

- Use of secure shell (SSH), a protocol similar to Telnet, but with encryption, for configuration.

- SNMP read-only access, so that SNMP's clear-text password cannot be used to make configuration changes.

- Possible use of SNMPv3 with encryption, on either the in-band or out-of-band management network.

- Private virtual LANs (VLANs) on the management module switches so that traffic cannot travel from one device to another over the management network; it instead goes to the firewall to ensure only authorized access.

Other design considerations for the network management module include the following:

- The number of network management systems required, depending on the number of end-user and other devices, the amount of data to be collected, and the capacity of the systems.

- The effect of Network Address Translation (NAT) (described in Chapter 3, "IPv4 Routing Design") and firewalls on management protocols. For example, SNMP is not compatible with NAT because addresses are embedded within the SNMP data.

- The bandwidth required for management data. For example, if a lot of syslog messages are sent across a WAN, the bandwidth can become a bottleneck.

Summary

In this chapter, you learned about network management design, including the following topics:

- Why effective and secure network management is critical

- The various protocols and tools available, including SNMP, MIB, RMON, NetFlow, syslog, and CiscoWorks

■ SLCs and SLAs, and the IP SLAs technology embedded in Cisco IOS that allows users to analyze service levels being experienced by IP applications

■ Network management design considerations, including security of this critical traffic

Endnotes

[1]"Cisco Management Information Base (MIB) User Quick Reference," http://www.cisco.com/univercd/cc/td/doc/product/software/ios112/mbook/index.htm.

[2]"NetFlow Services Solutions Guide," http://www.cisco.com/en/US/customer/products/sw/net-mgtsw/ps1964/products_implementation_design_guide09186a00800d6a11.html.

[3]"CiscoWorks LAN Management Solution," http://www.cisco.com/en/US/products/sw/cscowork/ps2425/index.html.

[4]"Designing and Managing High Availability IP Networks," Networkers 2004 Session NMS-2T20, http://www.cisco.com/warp/public/732/Tech/grip/docs/deploymanage.pdf.

[5]Cisco Network Assistant information, http://www.cisco.com/go/NetworkAssistant.

[6]Hutton and Ranjbar, *CCDP Self-Study: Designing Cisco Network Architectures (ARCH)*, Indianapolis, Cisco Press, 2005.

[7]"Cisco IOS IP SLAs Configuration Guide, Release 12.4," http://www.cisco.com/en/US/products/ps6350/products_configuration_guide_book09186a008043be2d.html.

[8]"IP SLAs—Command-Line Interface (CLI)," http://www.cisco.com/en/US/products/sw/ioss-wrel/ps5207/products_feature_guide09186a008044d161.html.

[9]"SAFE: A Security Blueprint for Enterprise Networks," http://www.cisco.com/go/safe

[10]Ibid.

This chapter briefly discusses four technologies and includes the following sections:

- IP Multicast

- Increasing Network Availability

- Storage Networking

- IP Version 6

CHAPTER **10**

Other Enabling Technologies

This chapter briefly describes four technologies that can be incorporated into your network design. In addition to the information provided in this chapter and because these topics are only briefly covered here, references to additional information on each of these topics are also included.

The chapter first introduces how IP multicast technology enables networks to send data to a group of end stations in the most efficient way. Next, the chapter describes the factors that affect the availability of a network and ways that it can be improved. Storage networking, that is, enabling storage devices to be accessed over the network, is then explored. The chapter concludes with a discussion of IP version 6 (IPv6), the next generation of the Internet Protocol.

> **NOTE** Appendix B, "Network Fundamentals," includes material that we assume you understand before reading the rest of the book. Thus, we encourage you to review any of the material in Appendix B that you are not familiar with before reading the rest of this chapter.

IP Multicast

Many types of data can be transferred between devices over an IP network, including, for example, document files, voice, and video. However, a traditional IP network is not efficient when sending the same data to many locations; the data is sent in unicast packets and is therefore replicated on the network for each destination. For example, if a CEO's annual video address is sent out on a company's network for all employees to watch, the same data stream must be replicated for each employee. Obviously, this would consume many resources, including precious WAN bandwidth.

IP multicast technology enables networks to send data to a group of destinations in the most efficient way. The data is sent from the source as one stream; this single data stream travels as far as it can in the network. Devices only replicate the data if they need to send it out on multiple interfaces to reach all members of the destination group.

Multicast groups are identified by Class D IP addresses, which are in the range from 224.0.0.0 to 239.255.255.255. IP multicast involves some new protocols for network devices, including two for informing network devices which hosts require which multicast data stream and one for determining the best way to route multicast traffic. These three protocols are described in the following sections.

Internet Group Management Protocol (IGMP) and Cisco Group Management Protocol (CGMP)

IGMP is used between hosts and their local routers. Hosts register with the router to join (and leave) specific multicast groups; the router is then aware that it needs to forward the data stream destined to a specific multicast group to the registered hosts.

In a typical network, hosts are not directly connected to routers but are connected to a Layer 2 switch, which is in turn connected to the router. IGMP is a network layer, Layer 3, protocol. Thus, Layer 2 switches do not participate in IGMP and are therefore not aware of which hosts attached to them might be part of a particular multicast group. By default, Layer 2 switches flood multicast frames to all ports (except the port from which the frame originated), which means that all multicast traffic received by a switch would be sent out on all ports, even if only one device on one port required the data stream. Cisco therefore developed CGMP, which is used between switches and routers. The routers inform each of their directly connected switches of IGMP registrations that were received from hosts through the switch, in other words, from hosts accessible through the switch. The switch then forwards the multicast traffic only to ports that those requesting hosts are on, rather than flooding the data to all ports. (Switches, including non-Cisco switches, can alternatively use *IGMP snooping* to eavesdrop on the IGMP messages sent between routers and hosts to learn similar information.)

Figure 10-1 illustrates the interaction of these two protocols. Hosts A and D register, using IGMP, to join the multicast group to receive data from the server. The router informs both switches of these registrations, using CGMP. When the router forwards the multicast data to the hosts, the switches ensure that the data only goes out of the ports on which hosts A and D are connected. The ports on which hosts B and C are connected do not receive the multicast data.

Figure 10-1 *GMP and CGMP Inform Network Devices About Which Hosts Want Which Multicast Data*

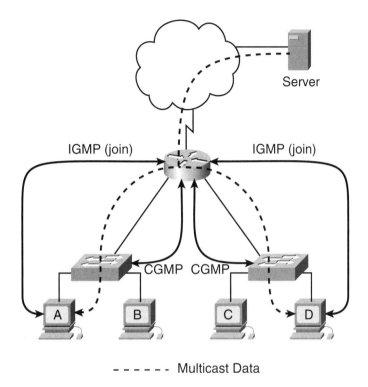

Protocol Independent Multicast (PIM) Routing Protocol

PIM is used by routers that are forwarding multicast packets. The "protocol independent" part of the name indicates that PIM is independent of the unicast routing protocol (for example, Enhanced Interior Gateway Routing Protocol [EIGRP] or Open Shortest Path First [OSPF]) running in the network. PIM uses the normal routing table, populated by the unicast routing protocol, in its multicast routing calculations.

NOTE   EIGRP, OSPF, and so forth are called *unicast routing protocols* because they are used for creating and maintaining unicast routing information in the routing table. Recall, though, that they use multicast packets (or broadcast packets in some protocols) to send their routing update traffic.

(Note that a variant of OSPF, called multicast OSPF, supports multicast routing. Cisco routers do not support multicast OSPF.)

> **NOTE**   Unlike other routing protocols, no routing updates are sent between PIM routers.

When a router is forwarding a unicast packet, it looks up the destination address in its routing table and forwards the packet out of the appropriate interface. However, when forwarding a multicast packet, the router might have to forward the packet out of multiple interfaces, toward all the receiving hosts. Multicast-enabled routers use PIM to dynamically create distribution trees that control the path that IP multicast traffic takes through the network to deliver traffic to all receivers. The following two types of distribution trees exist:

- **Source tree**—A source tree is created for each source sending to each multicast group. The source tree has its root at the source and has branches through the network to the receivers.

- **Shared tree**—A shared tree is a single tree that is shared between all sources for each multicast group. The shared tree has a single common root, called a *rendezvous point (RP)*.

Multicast routers consider the source address of the multicast packet as well as the destination address, and use the distribution tree to forward the packet away from the source toward the destination. Forwarding multicast traffic away from the source, rather than to the receiver, is called *Reverse Path Forwarding (RPF)*. To avoid routing loops, RPF uses the unicast routing table to determine the upstream (toward the source) and downstream (away from the source) neighbors and ensures that only one interface on the router is considered to be an incoming interface for data from a specific source. (For example, data received on one router interface and forwarded out another interface can loop around the network and come back into the same router on a different interface; RPF ensures that this data is not forwarded again.)

PIM operates in one of the following two modes:

- **Sparse mode**—This mode uses a "pull" model to send multicast traffic. Sparse mode uses a shared tree and therefore requires an RP to be defined. Sources register with the RP. Routers along the path from active receivers that have explicitly requested to join a specific multicast group register to join that group. These routers calculate, using the unicast routing table, whether they have a better metric to the RP or to the source itself; they forward the join message to the device with which they have the better metric.

- **Dense mode**—This mode uses a "push" model that floods multicast traffic to the entire network. Dense mode uses source trees. Routers that have no need for the data (because they are not connected to receivers that want the data or to other routers that want it) request that the tree is pruned so that they no longer receive the data.

> **NOTE**   Further information on IP multicast can be found at http://www.cisco.com/go/ipmulticast.

Increasing Network Availability

When we think of network availability, we must go back to the business objectives and requirements—the first step in the design process—to see what purpose the network has in the organization. For example, availability can mean that the online customer services must be available 24 hours a day, 7 days a week. Or, it can mean that the IP phone system must be as available as the public switched telephone network (PSTN) system.

Thus, when we think of increasing the network availability, or achieving high availability, we must also reference the business objectives. One definition of high availability is as follows:

> The ability to define, achieve, and sustain 'target availability objectives' across services and/or technologies supported in the network that align with the objectives of the business.[1]

Availability is usually measured as either the percentage of time that the network is up or by the amount of time the network is down. For example, two common formulas for availability are as follows:[2]

- Availability = MTBF / (MTBF + MTTR), where

  MTBF = Mean time between failure—the average amount of time that the network is up (between failures).

  MTTR = Mean time to repair—the average amount of time it takes to get the network functioning again after a failure has occurred.

  The type of network connections, for example, whether devices are connected in parallel or in series, can make this calculation more complex.

- Availability = (Total User Time – Total User Outage Time) / Total User Time, where

  Total User Time = Total amount of user time that the network should be accessible = Number of users * Total measurement time.

  Total User Outage Time = Sum of the amount of time that each user was unable to access the system during the measurement time.

Table 10-1 illustrates some availability percentages and describes how they translate to the amount of downtime in a year. High availability usually means that the network is down for less than 5 minutes in a year, which equates to a 99.999% availability (also known as *five nines* availability).

Table 10-1 *Availability Can Be Translated into Network Downtime*

Availability, %	Downtime per Year
99.000	3 days, 15 hours, 36 minutes
99.500	1 day, 19 hours, 48 minutes
99.700	26 hours, 17 minutes
99.900	8 hours, 46 minutes
99.950	4 hours, 23 minutes
99.990	53 minutes
99.999	5 minutes
99.9999	30 seconds

When you consider increasing the availability of your network, the cost of doing so should be weighed against the cost of downtime. For example, ensuring that an online ordering system is highly available avoids the opportunity costs of lost sales and therefore might be worth the expense. In contrast, ensuring that every user is always able to dial in to the corporate network without getting a busy signal might not be worth the loss in productivity of a few users having to retry making the connection.

The reasons for network problems must also be considered. Many times, only the design and the technologies used are considered in availability analysis; however, a network can experience problems for other reasons. For example, one study[3] found that the relative distribution of the common causes of network outages is as follows:

- User and process errors (including change management and process issues): 40%

- Software and applications (including software, performance, and load issues): 40%

- Technology (including design, hardware, and links): 20%

Thus, design and equipment issues should be considered, but other factors must also be taken into account. Therefore, increasing the availability of your network can include implementing the following measures:

- Using redundant links between devices, including between redundant devices

- Using redundant components within devices, for example, installing redundant network interface cards (NICs) in mission-critical servers or redundant processors in network devices

- Having a simple, logical network design that is easily understood by the network administrators and having processes and procedures for naming and labeling equipment, and for implementing changes to anything within the network

- Having processes and procedures in place for monitoring the network for potential problems and for correcting those problems before they cause the network to fail

- Ensuring the appropriate physical and environmental conditions for all equipment and the availability of appropriate spare parts

For redundancy, recall from Chapter 2, "Switching Design," that a Layer 2 switched network with redundant links can have problems because of the way that switches forward frames. Thus, the Spanning-Tree Protocol (STP) logically disables part of the redundant network for regular traffic while still maintaining the redundancy in case an error occurs. When multiple virtual LANs (VLANs) exist algorithms such as per-VLAN spanning tree (PVST) can also be implemented. With PVST, switches have one instance of STP running per VLAN. PVST can result in load balancing across the redundant links by allowing different links to be forwarding for each VLAN.

In Chapter 3, "IPv4 Routing Design," you see that routed (Layer 3) networks inherently support redundant paths, so a protocol such as STP is not required. All the IP version 4 (IPv4) routing protocols can load-balance over multiple paths of equal cost; EIGRP and Interior Gateway Routing Protocol (IGRP) can also load-balance over unequal-cost paths.

Some of the other protocols that can be enabled on network devices for increasing availability include the following:

- **Hot Standby Router Protocol (HSRP)**—The Cisco HSRP allows a group of routers to appear as a single virtual router to the hosts on a LAN. The group is assigned a virtual IP address (and is either assigned or autoconfigures, based on the group number, a virtual Media Access Control [MAC] address); hosts on the LAN have the virtual address as their default gateway. One router is elected as the active router and processes packets addressed to the virtual address. If the active router fails, another router takes over this responsibility, and routing continues transparently to the hosts.

> **NOTE**   HSRP supports load sharing, using the multiple HSRP (MHSRP) groups feature. However, hosts on the LAN must be configured to point to routers in the different groups as their default gateways.

- **Virtual Router Redundancy Protocol (VRRP)**—VRRP is a standard protocol, similar to the Cisco HSRP. A group of routers represent a single virtual router; the IP address of the virtual router is the same as configured on one of the real routers. That router, known as the *master virtual router,* is initially responsible for processing packets addressed to the IP address. If the master virtual router fails, one of the backup virtual routers (as determined by a priority) takes over, and routing continues transparently to the hosts.

- **Gateway Load Balancing Protocol (GLBP)**—GLBP is another protocol that allows redundancy of routers on a LAN, similar to HSRP. The difference is that GLBP allows load balancing over the redundant routers, using a single virtual IP address and multiple virtual MAC addresses, so that all hosts are configured with the same default gateway. All routers in the group participate in forwarding packets simultaneously, making better use of network resources.

- **Nonstop Forwarding (NSF) with Stateful Switchover (SSO)**—In Cisco devices that support two route processors, the SSO feature allows one to be active while the other is in standby mode. Configuration data and routing information are synchronized between the two, and if the active route processor fails, the other takes over. During the switchover, the NSF feature ensures that packets continue to be forwarded along the previous routes, with no packet loss.

- **Server Load Balancing (SLB)**—The Cisco SLB feature provides IP server load balancing. A virtual server address represents a group of real servers. When a client initiates a connection to the virtual server address, the SLB function chooses a real server for the connection, based on a load-balancing algorithm.

> **NOTE** Further information on increasing network availability can be found at http://www.cisco.com/go/availability.

Storage Networking

Storage networking can be defined as "the hardware and software that enables storage to be consolidated, shared, and accessed over a networked infrastructure."[4]

As networks are being used for more functions by more organizations and individuals, the amount of data that is created and must be stored is quickly increasing. This data includes documents, online transaction details, financial information, e-learning courses, corporate videos, and so forth.

Before storage networking, data was stored either on embedded disks within servers or on separate disks directly attached to servers, known as directly attached storage (DAS). Neither of these solutions is scalable because they are limited by the capacity of the server. They are also not reliable because access to the data depends on the server being available.

Storage networking allows data to be accessed over the network and is therefore not restricted by or dependent on a particular server.

Two complementary storage networking models exist:

■ Network-attached storage (NAS)

■ Storage area network (SAN)

An NAS device is considered an "appliance" that is installed directly onto a LAN and provides file-oriented access to data. The data stored on these high-performance devices is physically separate from the servers themselves and thus can be accessed by many different protocols. For example, files can be accessed with IP applications (such as Hypertext Transfer Protocol [HTTP] and File Transfer Protocol [FTP]), and the devices can also support file-sharing protocols such as the Network File System (NFS). NAS provides scalability and reliability but can also produce a lot of traffic because data travels between the NAS device, the server, and the client requesting it, all on the LAN.

In contrast, a SAN is a dedicated, high-performance network infrastructure that is deployed between servers and disks (called *storage resources*), as illustrated in Figure 10-2. The disks are interconnected in a separate network that is accessible from the servers. Clients communicate with servers over the LAN (and over a WAN), while servers communicate with disks over the SAN.

Figure 10-2   *A SAN Is Deployed Between Servers and Disks*

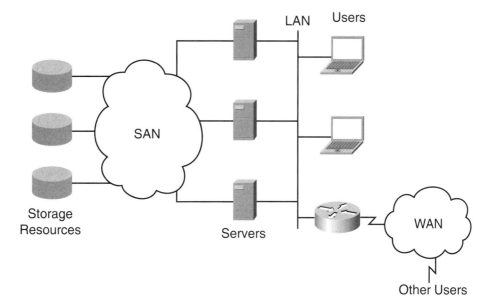

SAN technology allows a mixture of server platforms and storage devices. Within a SAN, a Fibre Channel infrastructure is typically used. Fibre Channel provides high-speed connectivity over relatively long distances, allowing functions such as backups to be performed quickly on a dedicated network.

Because Fibre Channel is not a well-known technology and is expensive to implement, the following two alternative SAN protocols, which use IP, have been developed:

- Fibre Channel IP (FCIP)

- Small Computer Systems Interface over IP (iSCSI)

FCIP interconnects SAN islands over an IP network by providing a transparent connection between the Fibre Channel networks. With FCIP, Fibre Channel frames are encapsulated within IP packets, creating a tunnel between two Fibre Channel devices connected to the IP network. The IP network provides the connectivity between the SAN islands, including over a WAN. The IP network uses the Transmission Control Protocol (TCP) to provide reliable delivery.

The iSCSI protocol is based on the Small Computer Systems Interface (SCSI) standard that has been around for a long time for communication between PCs and their attached devices, such as printers, disk drives, and so forth. SCSI uses *block-oriented* access, in which data is formatted into blocks before being sent. SCSI commands, for example, for reading and writing blocks of data, are also used in Fibre Channel technology.

The iSCSI protocol enables servers to communicate with Fibre Channel storage over an IP infrastructure by encapsulating the SCSI commands and data into IP packets and using TCP's reliable services. Routers with iSCSI capabilities connect iSCSI devices to Fibre Channel storage.

NOTE Further information on storage and SANs can be found at http://www.cisco.com/go/san and http://www.cisco.com/go/storage, and in the Cisco Press books *Storage Networking Fundamentals: An Introduction to Storage Devices, Subsystems, Applications, Management, and File Systems,* by Farley, and *Storage Area Network Fundamentals,* by Gupta.

IP Version 6

IPv6 is the next generation of IP, created to overcome the limitations of IPv4. Although IPv4 has served the Internet well, IPv4 addresses were not allocated efficiently—a global shortage of addresses exists, especially in the developing world. The use of private IPv4 addresses and Network Address Translation (NAT) (explained in Chapter 3) has meant that we have been able to cope so far. However, as more people become connected to the Internet with more devices, the ever-increasing need for IP addresses isn't about to disappear.

IPv4 and IPv6 have some similarities and some differences. To compare them, we start with the IPv6 packet header, as illustrated in Figure 10-3.

Figure 10-3 *IPv6 Header Includes 128-Bit Source and Destination Addresses*

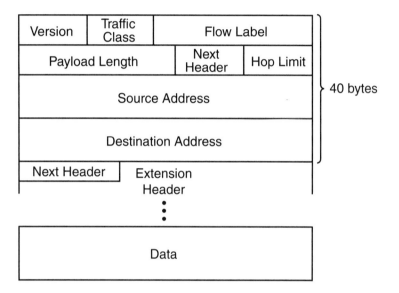

One noticeable difference between the two versions of the Internet Protocol is the size of the address: IPv6 addresses are 128 bits long, four times larger than IPv4 addresses. Those network administrators who struggled with calculating IPv4 subnet masks might wonder how they will cope with 128-bit IPv6 addresses. However, there is good news—these 128-bit addresses don't have to be typed into devices; rather, IPv6 devices can automatically configure their own addresses (with minimal typing on your part). IPv6 devices can even have multiple addresses per interface.

Other fields of note in the IPv6 header are as follows:

■ **Traffic class**—This 8-bit field is similar to IPv4's type of service (ToS) field, which marks traffic for quality of service (QoS).

■ **Flow label**—This 20-bit field is new in IPv6. It can be used by the source of the packet to tag the packet as being part of a specific flow. This feature allows routers to handle traffic on a per-flow basis, rather than per-packet, providing faster processing. The flow label can also be used to provide QoS.

■ **Hop limit**—This 8-bit field is similar to the IPv4 Time to Live (TTL) field. It is decremented by each router that the packet passes through; if it ever reaches 0, a message is sent back to the source of the packet and the packet is discarded.

Rather than using dotted decimal format, IPv6 addresses are written as hex numbers with colons between each set of four hex digits (which is 16 bits); we like to call this the "coloned hex" format. An example address is as follows:

2035:0001:2BC5:0000:0000:087C:0000:000A

Fortunately, you can shorten the written form of IPv6 addresses. Leading 0s within each set of four hex digits can be omitted, and a pair of colons can be used, once within an address, to represent any number of successive 0s. For example, the previous address can be shortened to the following:

2035:1:2BC5::87C:0:A

Similar to how IPv4 subnet masks can be written as a prefix (for example, /24), IPv6 uses prefixes to indicate the number of bits of network or subnet.

The following are the three main types of IPv6 addresses:

- **Unicast**—Similar to an IPv4 unicast address, an IPv6 unicast address is for a single interface. A packet that is sent to a unicast address goes to the interface identified by that address.

- **Anycast**—An IPv6 anycast address is assigned to a set of interfaces on different devices. A packet that is sent to an anycast address goes to the *closest* interface (as determined by the routing protocol being used) identified by the anycast address.

- **Multicast**—An IPv6 multicast address identifies a set of interfaces on different devices. A packet sent to a multicast address is delivered to *all* the interfaces identified by the multicast address.

Broadcast addresses do not exist in IPv6.

There are three main types of unicast addresses,[5] as follows:

- **Global unicast address**—Similar to IPv4 public unicast addresses, IPv6 global unicast addresses can be used on any network. Addresses in this group are defined by the prefix 2000::/3—in other words, the first 3 bits of the hex number 2000, which is binary 001, identify this group of addresses. A global unicast address typically has three fields: a 48-bit global prefix, a 16-bit subnet ID, and a 64-bit interface identifier (ID). The interface ID contains the 48-bit MAC address of the interface, written in an extended universal identifier 64-bit (EUI-64) format.

EUI-64 Format

The EUI-64 format interface ID is created by inserting the hex number FFFE between the upper 3 bytes (the Organizational Unique Identifier [OUI] field) and the lower 3 bytes (the serial number) of the MAC address. The seventh bit in the high-order byte is also set to 1 (equivalent to the IEEE G/L bit) to indicate the uniqueness of the 48-bit address.

- **Site-local unicast address**—These addresses are similar to IPv4 private addresses. They are identified by the FEC0::/10 prefix (binary 1111 1110 11), and they have a 16-bit subnet and a 64-bit interface ID in EUI-64 format.

- **Link-local unicast address**—This type of address is automatically configured on an interface by using the link-local prefix FE80::/10 (binary 1111 1110 10) and the interface ID in the EUI-64 format. Link-local addresses allow multiple devices on the same link to communicate with no address configuration required.

The IPv6 stateless autoconfiguration process allows IPv6 devices to be automatically configured and renumbered. Routers send out advertisements that include the prefix (/64) to be used on the network. The device then automatically concatenates its MAC address, in EUI-64 format, with this prefix to create its own address.

A few other types of unicast addresses exist; they are used for communicating between IPv4 and IPv6 devices or transporting IPv6 packets over an IPv4 network. These addresses would be used when migrating from IPv4 to IPv6.

NOTE   Further information on IPv6 can be found at http://www.cisco.com/go/ipv6.

Summary

In this chapter, you learned about four technologies that can be useful in your networks; the following topics were presented:

- IP multicast, which enables data to be sent from a source to a group in the most efficient way. The data travels from the source as one stream as far as it can in the network. Devices only replicate the data if they need to send it out on multiple interfaces to reach all members of the destination group.

- Increasing network availability, based on the business objectives, by using redundancy and having the appropriate processes and procedures in place.

- Storage networking, which allows data to be accessed over the network instead of being embedded in or directly attached to servers.

- IPv6, the next generation of IP, which was created to overcome the limitations of IPv4.

Endnotes

[1]"Designing and Managing High Availability IP Networks," Networkers 2004 Session NMS-2T20, http://www.cisco.com/warp/public/732/Tech/grip/docs/deploymanage.pdf.

[2]"Availability Measurement," Networkers 2004 Session NMS-2201, http://www.cisco.com/warp/public/732/Tech/grip/docs/availmgmt.pdf.

[3]Gartner Group, as reported in "Availability Measurement," Networkers 2004 Session NMS-2201, http://www.cisco.com/warp/public/732/Tech/grip/docs/availmgmt.pdf.

[4]"Cisco AVVID Network Infrastructure for Storage Networking," http://www.cisco.com/warp/public/cc/so/neso/stneso/tech/avvis_wp.pdf.

[5]"The ABCs of IP Version 6," http://www.cisco.com/application/pdf/en/us/guest/products/ioss-wrel/c1127/cdccont_0900aecd8018e369.pdf.

Part III: Designing Your Network: How to Apply What You Know

This chapter introduces the case study and includes the following sections:

- Background Information and Context

- Network Requirements After Acquisitions Are Complete

CHAPTER 11

Case Study Context: Venti Systems

This first chapter in Part III, "Designing Your Network: How to Apply What You Know," introduces a case study of a fictitious company called Venti Systems. The design methodologies discussed in Part I and the technologies discussed in Part II are applied to this case network, as appropriate.

This chapter provides background information and context for the case study, introduces assumptions made, and discusses the requirements for the new and redesigned networks. These requirements are developed in the next chapter, building to a comprehensive network design.

For the purposes of this case study, assume that you have been contracted by Venti Systems to design an upgraded/new network as it completes its acquisition of two complementary companies and moves to new facilities.

Background Information and Context

Venti Systems is a manufacturer of high-end automotive power modules. The company is based in the west side of Toronto, in central Canada, and has a sales home office in Tokyo, Japan. Venti Systems is in the process of acquiring two other companies: Grandics Corporation, which is also in Toronto (but on the east side of the city), and Konah Power, based in Seattle, in the north-western United States.

Grandics Corporation manufactures electronic components and has a sales home office in New Delhi, India, while Konah Power manufactures powertrains and has a sales office in Frankfurt, Germany.

The locations of all the offices are shown in Figure 11-1.

Figure 11-1 *Venti Systems and Its Acquisitions Have a Global Presence*

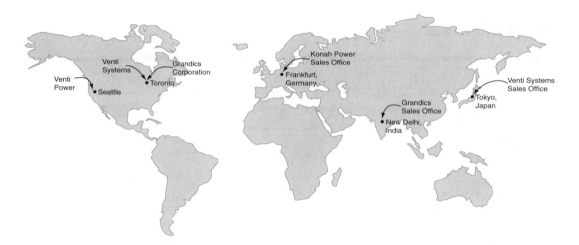

Venti Systems, including its two acquisitions, produces a low-volume, high-value-added product. The company expects to grow both organically and by acquisition.

Currently in North America, Venti Systems has 100 people, while Grandics Corporation and Konah Power have 60 people each. One person is located in each of the India and Japan locations; those two employees work from home. The two-person sales staff located in Germany works from a small remote office.

The current network at Venti Systems, as illustrated in Figure 11-2, includes 10BaseT to the desktops and 100BaseT to the servers. All wiring is unshielded twisted-pair (UTP). The company has one e-mail server and two file servers—one for business applications and one for computer-aided design/computer-aided manufacturing (CAD/CAM). A fourth server backs up the business application file server for redundancy. A backup of each server is done daily, and the backup tapes are stored off-site. The network is Layer 2 switched, using Cisco Catalyst 1924 switches and one 2950T-24 switch. Each port on the 1900 switches is attached to only one device; hubs were removed a few years ago. Virtual LANs (VLANs) are not used in this network. One Cisco 2514 router, which includes two 10-Mbps Ethernet interfaces and the firewall feature set, is used for Internet connectivity through a digital subscriber line (DSL) connection of greater than 1 Mbps. No backup Internet connectivity exists.

Figure 11-2 *Venti Systems' Current Network Topology*

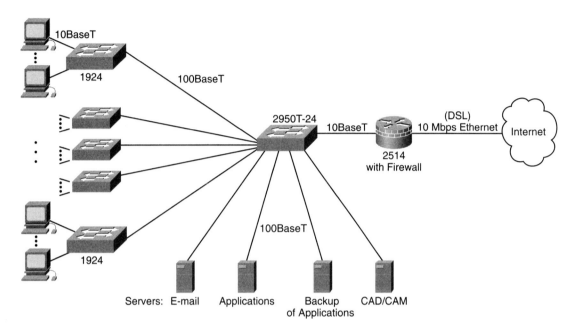

Because the Venti Systems network is Layer 2 switched without VLANs, it has a flat IP addressing scheme. Private IP addresses, in the 10.0.0.0 network, are used, with Network Address Translation (NAT) on the Internet router translating all addresses to the registered address configured on the external Ethernet interface. The external Ethernet interface connects to the Internet service provider (ISP) DSL network, which offers Point-to-Point Protocol over Ethernet (PPPoE) connectivity.

PPPOE

PPPoE capitalizes on two well-known standards: PPP and Ethernet. PPPoE provides connectivity using an Ethernet link for Internet access through a broadband medium, such as a DSL connection or a cable modem.

Venti Systems employees do not tend to send or download much data over the Internet connection, so no performance issues exist there. Internally, however, slow responsiveness has been reported, especially by the research and development (R&D) engineers.

Virtual private networks (VPNs) are used to allow remote employees, including the one working in a home office in Tokyo, to access files and their e-mail. Security is provided by the Internet router and with virus-checking software installed on all devices.

Telephone service is provided by a relatively old private branch exchange (PBX) system.

All three companies use the same CAD/CAM system and a common suite of office applications (for word processing and so forth). Some differences exist in the financial and other business applications used.

The current Grandics Corporation network is similar to Venti Systems' network. The current Konah Power building includes a low-tech industrial-grade network with shielded twisted-pair (STP) wiring, preventing signal attenuation because of electromagnetic interference produced by the heavy machinery. Konah outsources its Internet connectivity, telephone, and e-mail services.

Table 11-1 summarizes the current state of the three companies and their networks.

Table 11-1   *Current State of the Three Companies*

	Venti Systems	**Grandics Corporation**	**Konah Power**
Product	Power modules	Electronics	Powertrain
Location	Toronto-West	Toronto-East	Seattle
Number of Employees	100 (plus 1 in the home office in Japan)	60 (plus 1 in the home office in India)	60 (plus 2 in the small office in Germany)
Main Duties	Office workers and engineering	Engineering	Laborers
Network			
Topology	Flat, switched	Flat, switched	Flat, switched
Connectivity	UTP	UTP	STP
IP Addressing	Flat, private	Flat, private	Flat, private
Proprietary Systems/ Protocols	None—IP only	None—IP only	None—IP only
Servers	Applications (and another to backup this applications server), e-mail, and CAD/CAM	Applications, e-mail, and CAD/CAM	Applications and CAD/CAM
Redundancy	Application server backup only	—	—
Applications	Business applications, e-mail, and CAD/CAM	Business applications, e-mail, and CAD/CAM	Business applications and CAD/CAM
E-Mail	Corporate e-mail access	Corporate e-mail access	Outsourced

Table 11-1   *Current State of the Three Companies (Continued)*

	Venti Systems	Grandics Corporation	Konah Power
Edge Device	Cisco 2514 router with firewall feature set	Other vendor's router with integrated firewall	Leased from ISP
Internet Connectivity	DSL	DSL	DSL
Internet Connectivity Backup	—	—	—
Business Continuity	Application backup automatic. Backup done daily; tapes stored off site.	Backup done daily; tapes stored on site.	Backup done daily; tapes stored on site.
Remote Users (Including International Offices)	VPN to router for e-mail and file sharing.	VPN to router for e-mail and file sharing.	No remote access supported. E-mail is outsourced and file sharing is done through e-mail.
Voice	Old PBX	New PBX	Outsourced Centrex
Security	Virus check and firewall router	Virus check and firewall router	Virus check and ISP firewall
QoS	—	—	—
Network Management	Telnet to devices	Telnet to devices	Telnet to devices

Network Requirements After Acquisitions Are Complete

As described in Chapter 1, "Network Design," determining the requirements is the first step that should be taken when designing a new or updated network. This section examines the requirements for the Venti Systems networks.

After the acquisition, the two Toronto-based companies will be moving together to a new head-office location on the west side of the city, to achieve better synergy and to consolidate personnel and manufacturing facilities. The new location currently has one building, and the company has an option to lease the neighboring building if its current growth trend continues. The Seattle office will remain and will become a branch office of the Venti head office. All the international sales offices will remain in operation.

The 100 people in the original Venti Systems office will combine with the 60 Grandics Corporation employees; 15 people are expected to be laid off immediately because of redundancies. The company then expects to hire another 40 people over the next 18 months commensurate with growth. The number of Seattle staff will go from 60 to 45 through natural attrition and departure incentives after the acquisition.

The new organization structure of Venti Systems includes a chief executive officer (CEO) with the following four departments reporting to her, as illustrated in Figure 11-3:

■ Finance

■ Marketing and Sales

■ Operations

■ Human Resources (HR)

Figure 11-3 *Organization Structure of the Merged Company*

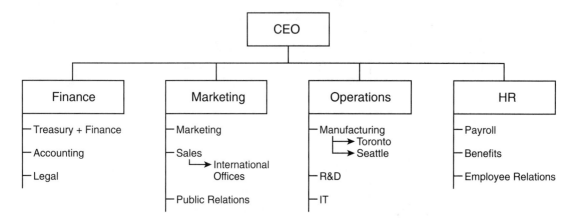

The CEO is technology-savvy and has declared that the new head office is to be state of the art. However, even though she would like to have the latest and greatest "bells and whistles" in the new network, she has advised the designers to recognize that, in the real world, the company has requirements and constraints that must be adhered to. Thus, the company can take advantage of new technologies only when they meet requirements and are cost effective. For example, IP telephony/Voice over IP (VoIP) will be implemented in the new Toronto office, but the low volume of calls between offices does not warrant the expense of changing to VoIP in Seattle, in the international offices, or between offices at this time. Because of time differences, most of the communication exchange with the international offices is through e-mail.

With a larger management team and for the sake of efficiency, the new Toronto office is to have a network that takes advantage of wireless connections and VPNs, as well as IP telephony.

Within the new Toronto office network, voice will be given priority over other traffic. IP telephony will replace the outdated PBX system and allow the company to take advantage of other benefits, including unified messaging (using the Cisco Unity product). Calls between offices and to outside locations will be done over the PSTN. A call center is not required at Venti Systems, because of the nature of the business.

Server and infrastructure redundancy will be implemented as necessary. A backup Internet connection is not initially required, because no mission-critical applications are running over the Internet, and the additional cost and complexity are not deemed necessary at this time.

The offices will keep their DSL connections, and all interoffice and remote-user communication will be through VPNs over the Internet.

All e-mail will be processed in the Toronto office, which will include two mail servers: an internal mail server and a mail relay server. The mail relay server will be located in the demilitarized zone (DMZ) and will sanitize e-mail messages before transmitting them to the internal mail server. The branch office, international offices, and remote users will access their e-mail and files through VPN connectivity to the head-office servers. A third personal digital assistant (PDA) e-mail synchronization server will provide push-based e-mail wireless services.

For ease of troubleshooting, the data on separate servers will be segmented as follows:

- Two Cisco CallManager servers (subscriber and publisher, for IP telephony)

- A Cisco unified messaging server

- Three e-mail servers (one internal, one on the DMZ, and one for PDA synchronization)

- A finance server

- A CAD/CAM server

- A general office server

- Network management servers (the number of these servers will be determined during the design process)

The internal e-mail, finance, and CAD/CAM servers each will be clustered for backup. Sensitive data will be encrypted on servers as necessary. All servers will be equipped with intrusion prevention system (IPS) software, and the network will include intrusion detection systems (IDSs).

To improve performance within the Toronto office, a switched and routed environment will be implemented. Private IP addresses in the 10.0.0.0 range will still be used, but multiple subnets will be required. NAT will still be used on the Internet router, translating all addresses to the registered address configured on the external Ethernet (DSL) interface.

The Toronto office will have a wireless network, to allow complete mobility within the building.

All employees who need a computer will be given a wireless-enabled laptop; all of these laptops will be from one manufacturer, with one operating system, and with a standard suite of programs installed. Any employee with a laptop, including those in the international sales offices, can then become a remote user. All computers, including laptops and engineering workstations, will run the latest generation of antivirus software, which also includes antispyware software.

Because all three companies use the same CAD/CAM system and a common suite of office applications, the merged company will continue to use these same systems. However, some differences exist in the financial and other business applications used in the three offices; these will be standardized to use Venti Systems' original applications. The data from the systems in the other offices needs to be translated and incorporated into the new system; a task force will be created for each application to be responsible for migrating the data and integrating the systems.

Within the Seattle location, few changes are required to the network because the work done there is not information-intensive. Communication between this office and other offices is mainly done through e-mail, which will be under the merged company domain through the e-mail server in Toronto. The Seattle office will remain as Layer 2 switched only because of the small number of people and the simplicity of the network. The office will have a VPN-enabled router to connect to Toronto. (The Cisco 2514 router, upgraded if necessary to at least the Internet Operating System [IOS] Release 12.2[29] firewall feature set, currently used by the Venti office will be moved to Seattle for this purpose; a new, more feature-rich router will be installed in the Toronto office.)

Management of devices within the network will be updated to include a more secure protocol, secure shell (SSH), for in-band connections.

Two other technologies were examined to see whether they would be useful for Venti Systems: content networking and storage networking. Venti decided that content networking is not required because the company is not involved in either e-commerce or high-volume file access. Storage networking, in the form of network-attached storage (NAS) appliances, might be considered in the future to help improve the performance, scalability, and reliability of access to the R&D data. At this time, NAS will not be implemented, but this decision will be revisited as the need warrants.

Business-related requirements and constraints for Venti Systems include the following:

- **Budget**—You can assume that sufficient budget is available for both capital and operating expenses for the new Toronto network, including IP telephony, wireless, and VPN, for new laptops, and for the minor upgrades to the Seattle network.

- **Schedule**—The move to the new office is to be completed within two months; the new network must therefore be in place and functioning by that time. The IP telephony network must be working in the new building because the PBX will not be moved. The business applications must also be merged by then, with integration phased in as defined by the assigned task forces.

> **NOTE**   Venti Systems' managers have decided to merge the acquired companies quickly, because they realize that if the merging of personnel takes too long, they will only "prolong the pain and defer the gain." Thus, when the merger/acquisition is announced, the corporate leaders will move at full speed to integrate the two operations.

- **People**—Training of existing (or newly hired) network personnel on VoIP and IP telephony must be undertaken and completed in time for the implementation to be completed and tested.

- **Legal**—Venti Systems has no contractual obligations related to the network that must be upheld. New laws require IT governance best practices and the privacy and security of customer and financial data be assured, including a secure backup of such data. Examples of such regulations are Sarbanes-Oxley (SOX) and the California Law on Notice of Security Breaches (Senate Bill [SB] 1386) in the United States, and the Personal Information Protection and Electronic Documents Act (PIPEDA) in Canada.

- **History**—Because the Seattle plant belongs to the heavy-industry sector, its employees tend to be less high-tech-savvy. This is another reason that VoIP is not being implemented in Seattle at this time. With the culture shock of merging with the other companies, the acquisition of new laptops, and so forth, introducing new phones and a new phone system would probably be too disruptive at this time. In the future, if the benefits that VoIP would bring to this office are warranted, its implementation will be revisited.

- **Policies**—No policies are in place that might restrict the network design. Venti Systems has no issues related to the use of proprietary technologies. However, policies need to be implemented for things such as Internet access, network and laptop security, and so forth.

Table 11-2 summarizes the requirements for the merged company and its networks.

Table 11-2   *Requirements for the Merged Company*

	Venti Systems—Toronto	**Venti Systems—Seattle**
Product	Power modules and electronics.	Powertrain.
Location	Toronto-West.	Seattle.
Number of Employees	145 (185 within 18 months following the merger, plus 1 each in the home offices in Japan and India).	45 (plus 2 in the small office in Germany).

continues

Table 11-2   *Requirements for the Merged Company (Continued)*

Main Duties	Office workers and engineering.	Laborers.
	Venti Systems—Toronto	**Venti Systems—Seattle**
Network		
Topology	Switched and routed	Switched.
Connectivity	UTP, wireless.	STP.
IP Addressing	Hierarchical, private.	Flat, private.
Proprietary Systems/Protocols	None—IP only.	None—IP only.
Servers	Cisco CallManager (one publisher and one subscriber), unified messaging, e-mail servers (one internal, one on the DMZ, and one for PDA synchronization), finance server, CAD/CAM server, general office server, and network management servers. Servers to be clustered: internal e-mail, finance, and CAD/CAM.	Office server and a CAD/CAM server. E-mail processed by head-office server.
Redundancy	Server and infrastructure redundancy.	—
Applications	Business applications, e-mail, and CAD/CAM.	Business applications and CAD/CAM.
E-Mail	Enterprise e-mail with PDA message-forwarding capability.	In-house, using head-office server.
Edge Device	Firewall and VPN concentrator.	Cisco 2514 with firewall feature set (previously in the Toronto office).
Internet Connectivity	DSL.	DSL.
Internet Connectivity Backup	—	—
Business Continuity	Backup done daily; tapes stored off-site.	Backup done daily; tapes stored off-site.
Remote Users (Including International Offices)	VPN tunnel to head office for mail and file access.	Seattle office and remote users access head office through VPN.

Table 11-2   *Requirements for the Merged Company (Continued)*

Voice	IP telephony with unified messaging, and voice gateway to PSTN provider. The voice-enabled router will be equipped with the firewall feature set.	New PBX (from Grandics Corporation).
	Venti Systems—Toronto	**Venti Systems—Seattle**
Security	Advanced virus-checking software, IPS, IDS, firewall, and firewall router.	Advanced virus-checking software and firewall router.
QoS	Voice traffic will be given priority.	—
Network Management	SSH for in-band connections.	SSH for in-band connections.
Support for Applications	Business applications software will be standardized on head-office current applications. Task forces will be named to plan and implement the integration of each application.	

Summary

This chapter introduced the Venti Systems case study, including a description of its current state and that of the two companies that it is in the process of acquiring. The requirements for the upgraded network and the network in the new building were developed, in preparation for the rest of the design steps in the following chapter.

This chapter provides a solution to the case study introduced in the previous chapter and includes the following sections:

- Design Model

- Switching

- Security

- IP Addressing and Routing Protocol

- E-Mail

- QoS and Voice

- Wireless

- Network Management

- Future Considerations

CHAPTER 12

Case Study Solution: Venti Systems

This chapter provides a comprehensive network design solution for the case study of a fictitious company called Venti Systems, as introduced in Chapter 11, "Case Study Context: Venti Systems."

For the purposes of this case study, assume that you have been contracted by Venti Systems to design an upgraded/new network as it completes its acquisition of two complementary companies and moves to new facilities.

Design Model

Recall from Chapter 1, "Network Design," that when designing a network, the following tasks should be considered:

- Determine requirements

- Analyze the existing network, if one exists

- Prepare the preliminary design

- Complete the final design development

- Deploy the network

- Monitor, and redesign if necessary

- Maintain documentation (as a part of all the other tasks)

Chapter 11 provides the background for the case study, including the details of the existing network and the requirements for the new and updated network. In this chapter, we produce the design. For the purposes of this case study, we assume that the relevant personnel at Venti Systems are being consulted along the way and that they are approving the design as we go. We do not go into the deployment or monitoring steps for this case study, but we provide all the details that would be necessary to produce the design documentation.

We use the Enterprise Composite Network Model, including hierarchical layers as appropriate (as detailed in Chapter 1), for this case study design. The three functional areas of the model are Enterprise Campus, Enterprise Edge, and Service Provider Edge. Each of these functional areas can be further divided into various modules, as illustrated in Figure 12-1. Each of the modules can include the hierarchical core, distribution, and access layer functionality.

Figure 12-1 *Modules of the Enterprise Composite Network Model[1]*

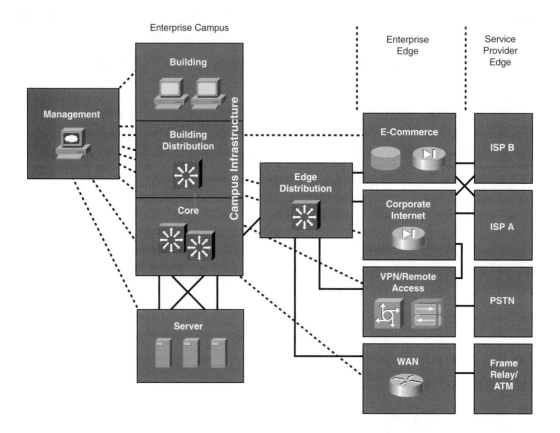

Venti Systems has no e-commerce, and communication between offices and remote users will be through virtual private networks (VPNs) over the Internet. We therefore do not include the e-commerce, WAN, or Frame Relay/Asynchronous Transfer Mode (ATM) modules.

The following sections provide the design models for the head office (in Toronto), branch office (in Seattle), and remote users (including the international sales personnel). Following those sections is a description of the users' devices and the servers.

Head Office

The new Toronto office will initially have one building, with an option to acquire a second building. Up to 185 people will be at this location within 18 months, and IP telephony is to be used for all internal calls. Redundancy is required, both at the infrastructure level and for some servers. VPN connectivity to the Seattle office and for remote users is to be used and wireless connectivity within the building is to be implemented.

Enterprise Campus

The Campus Infrastructure and Server modules of the Enterprise Campus for the head office are illustrated in Figure 12-2.

Figure 12-2 *Part of the Venti Systems Head-Office Enterprise Campus*

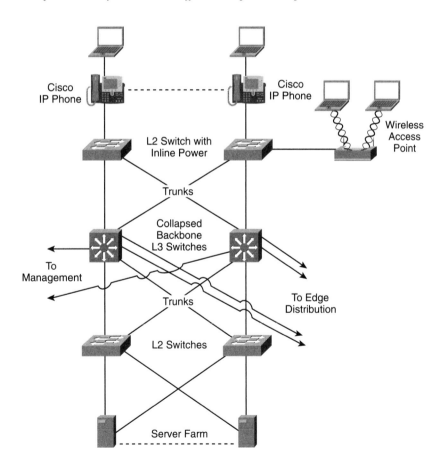

NOTE   IP phones and wireless access points are shown in Figure 12-2; the details of how these technologies are integrated within the network are described in the "QoS and Voice" and "Wireless" sections, respectively, later in this chapter.

The Management module is described in the "Network Management" section, later in this chapter.

The Campus Infrastructure module includes Layer 2 access switches for connectivity between the end-users' laptops and IP phones and the rest of the network. These switches provide inline power for the IP phones as well as user authentication and quality of service (QoS) marking. Redundancy for the laptops is provided through their wireless connections.

The collapsed backbone combines the Building Distribution and Core functionality in Layer 3 switches. Routing, route filtering, route summarization, and filtering are performed here. Redundancy to the Building access switches, to the Server access switches, to the Edge Distribution module, and to the Management module is provided to ensure a highly available and reliable backbone.

The centralized Server module contains the internal servers, including e-mail and file servers, and Cisco CallManager (CCM) servers for IP telephony. Redundancy is implemented to the collapsed backbone so that users always have access to the servers they need. Layer 2 access switches are used in this module to connect to the collapsed backbone.

The Edge Distribution module, shown as part of Figure 12-3, is the interface between the Enterprise Campus (through the Core) and the Enterprise Edge functional areas. This module uses Layer 3 switching to provide high-performance routing; redundancy is also implemented to ensure that campus users always have access to the Enterprise Edge.

NOTE   Figure 12-3 shows the physical network topology, including redundant devices and connections. Subsequent figures might show the logical topology, without the redundancy, for ease of understanding concepts.

Enterprise Edge and Service Provider Edge

The modules of the Enterprise Edge and Service Provider Edge for Venti Systems' head office are also shown as part of Figure 12-3. The Enterprise Edge's VPN/Remote Access module is collapsed into the Corporate Internet module because all external traffic will be converging from the Internet to the head office.

Figure 12-3   *Venti Systems' Enterprise Collapsed Edge: Corporate Internet, VPN Access, and PSTN*

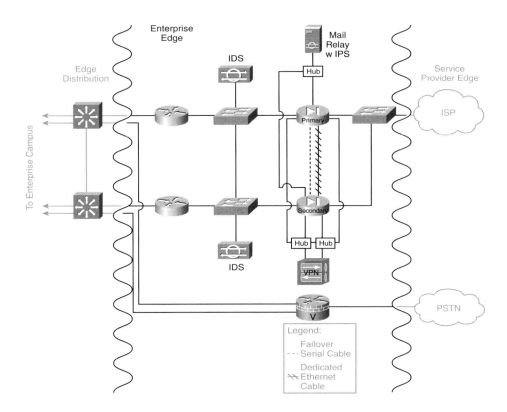

The Corporate Internet module provides Internet access for the users (and usually passes VPN traffic from remote users to the VPN/Remote Access module). This module includes an e-mail relay server (as detailed in the "E-Mail" section, later in this chapter). Security systems include firewalls and intrusion detection systems (IDSs) to ensure that only legitimate Internet traffic is allowed into the enterprise. (Security is described further in the "Security" section, later in the chapter.) The Domain Name Service (DNS) of the Internet service provider (ISP) will be used.

A VPN/Remote Access module usually terminates VPN traffic from external users. Devices in this module include VPN concentrators to terminate the remote user connections, and firewalls and IDS appliances to provide security. In our Venti Systems design, this functionality is collapsed with the Corporate Internet module. A VPN concentrator is attached behind the redundant firewalls to initiate and terminate VPN tunnels to and from the branch office and remote users.

The ISP module represents the connection to the Internet. Venti Systems connects to the ISP through a digital subscriber line (DSL) connection. A backup Internet connection is not initially required, because no mission-critical applications are running over the Internet, and the additional cost and complexity are not deemed necessary at this time. Venti Systems will negotiate with its ISP a comprehensive service-level agreement (SLA), including availability above 99.997 percent.

The public switched telephone network (PSTN) module is shown in Figure 12-3 because all external calls will be through the PSTN, not through IP telephony. Recall, though, that remote users will not dial in; rather, they will connect through a VPN, so PSTN access is not required for dial-in functionality. As is common for enterprises, PSTN redundancy is not required. Venti Systems will negotiate with its PSTN provider a comprehensive SLA, including a 99.999 percent availability.

Branch Office

As indicated in Chapter 11, few changes are required to the network in the Seattle office because the work done there is not information-intensive. The Seattle office originally outsourced its Internet connectivity, telephone, and e-mail services.

E-mail will be accessed using the server at the Toronto office, through the VPN connection. Internet connectivity will be through DSL.

The Seattle office will remain Layer 2 switched only because of the small number of people and the simplicity of the network. The office will connect to the Internet through the Cisco 2514 router that was decommissioned from Toronto and on which the Internet Operating System (IOS) will be upgraded to the latest IOS firewall feature set (at least to Release 12.2[29]). This router will be then able to route traffic and to terminate VPN tunnels.

Figure 12-4 illustrates the network at the Seattle office.

Figure 12-4   *Seattle Office Network: A Router with Integrated Firewall Will Provide VPN Access to the*
Head Office

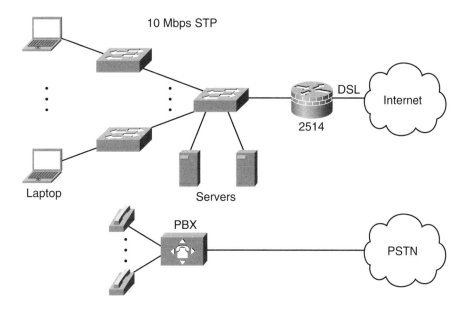

As also shown in Figure 12-4, the Seattle office will get a new private branch exchange (PBX)
(from the old Grandics Corporation office); IP telephony will not be implemented at this time.

Remote Users

All remote users will access the network through a VPN connection to the Toronto office. All
employees, in all offices, who need a computer will be given a wireless-enabled laptop; all of these
laptops will be from the same vendor, running the same operating system, with a standard suite of
programs installed. (Existing desktop PCs and any laptops that are not compatible with the new
standard will be replaced.) The laptops will be configured with VPN client software that provides
connectivity to the head office. A significant advantage of running a software VPN client is that
the encrypted tunnel originates from the laptop so that the data traveling on the home-area network
(HAN) toward the head office is encrypted, making the transmission safer. A typical connection
from a remote user is illustrated in Figure 12-5.

Figure 12-5 *Typical Remote User Connection*

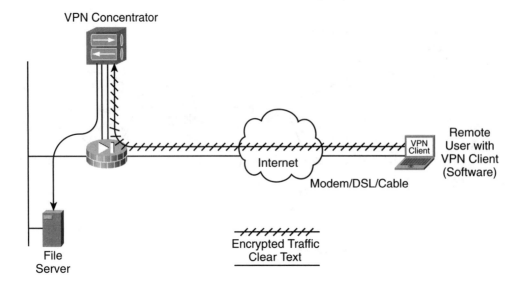

The users' laptops are as described in the following section.

User Devices

All users' laptops will have the following features:

- Wireless, PSTN, and Ethernet connectivity.

- Automatic operating system updates configured so that the latest service packs and security patches are always installed.

- Automatic application updates configured so that any security-critical updates are always installed.

- Advanced antivirus software, including antispyware software, installed, with automatic updates configured.

- VPN client software, to allow VPN with IP security (IPsec) connections to the head office. This software also allows policies to be pushed down from the head office after the connection is made. An example of such a policy is to disallow split tunnels so that after the laptop's VPN client is connected to the corporate network, the laptop can only send data to the corporate network and cannot simultaneously directly surf the Internet.

- Personal firewall software.

- Trust agent software, as described in the "Network Management" section, later in this chapter.

Servers

All servers will include management software so that they can be remotely managed. The servers will also be equipped with intrusion prevention system (IPS) software.

The internal e-mail, finance, and computer-aided design/computer-aided manufacturing (CAD/CAM) file servers will be installed as clusters. As its name implies, a cluster is a group of identical servers interconnected and accessible as a common storage pool. Clustering prevents the failure of a single file server from denying access to data. Should Venti Systems grow, an additional benefit of clustering is that it adds computing power to the network for large numbers of users.

The financial and other business applications used in the three offices will be standardized to use Venti Systems' applications. The data from the systems in the other offices needs to be converted and incorporated into the new system; a task force will be created for each application to be responsible for migrating the data and integrating the systems.

Switching

Layer 2 and Layer 3 switches are used in both the Toronto and Seattle offices, as described in the following sections. (The security features implemented on the switches are described in the "Security" section, later in the chapter.)

Head-Office Switching

Within the Toronto office, Layer 2 switches are used in the Building access layer to provide connectivity for the users' laptops and IP phones. These access switches have inline power for the IP phones, and they redundantly connect to the collapsed backbone Layer 3 switches. The Spanning Tree Protocol (STP) is therefore not required, because no Layer 2 loop exists between the switches. As is normally recommended, though, STP should not be turned off, just in case a loop is configured in the future. To shorten the time it takes for the ports to come up, PortFast should be configured on each switch port that is connected to a laptop/IP phone combination.

IP phones with a built-in switch will be used; one port connects to the access switch and another connects to the laptop, as illustrated in Figure 12-6. The IP phone and laptop send traffic on two separate virtual LANs (VLANs); the connection to the access switch is an Institute of Electrical and Electronics Engineers (IEEE) 802.1q trunk, with the laptop on the native VLAN.

Figure 12-6 *IP Phone with a Built-In Switch Connects to the Access Switch and User's Laptop*

NOTE In Figure 12-6, the connection between the laptop and the IP phone is not an IEEE 802.1q trunk. Data on this connection is all in a single VLAN; that VLAN is the native VLAN on the IEEE 802.1q trunk between the laptop and the access switch.

The Server module has Layer 2 access switches connected directly to the collapsed core.

The Toronto office also has Layer 3 switches, as shown earlier in Figure 12-2; the routing functionality required of these devices is described further in the "IP Addressing and Routing Protocol" section, later in the chapter. Because these switches are connected redundantly, the Gateway Load Balancing Protocol (GLBP) (as described in Chapter 10, "Other Enabling Technologies") should be used to allow both load sharing and redundancy.

Branch-Office Switching

The Seattle office also has Layer 2 switches, but because IP telephony is not used in this office, no special requirements exist for the switches. STP is again not required, because no Layer 2 loop exists between the switches. Just as in Toronto, STP should not be turned off, and PortFast should be configured on each switch port that is connected to a laptop.

Remote User Switching

The remote users do not require switches. However, users might have a router with a built-in switch (for example, a wireless broadband router with a built-in four-port switch can be used in an employee's home office).

Security

The head-office and branch-office networks will both be located behind a firewall. The basic rules of a firewall are that traffic that originates from the inside network is allowed to return; however, traffic that originates from outside is not allowed to penetrate the corporate network. As with most rules, these basic firewall rules are often broken, but with add-on precautions.

As an example, we examine Venti Systems' VPN connectivity, illustrated in Figure 12-7. When a remote user wants to connect to the head office, he launches his VPN client software, which in turn attempts to build a VPN tunnel with the destination as the firewall. By default, a firewall drops all packets that originate from the outside. But a VPN connection needs to terminate on the VPN concentrator, and therefore must transit through the firewall to the VPN concentrator. For VPN connectivity to work, the firewall must be configured with a rule stipulating that incoming IPsec traffic will be allowed in. This traffic must make its way to the VPN concentrator, which is in the demilitarized zone (DMZ), on interface E3 of the firewall in this network. Any other traffic—traffic that is not IPsec data—is refused entry at the E0 interface on the firewall. This exception to the firewall rule is sometimes referred to "punching a hole" in the firewall.

Figure 12-7 *Firewall Rules Allow VPN Tunnels*

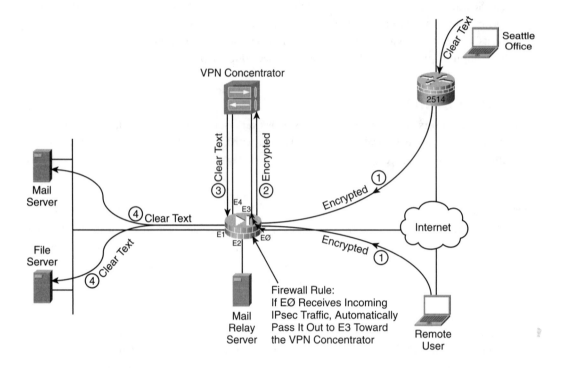

If the VPN concentrator succeeds at decrypting the data, it treats this as an indication that the originator is a safe source. However, when the remote user's data first transited through the firewall, it was encrypted, and therefore the firewall could not do a deep packet inspection. So that no chances are taken, the VPN concentrator is therefore configured to send the data that it just unencrypted back through the firewall (on interface E4 in the figure) for a deep inspection, before allowing it access to the internal head-office network (interface E1 in Figure 12-7).

Venti Systems, like any corporation, needs to create and disseminate its acceptable usage and security policies and procedures to all employees. These policies apply to the following items:

- Users' laptops

- Network usage

- Wireless usage

- Internet usage

- E-mail

- Instant messaging (IM)

> **NOTE**   IM programs typically tunnel through other protocols, bypassing firewalls, thus leaving the network open to viruses and other security problems. Corporate confidential information (such as financial spreadsheets or staffing details) can also be sent in an IM message, so policies similar to those for e-mail should be in place. Employees should be made aware that IM, like e-mail, is neither secure
> nor private.

> **NOTE**   A more extensive discussion on security policies and best practices can be found in *The Business Case for Network Security: Advocacy, Governance, and ROI*, by Paquet and Saxe, Cisco Press, 2005.

Strong authentication will be implemented for local and remote access to all managed devices, through an access control server (ACS). The ACS is located in the Management module, as discussed in the section "Network Management," later in this chapter. Strong authentication requires a two-factor authentication method, including two items from the following list:

- What a user knows

- What a user has

- What a user is

- What a user does

A password or personal identification number (PIN) is something a user knows, while a token (for example, a bank card or small device with an LCD) is something a user has. As an example, to be granted remote access at an automated teller machine (ATM), a customer must produce something he has—his bank card—along with something he knows—his PIN. In this design, we will use a security token as part of a two-factor, one-time password (OTP) authentication. Tokens (keychain-size devices) will be provided to users. The LCD on the tokens shows OTPs, one at a time, in a predefined order, for about 1 minute before the next password in the sequence appears. The token is synchronized with a token server that has the same predefined list of OTPs for that one user. Therefore, at any given time, only one valid password exists between the server and each token. The user must enter both the OTP (from something he has) and his PIN (something he knows) to be granted access to the network.

Within the new design, data will be encrypted while stored on a server, because static data located on a server is vulnerable. (Some pundits equate the encrypted WAN transmission of data, which is otherwise clear text while stored on a server, to using an armored truck to transfer money from a paper bag to a cardboard box.)

For server backup, the company is considering using a third-party backup service in which a service provider backs up data onto its disks over a WAN connection, eliminating issues such as dealing with tapes, off-site storage, and so forth. However, this also means that the data is now on the disks of another company, so the security and privacy of such data must be ensured. For example, if sensitive data were encrypted on the main servers, it would also be encrypted on the backup server, which would provide one level of protection. The service provider should be investigated thoroughly to ensure that it meets the policies and procedures required by the company.

NOTE   Storing off-site data is also part of the company's disaster recovery plan.

Head-Office Security

All the standard security best practices will be implemented at the head office, including changing default passwords on network devices, locking access to the server room and wiring closet, deactivating unused switch ports, and so forth.

Best practices call for redundancy of critical infrastructure. Because the firewall bridges the head office to the Internet and to the company's other facilities, redundancy of this deep-inspection device is a must.

The Cisco PIX Firewall allows two firewalls, a primary and a secondary, to implement failover mode, as shown earlier in Figure 12-3. Provided that the secondary firewall is identical to the primary, Cisco charges only for the hardware, so the cost for the secondary unit is minimal. The secondary firewall is configured exactly the same as the primary firewall and maintains an identical copy of the connections table used by the primary firewall, to monitor the status of individual data sessions. This connections table is synchronized over a dedicated Ethernet cable. The secondary firewall monitors the health of the primary firewall through the failover serial cable, and will be ready to take over should the primary unit experience significant performance issues.

To use failover mode, you need two identical PIX Firewalls. They must have the following characteristics:

- They must be running the same version of the PIX OS.

- They must have the same number and type of interfaces in the same slots.

- The primary must be running an unrestricted license of the PIX OS.

■ The secondary must run either an unrestricted license or a failover license of the PIX OS.

■ If the primary has a Data Encryption Standard (DES) or Triple Data Encryption Standard (3DES) license, the secondary must also have one.

The critical network segments and devices will be equipped with IDS sensors and IPS software, respectively, as shown in Figure 12-8. This figure shows the Server and Management modules of the Enterprise Campus functional area and the Enterprise Edge functional area.

Figure 12-8 *Intrusion Detection and Protection at Work*

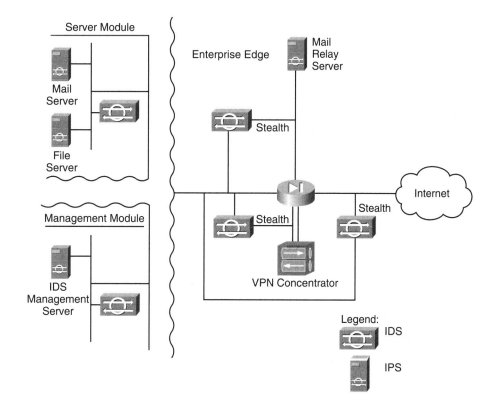

IDS sensors monitor traffic on a network and attempt to identify intrusions and hostile activity. IDS sensors can operate in stealth mode, meaning that their interfaces that connect to the DMZ or the outside network operate strictly at Layer 2, in promiscuous mode, copying the data, as it transits a network segment, to the IDS management server through its nonstealth interface. This is done either through a hub or by connecting to a Switched Port Analyzer (SPAN) port of a switch. Operating in stealth mode, sensors are not vulnerable to IP attacks from hackers because the interface is not reachable by IP. Sensors are configured to alert a management console should they detect suspicious activity, though invariably by the time the alert is delivered to the network administrator, the attack has already taken place.

> **NOTE** A SPAN port is a port on a switch that is configured to mirror the data passing through any other switch port or group of switch ports.

IPS software installed on critical devices scans incoming traffic and actively monitors all the devices' resources, such as memory, processes, and so forth.

Venti Systems will investigate the possibility of subcontracting the analysis of the data reported by its security systems, because the company believes in the saying, "If you log it, read it." Because Venti will have multiple IDS sensors potentially releasing many false positive alarms, the job of parsing through all those events will be subcontracted to a company that specializes in this field and uses sophisticated correlation tools. This firm will therefore inform the network administrator of a security event only when her intervention is warranted.

All servers will be equipped with IPS software to monitor all functions of the server—processes, memory usage, disk space, directory creation or deletion, and so forth—and to report suspicious activity to the IDS Management server. Depending on the configuration, these IPS systems should be able to shun a malicious user, that is, to report the malicious activity to the firewall and request that this particular source be denied further access to the network.

Port-level security will be implemented on all Layer 2 switch ports.

Wireless networks present security risks which must also be mitigated. Strategies include the following:

- Monitoring, in real time, of rogue access point detection, to ensure that only authorized access points are installed in the network

- Using IEEE 802.1x port-level authentication and Temporal Key Integrity Protocol (TKIP) encryption

- Changing the service set identifier (SSID), a unique identifier for a wireless access point or router, from the default (for example, from linksys or tsunami) to something difficult to guess, thereby prohibiting hackers from easily finding the access point

- Disabling SSID broadcasts so that drive-by hackers cannot detect an access point whose name they don't know

Branch-Office Security

The Seattle office router will be configured with the firewall feature set. The router-firewall configuration will be the default so that only traffic that originated from the inside network will be allowed to return. Traffic originating from outside will not be allowed to enter the network.

Remote User Security

Remote users' laptops will be configured with antivirus software, a personal firewall, and the corporate VPN client. Personnel will use strong authentication to be granted access to the corporate network.

IP Addressing and Routing Protocol

The network includes multiple VLANs and therefore multiple IP subnets. Private IP addresses, in the 10.0.0.0 range, will be used. Network Address Translation (NAT) will be used on the Toronto office perimeter firewall and on the Seattle office perimeter router.

Head-Office IP Addressing and Routing Protocol

The head office needs the following three registered IP addresses:

- Internal traffic to the Internet will be translated to address 1 (which is the perimeter firewall external interface registered address and will be overloaded by NAT).

> **NOTE**   NAT and overloading are explained in Chapter 3, "IPv4 Routing Design."

- The VPN concentrator will have static NAT to address 2.

- The mail relay server will have static NAT to address 3.

The perimeter firewall in Toronto has five subnets: one to the Internet, one to the mail relay server, two to the VPN concentrator, and one to the internal network.

The servers in the head office will all be in one VLAN, which will be configured as a private VLAN. As explained in Chapter 2, "Switching Design," a private VLAN ensures that if one server is compromised, the hacker would not be able to directly attack the other servers because traffic is restricted by the switch.

All VPN tunnels to the head office will be on one subnet, in the private 10.0.0.0 range. The VPN concentrator assigns the address that the VPN client will use on the VPN tunnel after they connect. The VPN concentrator keeps track of the addresses (the Outside Global address to the Outside Local address translation).

IP phone voice traffic will be put on a separate VLAN from the data traffic. Each VLAN will be present in only one access layer switch to limit the size of the broadcast domain and eliminate Layer 2 topological loops.

Because the private 10.0.0.0 addresses are being used, many host bits are available for subnetting. Thus, large ranges can be used, to allow easy subnet calculations and future growth. Table 12-1 provides the subnet allocations.

Table 12-1 *IP Subnet Allocation*

Subnet	Allocation
10.0.x.0/24	x = 0 through 31; Toronto data VLANs
10.0.x.0/24	x = 100 through 131; Toronto voice VLANs
10.1.y.0/24	y = 0 through 255; Toronto internal LANs
10.2.0.0/24S	Seattle VLAN
10.3.0.0/24	VPN VLAN
10.0.x.0/24	x = 0 through 31; Toronto data VLANs

The Dynamic Host Configuration Protocol (DHCP) assigns dynamic IP addressing information to users' laptops when they require them. DHCP server functionality will be from the collapsed backbone Layer 3 switches and the branch-office router.

The Enhanced Interior Gateway Routing Protocol (EIGRP) is chosen as the routing protocol for the new network because of its flexibility, fast convergence, simple configuration, and scalability features.

Branch-Office IP Addressing and Routing Protocol

The Seattle office router external interface will have a static IP address assigned by its ISP. This router will have a static route to the head office subnets over a VPN tunnel; it will dynamically create a VPN tunnel when traffic is to be sent to the head office. This VPN is considered to be a LAN-to-LAN connection.

The branch office is one VLAN. Branch users' laptops will use private addresses on the inside network. These private addresses will be translated by the edge router if the traffic is destined to an external network on the Internet. If the traffic is destined to the head office, the packets, including the private addresses, will be encapsulated inside a VPN tunnel.

The servers within the branch office will also be configured on a private VLAN, to provide additional security.

Remote User IP Addressing and Routing Protocol

Remote users will be assigned an IP address, either from their HAN if they are located behind a router or firewall at home or from their ISP if they connect directly on the Internet. The VPN concentrator assigns the address that the VPN client will use on the VPN tunnel after they connect.

E-Mail

Basic Internet e-mail security calls for the corporate mail server to not be accessible directly from the Internet. Therefore, as shown in Step 1 of Figure 12-9, incoming e-mail messages transit through the DMZ to a mail relay server. The mail relay server "sanitizes" all messages of viruses, spam, and conspicuous attachments, prior to forwarding them to the corporate mail server located on the inside network, as shown in Step 2 of Figure 12-9. This sanitizing of e-mail will be accomplished for now by software that resides on the mail relay server; a hardware-based solution will be considered in the future if the volume of e-mail warrants it.

Figure 12-9 *A Mail Relay Server Sanitizes Incoming E-Mail*

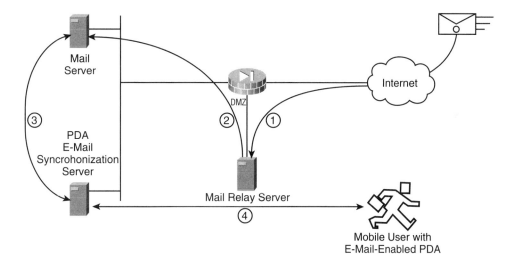

Head-Office E-Mail

Head office users will access their e-mail directly from the corporate e-mail server. See the "Remote User E-Mail" section for an explanation on how users will access their e-mail from home or while on business trips.

In addition to accessing e-mail through their laptops, senior executives and sales staff will be provided with personal digital assistants (PDAs) to extend the benefits of corporate e-mail. As shown in Step 3 of Figure 12-9, the PDA e-mail synchronization server maintains a Messaging Application Programming Interface (MAPI) connection on the user's mailbox, and automatically synchronizes its content to the user's hand-held device, as shown in Step 4 of Figure 12-9.

Branch-Office E-Mail

The branch office, international offices, and remote users will access their e-mail and files through VPN connectivity back to the head-office servers, as shown earlier in Figure 12-7.

Branch office users' mail software will attempt to poll the corporate mail server at its 10.0.0.0 subnet address. The branch-office router, upon seeing the request for the corporate head-office subnet, will initiate a VPN tunnel terminating at the head-office VPN concentrator (if no VPN tunnels are currently live), transiting through the firewall on its way.

Remote User E-Mail

Remote users, whether connecting from home or from a hotel room, will require the activation of their VPN client prior to accessing the corporate e-mail server, which is located on the inside network at the head office.

Most organizations do not permit their staff to simultaneously establish a VPN tunnel to the corporate head office and connect directly to the Internet. Allowing both Internet and VPN connections is known as *split tunneling* (as mentioned earlier) and is rarely permitted because, while the laptop's VPN session is up, that laptop would provide too much exposure to the corporate network. If split tunneling were allowed, a hacker could compromise the laptop, and then after he is inside the user's laptop, the hacker could make his way back to the corporate network through the VPN tunnel. Therefore, as long as the VPN tunnel that terminates at the head-office concentrator is up, the remote user cannot browse the Internet.

QoS and Voice

Venti Systems will implement IP telephony in the head office only.

Head-Office QoS and Voice

Because IP telephony is included in the Venti Systems design, you must also consider managing the quality of service that the traffic experiences. Recall that although you typically think of applying queuing only to slow WAN links, LAN links can also be congested, so queuing should be deployed on any link that could potentially experience congestion, to provide the needed services to the network traffic. Queuing policies—in other words, how each traffic class is handled—should be consistent across the enterprise.

Venti Systems will use IP phones to digitize and packetize the voice traffic. As illustrated earlier in Figure 12-6, IP phones with a built-in switch will be used; one port will connect to the access switch and another will connect to the user's laptop. Access switches will provide inline power for the IP phones, using power over Ethernet (PoE).

The voice and data traffic will be on separate VLANs to allow easier implementation of QoS tools; the connection to the access switch is an 802.1q trunk, with the laptop on the native VLAN.

Classification and marking of voice traffic will be done by the IP phone. Recall that the point within the network where markings are accepted is known as the trust boundary; any markings made by devices outside the trust boundary can be overwritten at the *trust boundary*. A Cisco IP phone could be considered to be a trusted device because it marks voice traffic appropriately, while a user's laptop would not usually be trusted because users could change markings (which they might be tempted to do to attempt to increase the priority of their traffic). Therefore, the access switches will mark the laptop traffic appropriately.

Classification and Marking

Recall that the type of service (ToS) field within an IPv4 packet header marks, or indicates, the kind of traffic that is in the packet. This marking can then be used by other tools within the network to provide the packet the service that it needs. The first 6 bits in the ToS field of an IP packet are known as the DiffServ Code Point (DSCP) bits. Using Layer 3 DSCP QoS markings allows QoS to be provided end to end throughout the network. If some access switches support only Layer 2 {class of service [CoS]) markings, these markings must be mapped to the appropriate DSCP values. This would be a function performed by the distribution switches (in this case, by the collapsed core switches). The distribution switches must also apply DSCP values to traffic that has not been marked elsewhere.

As described in Chapter 6, "Quality of Service Design," Cisco created a QoS Baseline that provides recommendations to ensure that both its products, and the designs and deployments that use them, are consistent in terms of QoS. The baseline includes an 11-class scheme, and companies can evolve to this level of classification. Venti Systems will start with a 5-class scheme, as illustrated in Figure 12-10.

Figure 12-10 *Venti Systems' QoS Classes*

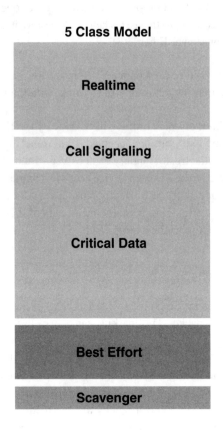

After traffic has been classified and marked and sent on its way through the network, other devices will then read the markings and act accordingly. Tools such as weighted random early detection (WRED) and low latency queuing (LLQ) will be used.

Cisco Automatic QoS (AutoQoS) provides a simple, automatic way to enable QoS configurations in conformance with the Cisco best-practice recommendations. Venti Systems will use AutoQoS to create configuration commands to perform such things as classifying and marking VoIP traffic and then applying strategies for that traffic. The configuration created by AutoQoS becomes part of the normal configuration file and can therefore be edited if required.

The call-processing function previously performed by the PBX will now be handled by a call-processing manager, CCM, a software-based system that provides functions such as setting up and terminating calls, routing to voice mail, and so forth. CCM is installed on a Cisco Media Convergence Server (MCS) and selected third-party servers. Because this is a relatively small IP telephony network (with less than 2500 phones), two CCM servers will be deployed: one to act as a publisher (and store the master copy of the database of configurations) and the other to act as a subscriber (the device with which phones register). The subscriber also acts as a backup to the publisher. The Cisco Unity unified messaging solution will be deployed to deliver e-mail, voice mail, and fax messages to a single inbox so that users can, for example, listen to their e-mail over the telephone, check voice messages from the Internet, and forward faxes to wherever they might be. The complete voice network architecture, with the redundant components removed for clarity, is illustrated in Figure 12-11.

Figure 12-11   *Venti Systems' IP Telephony Architecture*

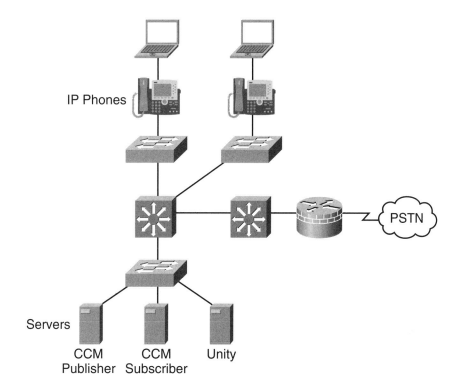

The voice gateway to the PSTN can be implemented with a variety of devices. For example, Cisco multiservice access routers communicate directly with CCM and support a wide range of packet telephony–based voice interfaces and signaling protocols. Alternatively, voice gateway modules can also be installed in Cisco switches.

If voice traffic travels across WAN links, the traffic should be compressed to reduce the required bandwidth. Currently, voice traffic is not going over WAN links in this design; if it does in the future, G.729 compression is recommended. RTP header compression, cRTP, would also be considered on these WAN links.

Another way that could be used to reduce the bandwidth required by voice calls is voice activity detection (VAD). Recall that, on average, about 35 percent of a call is in fact silence; when VoIP is used, this silence is packetized along with the conversation. VAD suppresses the silence, so instead of sending IP packets of silence, only IP packets of conversation are sent. The network bandwidth is therefore being used more efficiently and effectively.

Because voice is being transported in IP packets, security of voice traffic is inherent in the security provided for other data, as described earlier.

Branch-Office QoS and Voice

The Seattle office will have a PBX system installed to replace the outsourced Centrex solution. The PBX will be the one that was previously installed in the Grandics Corporation office.

Remote User QoS and Voice

Remote users will use their own phone and will use a company calling card for long-distance calls.

Wireless

Wireless access is provided at the head office through wireless laptops.

Head-Office Wireless

A site survey will be conducted to ensure proper provisioning of wireless access. Simultaneously, real-time wireless IDSs (such as AirDefense) will be installed, hoping to prevent wireless attacks such as a wireless denial of service attack in which frames are sent that force users off the access point with which they had registered.

Although Media Access Control (MAC) address filtering can somewhat improve wireless security, it is not an easily manageable solution. Therefore, security will be provided for wireless access by using IEEE 802.1x authentication and TKIP encryption.

Branch-Office Wireless

Wireless access is not provided at the branch office at this time.

Remote User Wireless

Remote users are not provided with wireless access points. However, employees can use their laptop's wireless card to access networks that they would otherwise access using their Ethernet connection.

Network Management

Network management will be provided throughout Venti Systems.

Head-Office Network Management

Management of devices within the Venti Systems network will be updated to include a more secure protocol, secure shell (SSH), for in-band connections. If the network is unavailable and SSH does not work, the network administrator can connect directly to the console ports of the devices. The Management module of the Enterprise Campus functional area is illustrated in Figure 12-12.

Figure 12-12 *Venti Systems' Management Module*

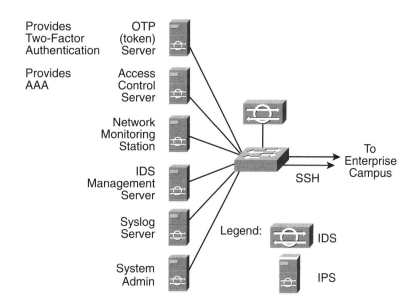

The Management module contains the following items:

- **OTP/token server**—Works with the users' tokens to provide strong user authentication.

- **Access control server**—Provides centralized command and control for all user authentication, authorization, and accounting (AAA).

- **Network monitoring station**—Is responsible for monitoring the devices in the network. The Simple Network Management Protocol (SNMP) is the main protocol used by this station.

- **IDS management server**—Provides configuration and viewing of alarms on IDS and IPS sensors deployed throughout the network. The IDS management server is alerted if suspicious activity is detected.

- **Syslog server**—Collects network events and traps.

- **System administration serve**r—Configures network management and other network devices.

Venti Systems will implement Network Admission Control (NAC) to ensure that users and their computers comply with the following corporate network policies:

- Host intrusion prevention

- Virus/spyware/adware protection

- Protection against buffer overflow attacks

- Operating system integrity assurance

- Application inventory

- Audit log consolidation

As described in Chapter 4, "Network Security Design," NAC requires a policy server, which is part of the network monitoring station; a network access device (NAD); and trust agent software installed on users' laptops. The NAD intercepts attempts to connect from local or remote users. The trust agent provides the NAD with pertinent information about the laptop's configuration, such as the version of antivirus software installed and the patch level of the operating system. The NAD passes this information to the policy server, which decides whether access will be granted to the laptop.

New laws require IT governance best practices and the privacy and security of customer and financial data to be assured, including a secure backup of such data. Examples of such regulations are Sarbanes-Oxley (SOX) and the California Law on Notice of Security Breaches (Senate Bill [SB] 1386) in the United States, and the Personal Information Protection and Electronic Documents Act (PIPEDA) in Canada. Reporting requirements under these regulations include identifying who can access data if critical information is secure (for example, if it is encrypted when it is stored), what information has been changed, and when the information was changed.

As part of security and network management, the company should also have auditing tools in place to collect and report on usage. A policy will be put in place so that someone looks at the collected data and compares it to what should be happening. For example, multiple attempts to access banned websites or services should be followed up on, as should invoices from service providers that are higher than the expected amounts.

The accounting function of the AAA server will provide monitoring of users' network activity.

Branch-Office Network Management

Critical devices within the Seattle office will also be managed through SNMP and accessed through SSH. This traffic will travel across the VPN. Syslog data will also be sent back to the head office through the VPN encrypted tunnel.

Remote User Network Management

Remote users' devices (for example, a home networking router) will be managed by the users themselves. Their laptops will be under the control of Venti Systems and protected by the implementation of NAC.

Future Considerations

Some enhancements that can be considered in the future for the Venti Systems network include the following:

- Implementing a disaster recovery plan and solution, which can include off-site network devices and servers hosted by a service provider

- Multihoming (having multiple connections) to the Internet

- Expanding IP telephony to the Seattle and sales offices

- Using wireless IP phones within the Toronto office

- Installing a software-based IP phone on users' laptops to allow VoIP calls

- Implementing a wireless solution in the Seattle office

- Using radio frequency identification (RFID) for an inventory system in Seattle

- Implementing storage networking, in the form of network-attached storage (NAS) appliances, to help improve the performance, scalability, and reliability of access to the research and development (R&D) data

Summary

This chapter provided a design for the Venti Systems case study, based on the requirements developed in the previous chapter.

Endnote

[1]Adapted from "SAFE: A Security Blueprint for Enterprise Networks," http://www.cisco.com/go/safe.

Part IV: Appendixes

This appendix lists websites and other external readings that are referred to throughout this book.

APPENDIX **A**

References

> **NOTE** The website references in this book were accurate at the time of writing; however, they might have since changed. If a particular uniform resource locator (URL) is unavailable, you might try conducting a search using the title as key words in a search engine such as Google (http://www.google.com).

AirDefense and Cisco integration information, http://www.airdefense.net/cisco/.

AutoQoS information, http://www.cisco.com/en/US/products/ps6656/
products_ios_protocol_option_home.html and http://www.cisco.com/en/US/tech/tk543/tk759/
tk879/tsd_technology_support_protocol_home.html.

"Availability Measurement," Networkers 2004 Session NMS-2201, http://www.cisco.com/
warp/public/732/Tech/grip/docs/availmgmt.pdf.

"Cisco ACNS Software Caching Configuration Guide for Centrally Managed Deployments
Release 5.3," http://www.cisco.com/application/pdf/en/us/guest/products/ps6049/c2001/
ccmigration_09186a00803b0ca7.pdf.

"Cisco AVVID Network Infrastructure for Storage Networking," http://www.cisco.com/warp/
public/cc/so/neso/stneso/tech/avvis_wp.pdf.

"Cisco Business Ready Campus Solutions," http://www.cisco.com/application/pdf/en/us/guest/
netsol/ns431/c654/cdccont_0900aecd800d8124.pdf.

"Cisco Content Engine 7320," http://www.cisco.com/en/US/products/hw/contnetw/ps766/
prod_release_note09186a00800d9f74.html.

"Cisco Content Engine and CDN Hardware Datasheet," http://www.cisco.com/en/US/
products/hw/contnetw/ps761/products_data_sheet09186a008014b5d4.html.

"Cisco Express Forwarding Overview," http://www.cisco.com/univercd/cc/td/doc/product/software/ios122/122cgcr/fswtch_c/swprt1/xcfcef.htm.

Cisco feature navigator site, http://www.cisco.com/go/fn.

"Cisco HWIC-AP WLAN Module for Cisco 1800 (Modular), 2800 and 3800," http://www.cisco.com/en/US/products/ps5949/products_data_sheet0900aecd8028cc7b.html.

"Cisco Integrated Wireless Network," http://www.cisco.com/en/US/netsol/ns340/ns394/ns348/ns337/networking_solutions_package.html.

"Cisco IOS IP SLAs Configuration Guide, Release 12.4," http://www.cisco.com/en/US/products/ps6350/products_configuration_guide_book09186a008043be2d.html.

"Cisco IOS Quality of Service Solutions Configuration Guide, Release 12.2," http://www.cisco.com/en/US/products/sw/iosswrel/ps1835/products_configuration_guide_book09186a00800c5e31.html.

Cisco IP phone information, http://www.cisco.com/en/US/products/hw/phones/ps379/index.html.

"Cisco IP Telephony Solution Reference Network Design (SRND) Cisco CallManager Release 4.0, November 2004," http://www.cisco.com/go/srnd.

"Cisco Management Information Base (MIB) User Quick Reference," http://www.cisco.com/univercd/cc/td/doc/product/software/ios112/mbook/index.htm.

"Cisco Network Assistant Information," http://www.cisco.com/go/NetworkAssistant.

Cisco router products home page, http://www.cisco.com/en/US/products/hw/routers/index.html.

"Cisco Structured Wireless-Aware Network (SWAN) Multimedia Presentation," http://www.cisco.com/en/US/netsol/ns340/ns394/ns348/ns337/networking_solutions_presentation0900aecd8022d512.shtml.

Cisco switch products home page, http://www.cisco.com/en/US/products/hw/switches/index.html.

"Cisco Wireless IP Phone 7920," http://www.cisco.com/en/US/partner/products/hw/phones/ps379/ps5056/index.html.

"CiscoWorks LAN Management Solution," http://www.cisco.com/en/US/products/sw/cscowork/ps2425/index.html.

"Designing and Managing High Availability IP Networks," Networkers 2004 Session NMS-2T20, http://www.cisco.com/warp/public/732/Tech/grip/docs/deploymanage.pdf.

"Designing Large-Scale IP Internetworks," http://www.cisco.com/univercd/cc/td/doc/cisintwk/idg4/nd2003.htm.

"Enterprise QoS Solution Reference Network Design Guide, Version 3.1," June 2005, http://www.cisco.com/univercd/cc/td/doc/solution/esm/qossrnd.pdf.

Erlang tables and calculators, http://www.erlang.com.

Farley, *Storage Networking Fundamentals: An Introduction to Storage Devices, Subsystems, Applications, Management, and File Systems,* Indianapolis, Cisco Press, 2004.

Gupta, *Storage Area Network Fundamentals,* Indianapolis, Cisco Press, 2002.

"Hierarchical Campus Design—At-A-Glance," http://www.cisco.com/application/pdf/en/us/guest/netsol/ns24/c643/cdccont_0900aecd800d8129.pdf.

High-availability information, http://www.cisco.com/go/availability.

Hutton and Ranjbar, *CCDP Self Study: Designing Cisco Network Architectures (ARCH),* Indianapolis, Cisco Press, 2005.

Internet Requests For Comments (RFCs), http://www.rfc-editor.org/rfc.html.

"Introducing the Content Routing Software," http://www.cisco.com/univercd/cc/td/doc/product/webscale/cr/crsw11/77509ov1.pdf.

IP communications/voice solutions information, http://www.cisco.com/go/ipc.

IP multicast information, http://www.cisco.com/go/ipmulticast.

"IP SLAs—Command-Line Interface (CLI)," http://www.cisco.com/en/US/products/sw/iosswrel/ps5207/products_feature_guide09186a008044d161.html.

"IP Summary Address for RIPv2," http://www.cisco.com/en/US/products/sw/iosswrel/ps1830/products_feature_guide09186a0080087ad1.html.

IPv6 information, http://www.cisco.com/go/ipv6.

Linegar, D. and Savage, D., Advanced Routing Protocol Deployment session, Cisco Technical Symposium 2004, Oct. 5, 2004, Toronto.

Myers, B., IP Telephony & Business Applications Productivity session, Cisco Technical Symposium 2004, Oct. 5, 2004, Toronto.

"Netflow Services Solutions Guide," http://www.cisco.com/en/US/customer/products/sw/ netmgtsw/ps1964/products_implementation_design_guide09186a00800d6a11.html.

"Network-Based Application Recognition and Distributed Network-Based Application Recognition," http://www.cisco.com/en/US/products/ps6350/ products_configuration_guide_chapter09186a0080455985.html.

Network management products and services page, http://www.cisco.com/en/US/products/sw/ netmgtsw/index.html.

Odom, *CCNA Self-Study: CCNA INTRO Exam Certification Guide,* Indianapolis, Cisco Press, 2004.

"OSPF Incremental SPF," http://www.cisco.com/univercd/cc/td/doc/product/software/ios120/ 120newft/120limit/120s/120s24/ospfispf.htm.

Paquet and Saxe, *The Business Case for Network Security: Advocacy, Governance, and ROI,* Indianapolis, Cisco Press, 2005.

Paquet and Teare, *CCNP Self-Study: Building Scalable Cisco Internetworks (BSCI), Second Edition,* Indianapolis, Cisco Press, 2003.

"Potential of IP Communications Takes Off at Toronto Pearson International Airport," http:// newsroom.cisco.com/dlls/partners/news/2004/f_hd_03-30.html.

"QoS Classification and Marking on Catalyst 6500/6000 Series Switches Running CatOS Software," http://www.cisco.com/en/US/products/hw/switches/ps700/ products_tech_note09186a008014f8a8.shtml.

Redford, R., "Intelligent Information Networks," Keynote Address at Cisco Technical Symposium 2004, Oct. 5, 2004, Toronto.

"SAFE: A Security Blueprint for Enterprise Networks," http://www.cisco.com/go/safe.

Storage networking information, http://www.cisco.com/go/san and http://www.cisco.com/go/ storage.

Szigeti, T., QoS Best Practices session, Cisco Technical Symposium 2004, Oct. 5, 2004, Toronto.

Szigeti and Hattingh, *End-to-End QoS Network Design: Quality of Service in LANs, WANs, and VPNs,* Indianapolis, Cisco Press, 2004.

Teare, *CCDA Self-Study: Designing for Cisco Internetwork Solutions (DESGN),* Indianapolis, Cisco Press, 2004.

"The ABCs of IP Version 6," http://www.cisco.com/application/pdf/en/us/guest/products/iosswrel/c1127/cdccont_0900aecd8018e369.pdf.

"Troubleshooting IP Multilayer Switching," http://www.cisco.com/en/US/products/hw/switches/ps700/products_tech_note09186a00800f99bc.shtml.

"Virtual LANs/VLAN Trunking Protocol (VLANs/VTP)," http://www.cisco.com/en/US/tech/tk389/tk689/tsd_technology_support_protocol_home.html.

Webb, *Building Cisco Multilayer Switched Networks,* Indianapolis, Cisco Press, 2001.

"White Paper: Scalable Content Switching," http://www.cisco.com/en/US/products/hw/contnetw/ps792/products_white_paper09186a0080136856.shtml.

"Wireless LANs At-A-Glance," http://www.cisco.com/application/pdf/en/us/guest/netsol/ns24/c643/cdccont_0900aecd800dc92e.pdf.

This appendix describes the fundamental concepts that relate to networks and includes the following sections:

- Introduction to Networks

- Protocols and the OSI Model

- LANs and WANs

- Network Devices

- Introduction to the TCP/IP Suite

- Routing

- Addressing

- Comprehensive Example

Network Fundamentals

The goal of this appendix is to introduce some fundamental concepts and terminology that are the foundation for the other material in the book. After a brief introduction to networks in general, we delve into the communication protocols that are used by network devices; this necessarily includes a discussion of the infamous Open Systems Interconnection (OSI) model. LANs and WANs are described, as are the various devices found in a network. This is followed by an introduction to the Transmission Control Protocol/Internet Protocol (TCP/IP), used extensively in the Internet. Routing and addressing, including IP addresses, are explored. The appendix concludes with a comprehensive example, tying together many of the concepts covered.

We encourage you to review any of the material in this appendix that you are not familiar with before reading the rest of the book, because these ideas are critical to the understanding of the more complex technologies covered in the other chapters.

Introduction to Networks

In the 1960s and 1970s, before the PC was invented, a company would typically have only one central computer, a mainframe. Users connected to the mainframe through terminals on their desks. These terminals had no intelligence of their own—their only function was to display a text-based user interface provided by the mainframe. Hence, they were usually called *dumb terminals.* The only network was the connection between the terminals and the mainframe.

In 1981, the IBM PC was released—this event changed the industry significantly. The PC had intelligence of its own, allowing users to do tasks on their desktops that previously required a mainframe. Networks were introduced to interconnect these distributed PCs.

The term *network* is used in many ways. For example, people network with one another, telephones are networked in the public telephone system, and data networks connect different computers. These uses of the term have a common thread: Networks provide the ability for people or devices to communicate with each other.

A *data network* is a network that allows computers to exchange data. The simplest data network is two PCs connected through a cable. However, most data networks connect many devices.

An *internetwork* is a collection of individual networks that are connected by networking devices and that function as a single large network. The public Internet is the most common example—it is a single network that connects millions of computers. *Internetworking* refers to the industry and products that design, implement, and administer internetworks.

The first networks were LANs; they enabled multiple users in a relatively small geographical area to exchange files and messages and to access shared resources such as printers and disk storage. WANs were introduced to interconnect these LANs so that geographically dispersed users could also share information. The "LANs and WANs" section, later in this appendix, further describes these two types of networks.

NOTE   Appendix D, "Abbreviations," lists many of the acronyms that appear in this book.

Protocols and the OSI Model

Consider that you are in Toronto and you want to send an e-mail to your friend in San Francisco. Successfully sending and receiving e-mail involves doing many things, including the following:

- You must type the message in your e-mail application.

- You must address the message in your e-mail application.

- You must click the **Send** button in your e-mail application to start sending the message.

- You must use the correct type of connections and wires to connect your PC to your local network.

- Your PC must put the data on the wire.

- Your PC must be able to connect to the Internet, and you must provide any necessary login information.

- Network devices must find the best path through the Internet so that the e-mail is received by the right person.

The following sections introduce the model that specifies all of these functions so that the system as a whole can work correctly.

The OSI Model

The International Organization for Standardization (ISO) standards committee created a list of all the network functions required for sending data (such as an e-mail) and divided them into seven categories. These categories are collectively known as the *OSI 7-layer model,* which was released in 1984. The model is illustrated in Figure B-1—no network book would be complete without a section on the OSI model.

Figure B-1   *Each of the Seven Layers of the OSI Model Represents Functions Required for Communication*

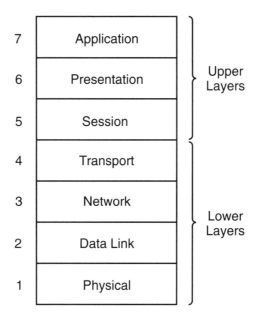

7	Application	Upper Layers
6	Presentation	
5	Session	
4	Transport	Lower Layers
3	Network	
2	Data Link	
1	Physical	

NOTE   You might also have heard people talk about OSI Layers 8 and 9. While they are not official, Layer 8 is commonly known as the political layer, and Layer 9 is the religious layer. These light-heartedly represent all the other issues you might encounter in an IT project.

KEY POINT   The OSI model represents everything that must happen to send data. The important thing to remember is that the OSI model does not specify *how* these things are to be done, just *what* needs to be done. Different protocols can implement these functions differently. For example, the open-standard Internet Protocol (IP) and Novell's Internetwork Packet Exchange (IPX) Protocol are different implementations of the network layer.

As also shown in Figure B-1, the seven layers can be thought of in two groups: the upper layers and the lower layers. The term *upper layers* often refers to Layers 5 through 7, and the term *lower layers* often refers to Layers 1 through 4, although this terminology is relative. The term *upper layer* also refers to any layer above another layer.

The upper layers are concerned with application issues—for example, the interface to the user and the format of the data. The lower layers are concerned with transport issues—for example, how the data traverses the network and the physical characteristics of that network.

Protocols

A *protocol* is a set of rules. The OSI model provides a framework for the communication protocols used between computers. Just as we need rules of the road—for example, so that we know that a red light means stop and a green light means go—computers also need to agree on a set of rules to successfully communicate. Two computers must use the same protocol to communicate. Computers that try to use different protocols would be like speaking Italian to someone who only understands English—it would not work.

Many different networking protocols are in use, in a variety of categories. For example, *LAN* and *WAN protocols* (at the lower three OSI layers) specify how communication is accomplished across various media types, *routed protocols* (at Layer 3) specify the format of and how data is carried throughout a network, and *routing protocols* (also at Layer 3) specify how routers communicate to indicate the best paths through the network.

KEY POINT | Many *protocol suites* define various protocols that correspond to the functions defined in the seven OSI layers, including routed protocols, a selection of routing protocols, applications, and so forth. Protocol suites are also known as *protocol stacks.*

The most widely used network protocol suite is the TCP/IP suite, named after two of the protocols within the suite; this protocol suite is used in the Internet. Novell's Netware is another example of a protocol suite.

KEY POINT | The OSI protocol suite is another suite. Although the OSI protocol suite uses the same names for its seven layers as the OSI 7-layer model does, the two OSI items are different—one is a protocol suite and the other is the model that all the protocol suites are based on.

The OSI Layers

The following sections briefly describe each of the seven layers of the OSI model, starting at the lowest layer.

Physical Layer (Layer 1)

The OSI physical layer defines specifications such as the electrical and mechanical conditions that are necessary for activating, maintaining, and deactivating the physical link between devices. Specifications include voltage levels, maximum cable lengths, connector types, and maximum data rates. The physical layer is concerned with the binary transmission of data. This binary data is represented as *bits* (which is short for *binary digits*). A bit has a single binary value, either 0 or 1.

> **NOTE**   Appendix C, "Decimal–Binary Conversion," provides information on binary numbers and explains how to convert between decimal and binary formats (and vice versa).

Data Link Layer (Layer 2)

Layer 2, the data link layer, defines the format of data that is to be transmitted across the physical network and indicates how the physical media is accessed, including physical addressing, error handling, and flow control. The data link layer sends *frames* of data; different media have different types of frames.

KEY POINT   A *frame* is a defined set of data that includes addressing and control information and is transmitted between network devices. A frame can contain a header field (in front of the data) and/or a trailer field (after the data); these two fields are said to frame the data.

For LANs, the Institute of Electrical and Electronics Engineers (IEEE) split Layer 2 into two sublayers: Logical Link Control (LLC) and Media Access Control (MAC), as illustrated in Figure B-2.

Figure B-2   *For LANs, the Data Link Layer Is Divided into the LLC and MAC Sublayers*

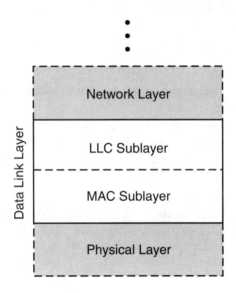

The LLC sublayer (defined by the IEEE 802.2 specification) allows multiple network layer (Layer 3) protocols to communicate over the same physical data link, by allowing the Layer 3 protocol to be specified in the LLC portion of the frame.

The MAC sublayer specifies the physical MAC address that uniquely identifies a device on a network. Each frame that is sent out specifies a destination MAC address; only the device with that MAC address should receive and process the frame.

Network Layer (Layer 3)

The network layer is responsible for routing, which allows data to be properly forwarded across a logical internetwork (consisting of multiple physical networks). Logical network addresses (versus physical MAC addresses) are specified at Layer 3. Layer 3 protocols include routed and routing protocols. The routing protocols determine the best path that should be used to forward the routed data through the internetwork to its destination.

The network layer sends *datagrams* (or *packets*); different routed protocols have different types of datagrams.

KEY POINT

A *datagram* is a defined set of data that includes addressing and control information and is routed between the source and the destination of the data. A datagram might contain a header field (in front of the data) and/or a trailer field (after the data).

If a datagram needs to be sent across a network that can only handle a certain amount of data at a time, the datagram can be fragmented into multiple *packets* and then reassembled at the destination.

Thus, a datagram is a unit of data, while a *packet* is what physically goes on the network. If no fragmentation is required, a packet is a datagram; the two terms are often used interchangeably.

Transport Layer (Layer 4)

Layer 4, the transport layer, is concerned with end-to-end connections between the source and the destination. The transport layer provides network services to the upper layers, including connection-oriented and connectionless transport, multiplexing, and error checking and recovery.

Connection-oriented reliable transport establishes a logical connection and uses sequence numbers to ensure that all data is received at the destination. Connectionless unreliable transport just sends the data and relies on upper-layer error detection mechanisms to report and correct problems. Reliable transport has more overhead than unreliable transport, just as using a courier company costs more than using regular mail to deliver your letters.

NOTE   The term *unreliable* as used here does not mean that the network isn't functioning properly or that the data won't be delivered. Rather, it means that the protocol will *not check* to see if the data was delivered intact; this function must be done by a higher level protocol, or the end-user.

Multiplexing allows many applications to use the same physical connection. For example, numbers identify different applications, and data is then tagged with the number that corresponds to the application from which it came. Both sides of the connection are then able to interpret the data in the same way.

The transport layer sends *segments*.

KEY POINT

A *segment* is a defined set of data that includes control information and is sent between the transport layers of the sender and receiver of the data. A segment can contain a header field (in front of the data) and/or a trailer field (after the data).

Upper Layers (Layers 5 through 7)

From the lower layers' perspective, the three upper layers represent the data that must be transmitted from the source to the destination; the network typically does not know nor care about the contents of these layers. For completeness, the following briefly describes the functions of these layers:

- The session layer, Layer 5, is responsible for establishing, maintaining, and terminating communication sessions between applications running on different hosts.

- The presentation layer, Layer 6, specifies the format, data structure, coding, compression, and other ways of representing the data to ensure that information sent from one host's application layer can be read by the destination host.

- Finally the application layer, Layer 7, is the closest to the end user; it interacts directly with software applications that need to communicate over the network.

KEY POINT | The OSI application layer is not the application itself; rather, the OSI application layer provides the communication services to the application.

For example, your e-mail application might use two OSI application layer protocols—Simple Mail Transfer Protocol (SMTP) and Post Office Protocol version 3 (POP3)—to send and retrieve e-mail messages.

Communication Among OSI Layers

This section describes how communication among the seven OSI layers is accomplished.

When you send an e-mail from Toronto to your friend in San Francisco, you can think of your e-mail application sending a message to the e-mail application on your friend's computer. In OSI model terms, information is exchanged between peer OSI layers—the application layer on your computer is communicating with the application layer on your friend's computer. However, to accomplish this, the e-mail must go through all the other layers on your computer (for example, it must have the correct network layer address, be put in the correct frame type, and so on), then go over the network, and then go back through all the layers on your friend's computer, until it finally arrives at her e-mail application.

Control information from each layer is added to the e-mail data before it passes to lower layers; this control information is necessary to allow the data to go through the network properly. Thus, the data at each layer is *encapsulated,* or wrapped in, the information that's appropriate for that layer, including addressing and error checking. The right side of Figure B-3 illustrates the following encapsulation process:

- At Layer 4, the e-mail is encapsulated in a segment.

- At Layer 3, this segment is then encapsulated in a packet.

■   At Layer 2, this packet is then encapsulated in a frame.

■   And finally at Layer 1, the frame is sent out on the wire (or air, if wireless is used) in bits.

Figure B-3   *Data Is Encapsulated as It Goes Down Through the Layers and Decapsulated as It Goes Up*

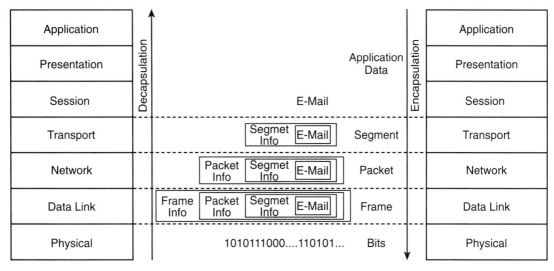

The grouping of data used to exchange information at a particular OSI layer is known as a protocol data unit (PDU). Thus, the PDU at Layer 4 is a segment, at Layer 3 is a packet, and at Layer 2 is a frame.

Notice how the overall size of the information increases as the data goes down through the lower layers.

When data is received at the other end of the network, this additional information is analyzed and then removed as the data is passed to the higher layers toward the application layer. Thus, the data is *decapsulated,* or unwrapped; this process is shown on the left side of Figure B-3.

NOTE   For simplicity, the example in Figure B-3 shows only two systems, one in San Francisco and one in Toronto, and does not show the details of e-mail protocols or e-mail servers. Later sections in this appendix describe what happens when intermediate devices, such as routers, are encountered between the two systems.

At each layer, different protocols are available. For example, the packets sent out by IP are different than those sent out by IPX, because different protocols (rules) must be followed. Both sides of peer layers that are communicating must support the same protocol.

LANs and WANs

LANs were first used between PCs when users needed to connect with other PCs in the same building to share resources. A LAN is a high-speed, yet relatively inexpensive, network that allows connected computers to communicate. LANs have limited reach (hence the term *local-area* network), typically less than a few hundred meters, so they can only connect devices that are in the same room or building, or possibly within the same campus.

A LAN is an always-on connection—in other words, you don't have to dial up or otherwise connect to it when you want to send some data. LANs also belong to the organization in which they are deployed, so no incremental cost is typically associated with sending data.

A variety of LAN technologies are available, some of which are shown in the center of Figure B-4 and briefly described here:

- Ethernet and IEEE 802.3, running at 10 megabits per second (Mbps), use a carrier sense multiple access collision detect (CSMA/CD) technology. When a CSMA/CD device has data to send, it listens to see whether any of the other devices on the wire (multiple access) are transmitting (carrier sense). If no other device is transmitting, this device starts to send its data, listening all the time in case another device erroneously starts to send data (collision detect).

- Fast Ethernet (at 100 Mbps), covered by the IEEE 802.3u specification, also uses the CSMA/CD technology.

- Gigabit Ethernet (running at 1 gigabit per second [Gbps]) is covered by the IEEE 802.3z and 802.3ab specifications and uses the CSMA/CD technology.

- Wireless LAN (WLAN) standards, defined by the IEEE 802.11 specifications, are capable of speeds up to 54 Mbps under the 802.11g specification.

Figure B-4 *A Variety of LAN and WAN Standards*

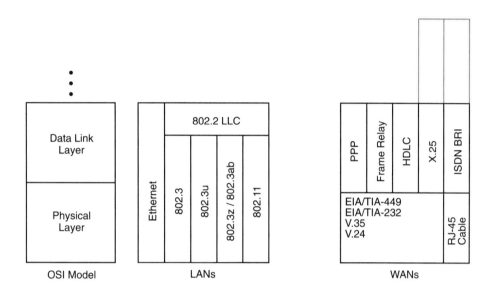

WANs interconnect devices (which are usually connected to LANs) that are located over a relatively broad geographical area (hence the term *wide-area* network). Compared to a LAN, a typical WAN is slower, requires a connection request when you want to send data, and usually belongs to another organization (called the *service provider*). You pay the service provider a fee (known as a *tariff*) for the use of the WAN; this fee could be a fixed monthly amount, or it could be variable based on usage and/or distance.

Just as you find many types of LANs, many types of WANs are also available, some of which are illustrated on the right side of Figure B-4. Like LANs, WANs function at the lower two layers of the OSI model (X.25 and Integrated Services Digital Network [ISDN] also function at Layer 3). The service you use depends on many factors, including what is available where you are and, of course, the cost of the service.

Some of the common WAN technologies include the following:

■ **Packet-switched network**—A network that shares the service provider's facilities. The service provider creates permanent virtual circuits (PVCs) and switched virtual circuits (SVCs) that deliver data between subscribers' sites. X.25 and Frame Relay are examples of packet-switched networks.

■ **Leased line**—A point-to-point connection that is reserved for transmission. Common data link layer protocols used in this case are Point-to-Point Protocol (PPP) and High-Level Data Link Control (HDLC).

■ **Circuit-switched network**—A physical path that is reserved for the duration of the connection between two points. ISDN Basic Rate Interface (BRI) is an example of this type of network.

Two other technologies, digital subscriber line (DSL) and cable, connect residential and business premises to service providers' premises; they are described as follows:

■ **DSL**—Utilizes unused bandwidth on traditional copper telephone lines to deliver traffic at higher speeds than traditional modems allow. The most common DSL implementation is asymmetric DSL (ADSL). ADSL allows regular telephone traffic to simultaneously share the line with high-speed data traffic so that only one telephone line is required to support both high-speed Internet and normal telephone services.

■ **Cable**—Utilizes unused bandwidth on cable television networks to deliver data at higher speeds than traditional modems allow.

Network Devices

The main devices that interconnect networks are hubs, switches, and routers, as described in the following sections.

> **NOTE** Many other devices can be used in networks to provide specific functionality; these devices are introduced in the appropriate chapters in this book. For example, security devices, including firewalls, are discussed in Chapter 4, "Network Security Design."

Terminology: Domains, Bandwidth, Broadcast, and Multicast

The following is some terminology related to the operation of network devices:

■ A *domain* is a specific part of a network.

■ *Bandwidth* is the amount of data that can be carried across a network in a given time period.

■ A *broadcast* is data meant for all devices; it uses a special broadcast address to indicate this.

■ A *multicast* is data destined for a specific group; again, a special address indicates this.

- A *bandwidth domain,* known as a *collision domain* for Ethernet LANs, includes all devices that share the same bandwidth.

- A *broadcast domain* includes all devices that receive each other's broadcasts (and multicasts).

Devices in the same bandwidth domain are also in the same broadcast domain; however, devices in the same broadcast domain can be in different bandwidth domains.

Hubs

A typical Ethernet LAN uses unshielded twisted-pair (UTP) cables with RJ-45 connectors (which are slightly bigger than telephone RJ-11 connectors). Because these cables have only two ends, you need an intermediary device to connect more than two computers. That device is a hub.

A *hub* works at Layer 1 and connects multiple devices so that they are logically all on one LAN.

Physical Interfaces and Ports

The physical connection point on a network device—a hub, switch, or router—is called an *interface* or a *port.*

Don't confuse this definition of *port* with the application layer *port numbers* that are discussed in the "TCP/IP Transport Layer Protocols" section, later in this appendix.

A hub has no intelligence—it sends all data received on any port to all the other ports. Thus, devices connected through a hub receive everything that the other devices send, whether it was meant for them or not. This is analogous to being in a room with lots of people—if you speak, everyone can hear you. If more than one person speaks at a time, everyone just hears noise.

All devices connected to a hub are in one collision domain and one broadcast domain.

NOTE   A hub just repeats all the data received on any port to all the other ports; thus, hubs are also known as *repeaters.*

Switches

Just as having many people in a room trying to speak can result in nobody hearing anything intelligible, using hubs in anything but a small network is not efficient. To improve performance, LANs are usually divided into multiple smaller LANs interconnected by a Layer 2 LAN *switch.* The devices connected to a switch again appear as they are all on one LAN, but this time, multiple conversations between devices connected through the switch can be happening simultaneously.

> **NOTE**   In this appendix, we discuss Layer 2 LAN switches. Chapter 2, "Switching Design," has more advanced switching topics, including virtual LANs (VLANs) and Layer 3 switching.

Switches are Layer 2 devices and have some intelligence—they only send data to a port if the data needs to go there. A device connected to a switch port does not receive any of the information addressed to devices on other ports. Thus, the main advantage of using a switch instead of a hub is that the traffic received by a device is reduced, because only frames addressed to a specific device are forwarded to the port on which that device is connected.

Switches keep track of who is where, and who is talking to whom, and only send data where it needs to go. If the switch receives a broadcast (information meant for everyone) though, by default it sends it out all ports (except for the one on which it was received).

All devices connected to one switch port are in the same collision domain, but devices connected to different ports are in different collision domains. By default, all devices connected to a switch are in the same broadcast domain.

Switches Versus Bridges

You might have also heard of bridges. Switches and bridges are logically equivalent. The main differences are as follows:

- Switches are significantly faster because they switch in hardware, whereas bridges switch in software.
- Switches can interconnect LANs of unlike bandwidth. A 10-Mbps Ethernet LAN and a 100-Mbps Ethernet LAN, for example, can be connected using a switch. In contrast, all the ports on a bridge support one type of media.
- Switches typically have more ports than bridges.

Switches do not allow devices on different logical LANs to communicate with each other; this requires a router, as described in the next section.

Routers

A *router* goes one step further than a switch. It is a Layer 3 device that has a lot more intelligence than a hub or switch. By using logical Layer 3 addresses, routers allow devices on different LANs to communicate with each other and with distant devices, for example, those connected through the Internet or through a WAN.

A device connected to a router does not receive any of the information meant just for devices on other ports, or broadcasts (destined for all networks) from devices on other ports.

The router keeps track of who is where, and who is talking to whom, and only sends data where it needs to go. It supports communication between LANs, but it blocks broadcasts (destined for all networks).

All devices that are connected to one router port are in the same collision domain, but devices connected to different ports are in different collision domains.

All the devices connected to one router port are in the same broadcast domain, but devices connected to different ports are in different broadcast domains. Routers block broadcasts (destined for *all* networks) and multicasts by default; routers only forward *unicast* packets (destined for a specific device) and packets of a special type, called *directed broadcasts*.

> **NOTE**   IP multicast technology, which enables multicast packets to be sent throughout a network, is described in Chapter 10, "Other Enabling Technologies."

> **NOTE**   An IP directed broadcast is an IP packet that is destined for all devices on an IP subnet, but which originates from a device on another subnet. IP subnets are described in the "Addressing" section, later in this appendix. On Cisco routers, the **ip directed-broadcast** interface command controls what the router connected to the destination subnet does with a directed broadcast packet; the behavior of this command is described in Chapter 2.

The fact that a router does not forward broadcasts (destined for all networks) is a significant difference between a router and a switch, and helps to control the amount of traffic on the network. For example, many protocols, such as IP, use broadcasts for routing protocol advertisements, discovering servers, and so on. These broadcasts are a necessary part of local LAN traffic, but they are not required on other LANs and can even overwhelm slower WANs. Routers can generate broadcasts themselves if necessary (for example, to send out a routing protocol advertisement) but do not pass on a received broadcast.

Routing operation is discussed further in the "Routing" section, later in this appendix.

> **NOTE**   The concepts of unicast, multicast, and broadcast apply to Layer 2 and Layer 3 separately. While a router does not forward any type of frame, it can forward a unicast, multicast, or directed broadcast packet (that it received in a frame). A switch, however, can forward a unicast, multicast, or broadcast frame.

Introduction to the TCP/IP Suite

As mentioned earlier, TCP/IP is the most widely used protocol suite. The relationship between the four layers of the TCP/IP suite and the seven layers of the OSI model is illustrated in Figure B-5.

Figure B-5   *TCP/IP Protocol Suite*

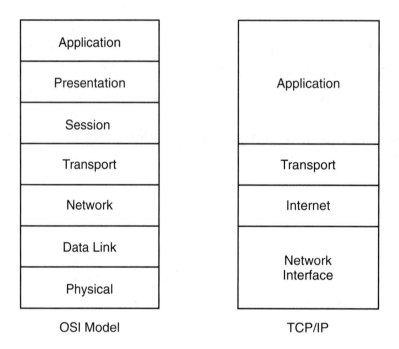

The four layers of the TCP/IP suite are the application layer, transport layer, Internet layer, and network interface layer.

The application layer includes the functionality of the OSI application, presentation, and session layers. Applications defined in the TCP/IP suite include the following:

- **FTP and TFTP**—Transfer files between devices.

- **SMTP and POP3**—Provide e-mail services.

- **HTTP**—Transfers information to and from a world wide web (WWW) server through web-browser software.

- **Telnet**—Emulates a terminal to connect to devices.

- **Domain Name System (DNS)**—Translates network device names into network addresses, and vice versa.

- **Simple Network Management Protocol (SNMP)**—Used for network management, including setting threshold values and reporting network errors.

- **DHCP**—Assigns dynamic IP addressing information to devices as they require it.

The network interface layer can support a wide variety of LANs and WANs (including those discussed in the "LANs and WANs" section, earlier in this appendix).

The transport layer and the Internet layer are detailed in the following sections.

TCP/IP Transport Layer Protocols

The TCP/IP transport layer includes the following two protocols:

- **TCP**—Provides connection-oriented, end-to-end reliable transmission. Before sending any data, TCP on the source device establishes a connection with TCP on the destination device, ensuring that both sides are synchronized. Data is acknowledged; any data that is not received properly is retransmitted. FTP is an example of an application that uses TCP to guarantee that the data sent from one device to another is received successfully.

- **User Datagram Protocol (UDP)**—Provides connectionless, best-effort unacknowledged data transmission. In other words, UDP does not ensure that all the segments arrive at the destination undamaged. UDP does not have the overhead of TCP related to establishing the connection and acknowledging the data. However, this means that upper-layer protocols or the user must determine whether all the data arrived successfully, and retransmit if necessary. TFTP is an example of an application that uses UDP. When all the segments have arrived at the destination, TFTP computes the file check sequence and reports the results to the user. If an error occurs, the user must send the entire file again.

TCP and UDP, being at the transport layer, send segments.

Figure B-6 illustrates the fields in a UDP segment and in a TCP segment.

Figure B-6   *UDP Segments Contain at Least 8 Bytes While TCP Segments Contain at Least 20 Bytes*

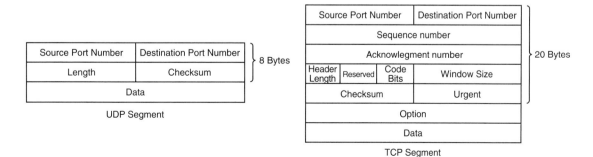

The UDP segment fields are as follows:

- **Source and destination port numbers** (16 bits each)—Identify the upper-layer protocol (the application) in the sending and receiving devices.

- **Length** (16 bits)—The total number of 32-bit words in the header and the data.

- **Checksum** (16 bits)—The checksum of the header and data fields, used to ensure that the segment is received correctly.

- **Data** (variable length)—The upper-layer data (the application data).

The TCP segment fields are as follows:

- **Source and destination port numbers** (16 bits each)—Identify the upper-layer protocol (the application) in the sending and receiving hosts.

- **Sequence and acknowledgment numbers** (32 bits each)—Ensure the correct order of the received data and that the data reached the destination.

- **Header length** (4 bits)—The number of 32-bit words in the header.

- **Reserved** (6 bits)—For future use, set to 0.

- **Code bits** (6 bits)—Indicates different types of segments. For example, the SYN (synchronize) bit sets up a session, the ACK (acknowledge) bit acknowledges a segment, and the FIN (finish) bit closes a session.

- **Window size** (16 bits)—The number of octets that the receiving device is willing to accept before it must send an acknowledgment.

NOTE   An *octet* is 8 bits of data.

- **Checksum** (16 bits)—The checksum of the header and data fields, used to ensure that the segment is received correctly.

- **Urgent** (16 bits)—Indicates the end of urgent data.

- **Option** (0 or 32 bits)—Only one option is currently defined: the maximum TCP segment size.

- **Data** (variable)—The upper-layer data (the application data).

Notice that the UDP header is much smaller than the TCP header. UDP does not need the sequencing, acknowledgment, or windowing fields because it does not establish and maintain connections.

Port number operation, which is the same for both TCP and UDP, is described in the next section. Following that section, the operation of sequence and acknowledgment numbers and windowing are described; these are key to understanding TCP operation.

Port Numbers

KEY POINT   TCP and UDP use protocol *port numbers* to distinguish among multiple applications that are running on a single device.

Well-known, or standardized, port numbers are assigned to applications so that different implementations of the TCP/IP protocol suite can interoperate. Well-known port numbers are numbers up to 1023; examples include the following:

- **FTP**—TCP port 20 (data) and port 21 (control)

- **TFTP**—UDP port 69

- **SMTP**—TCP port 25

- **POP3**—TCP port 110

- **HTTP**—TCP port 80

- **Telnet**—TCP port 23

- **DNS**—TCP and UDP port 53

- **SNMP**—UDP port 161

Port numbers from 1024 through 49151 are called *registered port numbers;* these are registered for use by other applications. The dynamic ports numbers are those from 49152 through 65535; these can be dynamically assigned by hosts as source port numbers when they create and end sessions. Figure B-7 illustrates a device in Toronto that is opening a Telnet session (TCP port 23) with a device in London. Note that the source port from Toronto is 50051. Toronto records this Telnet session with London as port 50051 to distinguish it from any other Telnet sessions it might have running (because you can have simultaneous multiple Telnet sessions running on a device). The London device receives port number 23 and therefore knows that this is a Telnet session. In its reply, it uses a destination port of 50051, which Toronto knows is the Telnet session it opened with London.

Figure B-7 *Source and Destination Port Numbers Indicate the Application Being Used*

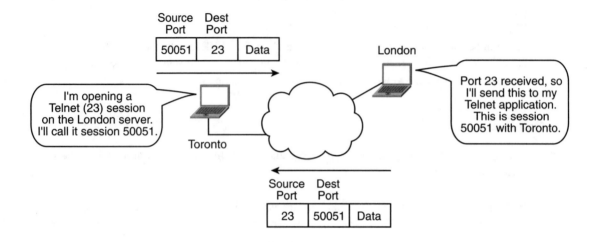

TCP Sequencing, Acknowledgment, and Windowing

To illustrate TCP operation, we follow a TCP session as it is established, data is sent, and the session is closed.

KEY POINT A TCP connection is established by a process called a *three-way handshake*. This process uses the SYN and ACK bits (in the code bits field in the TCP segment) as well as the sequence and acknowledgment number fields..

The TCP three-way handshake is shown in Figure B-8.

Figure B-8 *Three-Way Handshake Establishes a TCP Session*

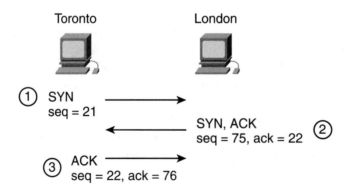

In this example, a user in Toronto wants to establish a TCP session with a device in London, for example, to start a Telnet session. The first step in the handshake involves the initiator, Toronto, sending a segment with the SYN bit set—this indicates that it wants to start a session and synchronize with London. This segment also includes the initial sequence number that Toronto is using—21 in this example. Assuming that the device in London is willing to establish the session, it returns a segment that also has the SYN bit set. In addition, this segment has the ACK bit set because London is acknowledging that it successfully received a segment from Toronto; the acknowledgment number is set to 22, indicating that London is now expecting to receive segment 22 and therefore that it successfully received number 21. (This is known as an *expectational acknowledgment.*) This new segment includes the initial sequence number that London is using— 75 in this example. Finally, Toronto replies with an acknowledgment segment, sequence number 22 (as London is expecting), and acknowledgment number 76 (indicating that it is now expecting number 76 and therefore it has successfully received number 75). The session is now established, and data can be exchanged between Toronto and London.

NOTE   The sequence and acknowledgment numbers specify octet numbers, not segment numbers. For ease of illustration purposes here, we are assuming a segment is 1 octet of data. This is not the case in real life, but it simplifies the example so that the concepts are easier to understand.

The window size field in the segment controls the flow of the session. It indicates the number of octets that a device is willing to accept before it must send an acknowledgment. Because each host can have different flow restrictions (for example, one host might be very busy and therefore require that a smaller amount of data be sent at one time), each side of the session can have different window sizes, as illustrated in the example in Figure B-9.

Figure B-9   *Window Size Indicates the Number of Octets a Device Is Willing to Accept Before It Sends an Acknowledgment*

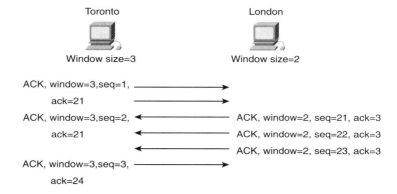

In this example, the window size on Toronto is set to 3, and on London, it is set to 2. When Toronto sends data to London, it can only send 2 octets before it must wait for an acknowledgment. When London sends data to Toronto, it can send 3 octets before it must wait for an acknowledgment.

> **NOTE** The window size specifies the number of octets, not the number of segments, that can be sent. For ease of illustration purposes here, we are assuming a segment is 1 octet of data. This is not the case in real life, but it again simplifies the example so that the concepts are easier to understand. The window sizes shown in the example are also small, for ease of explanation purposes. In reality, the window size would be much larger, allowing a lot of data to be sent between acknowledgments.

After all the data for the session is sent, the session can be closed. The process is similar to how it was established, using a handshake. In this case, four steps are used, as illustrated in Figure B-10.

Figure B-10 *Four-Way Handshake Closes a TCP Session*

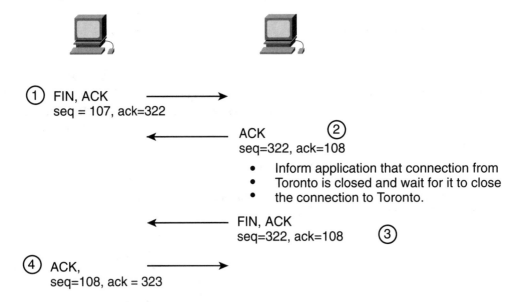

In this example, Toronto wants to close its Telnet session with London. The first step in the handshake involves Toronto sending a segment with the FIN bit set, indicating that it wants to finish the session. This segment also includes the sequence number that Toronto is currently using—107 in this example. London immediately acknowledges the request. This segment has the ACK bit set with the acknowledgment number set to 108, indicating that London successfully received number 107. This segment includes the sequence number that London is currently using—322 in this example. London then informs its Telnet application that half of the session, the connection from Toronto, is now closed. When the application on the London device requests that the other half of the connection (to Toronto) be closed, London sends a new segment with the FIN bit set, indicating that it wants to close the session. Finally, Toronto replies with an acknowledgment segment with acknowledgment number 323 (indicating that it has successfully received number 322). The session is now closed in both directions.

TCP/IP Internet Layer Protocols

The TCP/IP Internet layer corresponds to the OSI network layer and includes the IP routed protocol, as well as protocols for address resolution and message and error reporting.

Protocols

The protocols at this layer include the following:

- **IP**—Provides connectionless, best-effort delivery of datagrams through the network. A unique IP address—a logical address—is assigned to each interface of each device in the network. IP and IP addresses are introduced later in this appendix and are described in more detail in Chapter 3, "IPv4 Routing Design."

> **NOTE**   Two versions of IP currently exist, IP version 4 (IPv4) and the emerging IP version 6 (IPv6). In this book, the term *IP* refers to IPv4. IPv6 is introduced in Chapter 10.

- **Internet Control Message Protocol (ICMP)**—Sends messages and error reports through the network. For example, the ping application included in most TCP/IP protocol suites sends an ICMP echo message to a destination, which then replies with an ICMP echo reply message. Ping provides confirmation that the destination can be reached and gives a measure of how long packets are taking to travel between the source and destination.

- **Address Resolution Protocol (ARP)**—Requests the MAC address (the data link layer physical address) for a given IP address. The returned MAC address is used as the destination address in the frames that encapsulate the packets of data being routed to the destination IP address.

> **NOTE** These protocols are all at the TCP/IP Internet layer, corresponding to the OSI model network layer, Layer 3. They run on top of the TCP/IP network interface layer, corresponding to the OSI model Layers 1 and 2—the physical and data link layers.

> **NOTE** You might have heard people refer to IP as a LAN protocol; this is because they configure IP on their PCs, which are attached to LANs. In fact, however, IP is a network layer protocol—it runs on top of any LAN or WAN.

IP Datagrams

Figure B-11 illustrates the fields of an IP datagram.

Figure B-11 *An IP Datagram Contains at Least 20 Bytes*

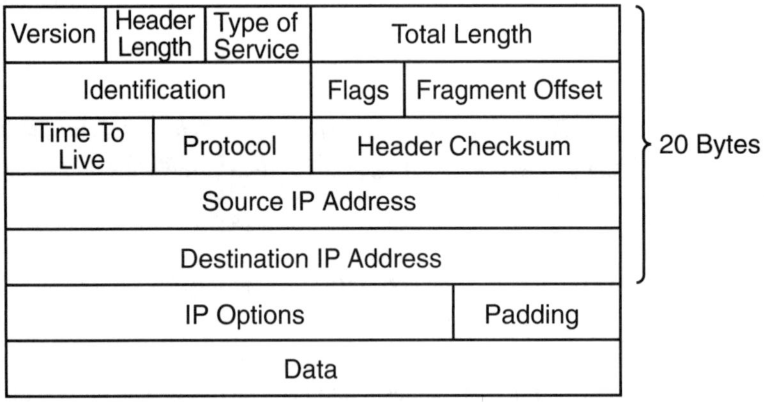

The IP datagram fields are as follows:

- **Version** (4 bits)—Identifies the IP version, in this case version 4.

- **Header length** (4 bits)—The number of 32-bit words in the header (including the options).

- **Type of service (ToS)** (8 bits)—Specifies how the datagram should be handled within the network. These bits mark traffic for a specific quality of service (QoS), which is further described in Chapter 6, "Quality of Service Design."

- **Total length** (16 bits)—The total number of octets in the header and data fields.

- **Identification** (16 bits), **flags** (3 bits), and **fragment offset** (13 bits)—Handle cases where a large datagram must be fragmented—split into multiple packets—to go through a network that cannot handle datagrams of that size.

- **Time to Live (TTL)** (8 bits)—Ensures that datagrams do not loop endlessly in the network; this field must be decremented by 1 by each router that the datagram passes through.

- **Protocol** (8 bits)—Indicates the upper-layer (Layer 4, the transport layer) protocol that the data is for. In other words, this field indicates the type of segment that the datagram is carrying, similar to how the port number field in the UDP and TCP segments indicates the type of application that the segment is carrying. A protocol number of 6 means that the datagram is carrying a TCP segment, while a protocol number of 17 means that the datagram is carrying a UDP segment.

- **Header checksum** (16 bits)—Ensures that the header is received correctly.

- **Source and destination IP addresses** (32 bits each)—Logical IP addresses assigned to the source and destination of the datagram, respectively. IP addresses are introduced later in this appendix, in the "Addressing" section.

- **IP options and padding** (variable length, 0 or a multiple of 32 bits)—Used for network testing and debugging.

- **Data** (variable)—The upper-layer (transport layer) data.

Routing

This section examines how routers work and introduces routing tables and routing protocols.

Routers work at the OSI model network layer. The main functions of a router are first to determine the best path that each packet should take to get to its destination and second to send the packet on its way. Thus, a router's job is much like that of a worker at a post office—she looks at the address label on the letter (the network layer address on the packet), determines which way the letter (the packet) should be sent, and then sends it. The comparison between the post office and a router is illustrated in Figure B-12.

Figure B-12 *A Router Behaves Much Like a Worker at a Post Office*

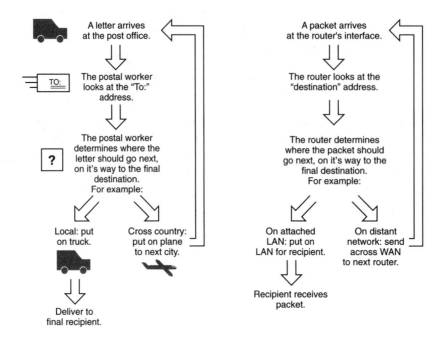

> **NOTE** This discussion of routers is concerned with the traditional role of routers in a network, at the OSI model network layer. Routers are now taking on more functions, for example, in QoS and security areas; these other functions are described in the relevant chapters throughout this book.

Routers Work at the Lower Three OSI Layers

The router doesn't care what is in the upper layers—what kind of data is in the packet—the router is just responsible for sending the packet the correct way. The router does have to be concerned with the data link and physical layers, though, because it might have to receive and send data on different media. For example, a packet received on an Ethernet LAN might have to be sent out on a Frame Relay WAN, requiring the router to know how to communicate on both of these types of media. In terms of layers, therefore, a router decapsulates received data up to the network layer and then encapsulates the data again into the appropriate frame and bit types. This process is illustrated in Figure B-13, where the PC on the left is sending data to the PC on the right. The routers have determined that the path marked with arrows is the best path between the PCs.

Figure B-13 *Router Works at the Network Layer*

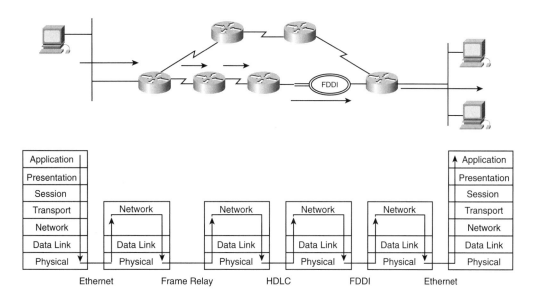

In this figure, notice that only the two PCs care about the upper layers, while all the routers in the path concern themselves with only the lower three layers.

Routing Tables

To determine the best path on which to send a packet, a router must know where the packet's destination network is.

KEY POINT Routers learn about networks by being physically connected to them, or by learning about them either from other routers or from a network administrator. Routes configured by network administrators are known as *static routes* because they are hard-coded in the router and remain there—static—until the administrator removes them. Routes to which a router is physically connected are known as *directly connected routes*. Routers learn routes from other routers by using a routing protocol.

However routes are learned, routers keep the best path (or multiple best paths) to each destination in a *routing table*. A routing table contains a list of all the networks that a router knows how to reach. For each network, the routing table typically contains the following items:

■   How the route to the network was learned (for example, statically or by using a routing protocol).

- The network address of the router from which the route to the network was learned (if applicable).

- The interface (port) through which the network can be reached.

- The metric of the route. The *metric* is a measurement, such as the number of other routers that the path goes through, that routing protocols use when determining the best path.

> **NOTE** The path that the router determines is the *best* depends on the routing protocol in use. For example, some routing protocols define *best* as the path that goes through the least number of other routers (the least number of hops), while others define *best* as the path with the highest bandwidth.

For example, in the network shown in Figure B-14, the metric used is hops—the number of other routers between this router and the destination network. Both routers know about all three networks. Router X, on the left, knows about networks A and B because it is connected to them (hence the metric of 0) and about network C from Router Y (hence the metric of 1). Router Y, on the right, knows about networks B and C because it is connected to them (hence the metric of 0) and about network A from Router X (hence the metric of 1).

Figure B-14 *Routers Keep Routing Information in Routing Tables*

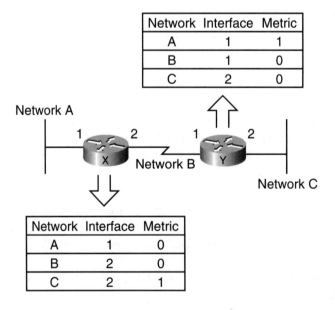

Routing Protocols

Routers use routing protocols to exchange routing information. *Routing protocols* allow routers to learn from other routers the networks that are available so that data can be sent in the correct direction. Remember that two routers communicating with each other must use the same routing protocol, or they can't understand each other.

The TCP/IP protocol suite includes the following routing protocols:

- Routing Information Protocol (RIP), versions 1 and 2 (RIPv1 and RIPv2)

- Interior Gateway Routing Protocol (IGRP)

- Enhanced Interior Gateway Routing Protocol (EIGRP)

- Open Shortest Path First (OSPF)

- Integrated Intermediate System-to-Intermediate System (IS-IS)

- Border Gateway Protocol (BGP) Version 4 (BGP4)

NOTE   These routing protocols are discussed further in Chapter 3.

The previous sections introduced the basics of routing and how routers learn about the networks that are available so that data can be sent along the correct path. Routers look at the destination address of the packet to determine where the packet is going so that they can then select the best route to get the packet there. The following section discusses these addresses.

Addressing

This section describes network layer addressing and compares it to the physical addresses discussed earlier. A discussion of how routers use these addresses follows; the section concludes with a brief introduction to IP addressing.

Physical and Logical Addresses

Earlier we discussed MAC addresses; recall that these are at the data link layer and are considered to be physical addresses. When a network interface card is manufactured, it is assigned an address, called a *burned-in address (BIA)*—it doesn't change when the network card is installed in a PC and is moved from one network to another. Typically, this BIA is copied to interface memory and is used as the MAC address of the interface. MAC addresses are analogous to social insurance numbers or social security numbers—each person has one assigned to him or her, and the numbers don't change as the person moves to a new house. These numbers are associated with the physical person, not where the person lives.

> **NOTE**   The BIA is a 48-bit value. The upper 24 bits are an Organizational Unique Identifier (OUI), representing the vendor of the device. The lower 24 bits are a unique value for that OUI, typically the serial number of the device.

Knowing the MAC address assigned to a PC or to a router's interface doesn't tell you anything about where it is or what network it is attached to—it can't help a router determine the best way to send data to it. For this we need logical network layer addresses; they are assigned when a device is installed on a network and should be changed when the device is moved.

> **NOTE**   Some organizations set the MAC addresses of their devices to something other than the BIA, for example, based on the location of the device in the network, for management purposes.

When you send a letter to someone, you have to know his postal address. Because every postal address in the world is unique, you can potentially send a letter to anyone in the world. Postal addresses are logical and hierarchical—for example, they include the country, province/state, street, and building/house number on the street. The top portion of Figure B-15 illustrates Main Street with various houses on it. All of these houses have one portion of their address in common— Main Street—and one portion unique—their house number.

Figure B-15   *Network Layer Addresses Are Similar to Postal Addresses*

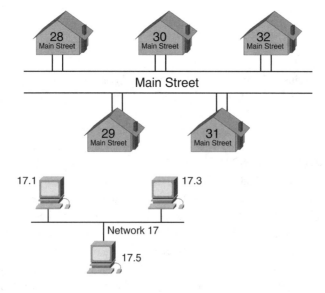

KEY POINT | Network layer addresses are also logical and hierarchical. They have two main parts: the network that the device is on (similar to the street, city, province, and so on) and the device number on that network (similar to the building number on the street).

> **NOTE** The terms *device, host,* and *node* are used interchangeably to represent the entity that is communicating.

The lower portion of Figure B-15 illustrates a network, 17, with various PCs on it. All of these PCs have one portion of their address in common—17—and one part unique—their device number. Devices on the same logical network must share the same network portion of their address and have different device portions.

Routing and Network Layer Addresses

A router typically only looks at the network portion of a destination address. It compares the network portion to its routing table, and if it finds a match, it sends the packet out of the appropriate interface, toward its destination.

A router only needs to concern itself with the device portion of a destination address if it is directly connected to the same network as the destination. In this case, the router must send the packet directly to the appropriate device, and it needs to use the entire destination address for this. (A router on a LAN uses ARP to determine the MAC address of the device with that IP address and then creates an appropriate frame with that MAC address as the destination MAC address.)

IP Addresses

IP addresses are network layer addresses. As you saw earlier, IP addresses are 32-bit numbers. As shown in Figure B-16, the 32 bits are usually written in *dotted decimal notation*—they are grouped into four octets (8 bits each), separated by dots, and represented in decimal format. Each bit in the octet has a binary weight (the highest is 128 and the next is 64, followed by 32, 16, 8, 4, 2, and 1). Thus, the minimum value for an octet is 0, and the maximum decimal value for an octet is 255.

Figure B-16 *32-bit IPv4 Addresses Are Written in Dotted Decimal Notation*

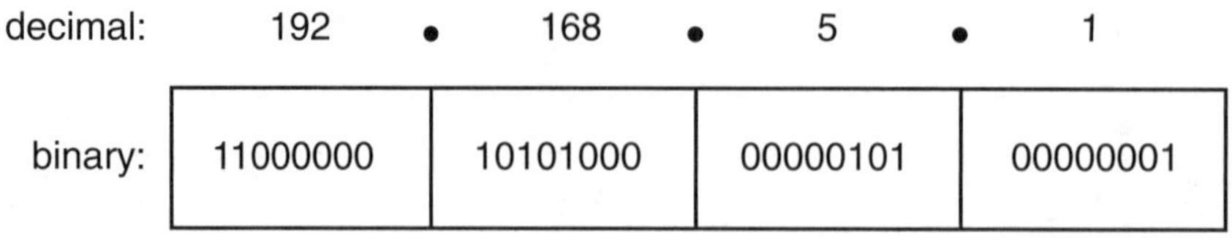

decimal:	192 •	168 •	5 •	1
binary:	11000000	10101000	00000101	00000001

> **NOTE** The maximum value of an octet is when all 8 bits are binary 1. The decimal value of an octet is calculated by adding all the weighted bits, in this case, 128 + 64 + 32 + 16 + 8 + 4 + 2 + 1 = 255.

> **NOTE** Appendix C details how to convert between decimal and binary formats (and vice versa) and provides a decimal-to-binary conversion chart.

IP Address Classes

IPv4 addresses are categorized into five classes: A, B, C, D, and E. Only Classes A, B, and C addresses are used for addressing devices; Class D is used for multicast groups, and Class E is reserved for experimental use.

The first octet of an IPv4 address defines which class it is in, as illustrated in Table B-1 for Class A, B, and C addresses. The address class determines which part of the address represents the network bits (N) and which part represents the host bits (H), as also shown in this table. The number of networks available in each class and the number of hosts per network are also shown.

Table B-1 *IP Address Classes A, B, and C Are Available for Addressing Devices*

Class	Format*	Higher-Order Bit(s)	Address Range	Number of Networks	Number of Hosts per Network
A	N.H.H.H	0	1.0.0.0 to 126.0.0.0	126	16,777,214
B	N.N.H.H	10	128.0.0.0 to 191.255.0.0	16,386	65,534
C	N.N.N.H	110	192.0.0.0 to 223.255.255.0	2,097,152	254

*N=network number bits; H=host number bits.

NOTE   Class A addresses are any addresses that have the higher-order bit set to 0; this would include 0 through 127 in the first octet. However, network 0.0.0.0 is reserved, and network 127.0.0.0 (any address starting with decimal 127) is reserved for loopback functionality. Therefore, the first octet of Class A addresses ranges from 1 to 126.

NOTE   Class D addresses have higher-order bits 1110 and are in the range of 224.0.0.0 to 239.255.255.255. Class E addresses have higher-order bits 1111 and are in the range of 240.0.0.0 to 255.255.255.255.

For example, 192.168.5.1 is a Class C address. Therefore, it is in the format N.N.N.H—the network part is 192.168.5 and the host part is 1.

Private and Public IP Addresses

The IPv4 address space is divided into public and private sections. Private addresses are reserved addresses to be used only internally within a company's network, not on the Internet. When you want to send anything on the Internet, private addresses must be mapped to a company's external registered address. Public IPv4 addresses are provided for external communication.

KEY POINT   Request For Comments (RFC) 1918, "Address Allocation for Private Internets," defines the private IPv4 addresses as follows:

- 10.0.0.0 to 10.255.255.255
- 172.16.0.0 to 172.31.255.255
- 192.168.0.0 to 192.168.255.255

The remaining addresses are public addresses.

NOTE   Internet RFC documents are written definitions of the Internet's protocols and policies. A complete list and the documents themselves can be found at http://www.rfc-editor.org/rfc.html.

Note that all the IP addresses used in this book are private addresses, to avoid publishing anyone's registered addresses.

Subnets

As illustrated in Table B-1, Class A addresses have little use in a normal organization—most companies would not want one network with over 16 million PCs on it! This would not be physically possible or desirable. Because of this limitation on addresses when only their class is considered (called *classful addressing*) and the finite number of such addresses, subnets were introduced by RFC 950, "Internet Standard Subnetting Procedure."

Class A, B, and C addresses can be divided into smaller networks, called *subnetworks* or *subnets,* resulting in a larger number of possible networks, each with fewer host addresses available than the original network.

The addresses used for the subnets are created by borrowing bits from the host field and using them as subnet bits; a subnet mask indicates which bits have been borrowed. A *subnet mask* is a 32-bit value that is associated with an IP address to specify which bits in the address represent network and subnet bits and which represent host bits. Using subnet masks creates a three-level hierarchy: network, subnet, and host.

KEY POINT

In binary format, a subnet mask bit of 1 indicates that the corresponding bit in the IP address is a network or subnet bit, and a subnet mask bit of 0 indicates that the corresponding bit in the IP address is a host bit.

Subnet mask bits come from the higher-order (the leftmost) bits of the host field; therefore, the 1s in the subnet mask are contiguous.

The default subnet masks for Class A, B, and C addresses are shown Table B-2.

Table B-2   *IP Address Default Subnet Masks*

Class	Default Mask in Binary Format	Default Mask in Decimal Format
A	11111111.00000000.00000000.00000000	255.0.0.0
B	11111111.11111111.00000000.00000000	255.255.0.0
C	11111111.11111111.11111111.00000000	255.255.255.0

When all of an address's host bits are 0, the address is for the subnet itself (sometimes called *the wire*). When all of an address's host bits are 1, the address is the directed broadcast address for that subnet (in other words, for all the devices on that subnet).

For example, 10.0.0.0 is a Class A address with a default subnet mask of 255.0.0.0, indicating 8 network bits and 24 host bits. If you want to use 8 of the host bits as subnet bits instead, you would use a subnet mask of 11111111.11111111.00000000.00000000, which is 255.255.0.0 in decimal format. You could then use the 8 bits to address 256 subnets. Each of these subnets could support up to 65,534 hosts. The address of one of the subnets is 10.1.0.0; the broadcast address on this subnet is 10.1.255.255.

Another way of indicating the subnet mask is to use a *prefix*. A prefix is a slash (/) followed by a numeral that is the number of bits in the network and subnet portion of the address—in other words, the number of contiguous ones that would be in the subnet mask. For example, the subnet mask of 255.255.240.0 is 11111111.11111111.11110000.00000000 in binary format, which is 20 1s followed by 12 0s. Thus, the prefix would be /20 for the 20 bits of network and subnet information, the number of 1s in the mask.

KEY POINT   The formula 2^n calculates the number of subnets created, where n is the number of subnet bits (the number of bits borrowed from the host field).

The formula $2^x - 2$ calculates the number of host addresses available on each subnet, where x is the number of host bits.

IP addressing is further explored in Chapter 3.

Comprehensive Example

This section presents a comprehensive example, tying together many of the concepts covered in the rest of this appendix. Figure B-17 illustrates the network used in this example.

Figure B-17   *PC1 in New York Is Sending FTP Data to FS1 in London*

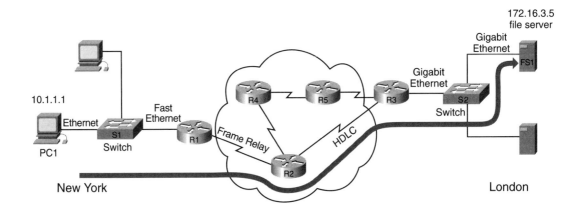

In this network, PC1, located in New York, has an FTP connection with the file server FS1 in London. PC1 is transferring a file, using FTP, to FS1. The path between PC1 and FS1 goes through switch S1; Routers R1, R2, and R3; and switch S2, as illustrated by the thick line in the figure. (The routers have communicated, using a routing protocol, to determine the best path between network 10.0.0.0 and network 172.16.0.0.) PC1 has an IP address of 10.1.1.1, and FS1 has an IP address of 172.16.3.5. When PC1 first needed to send data to a device on another network, it sent an ARP request; its default gateway R1 replied with its own MAC address, which PC1 keeps in its memory.

FTP data is now being sent from PC1 to FS1. Figure B-18 shows how this data flows within the devices in the network, and what the data looks like at each point within the network.

Figure B-18 *Data Is Encapsulated and Decapsulated as It Flows Through the Network*

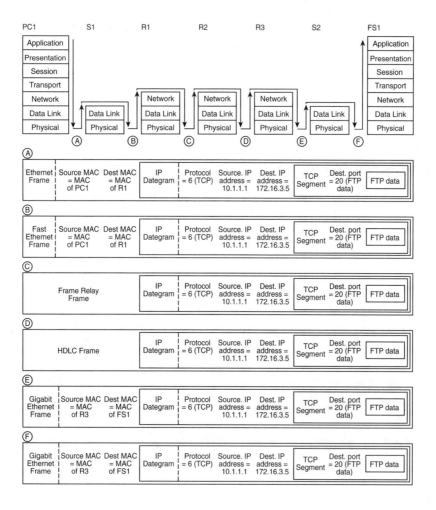

Starting at the left of Figure B-18, PC1 prepares the data for transport across the network, and the resulting frame is shown as point A in the figure. PC1 encapsulates the FTP data in a TCP segment; the destination port field of the segment is set to 20, indicating that it contains FTP data. This TCP segment is then encapsulated in an IP datagram. The protocol number of the datagram is set to 6, indicating that it contains a TCP segment. The source IP address is set to PC1's address, 10.1.1.1, while the destination IP address is set to FS1's address, 172.16.3.5. The IP datagram is encapsulated in an Ethernet frame, with the source MAC address set to PC1's MAC address and the destination MAC address set to R1's MAC address. PC1 then puts the frame on the Ethernet network, and the bits arrive at S1.

S1 receives the frame and looks at the destination MAC address—it is R1's MAC address. S1 looks in its MAC address table and sees that this MAC address is on its Fast Ethernet port. Therefore, S1 encapsulates the IP datagram in a Fast Ethernet frame, as shown at point B in the figure. Notice that the source and destination MAC addresses have not changed in this new frame type, and that the datagram, segment, and data all remain untouched by the switch. S1 then puts the frame on the Fast Ethernet network, and the bits arrive at R1.

R1 receives the frame, and because it is destined for R1's MAC address, R1 decapsulates the frame to Layer 3. R1 looks at the destination IP address 172.16.3.5 and compares it to its routing table. This network is accessible through R2, over a Frame Relay network, so R1 encapsulates the IP datagram in a Frame Relay frame, as shown at point C in the figure. Notice that the datagram, segment, and data all remain untouched by the router, but the frame type has changed. R1 then puts the frame on the Frame Relay network, and the bits arrive at R2.

R2 receives the frame and decapsulates it to Layer 3. R2 looks at the destination IP address 172.16.3.5 and compares it to its routing table. This network is accessible through R3, over an HDLC network, so R2 encapsulates the IP datagram in an HDLC frame, as shown at point D in the figure. Notice that the datagram, segment, and data all remain untouched by the router, but the frame type has changed again. R2 then puts the frame on the HDLC network, and the bits arrive at R3.

R3 receives the frame and decapsulates it to Layer 3. R3 looks at the destination IP address 172.16.3.5 and compares it to its routing table. This network is accessible through its Gigabit Ethernet interface—it is directly connected to that network. When R3 first needed to send data to FS1, it sent an ARP request; FS1 replied with its own MAC address, which R3 keeps in its memory. So R3 encapsulates the IP datagram in a Gigabit Ethernet frame, as shown at point E in the figure, with the source MAC address set to its own address and the destination MAC address set to FS1's address. Notice that the datagram, segment, and data all remain untouched by the router, but the frame type has changed. The bits arrive at S2.

S2 receives the frame and looks at the destination MAC address—It is FS1's MAC address. S2 looks in its MAC address table and sees that this MAC address is on another one of its Gigabit Ethernet ports. Therefore, the IP datagram can stay in a Gigabit Ethernet frame, as shown at point F in the figure. Notice that the source and destination MAC addresses have not changed in this frame, and that the datagram, segment, and data all remain untouched by the switch. S2 then puts the frame on the other Gigabit Ethernet network, and the bits arrive at FS1. FS1 receives the frame, and because it is destined for FS1's MAC address, FS1 decapsulates the frame to Layer 3. FS1 looks at the destination IP address and determines that it is its own address. Therefore, FS1 decapsulates the segment and the FTP data and then sends it to its FTP application. The FTP data is now at its destination.

KEY POINT

At each communication layer, the same protocol must be used at each side of a connection.

For example, PC1 is sending data to FS1 using FTP, so both PC1 and FS1 must support FTP at the application layer. If they don't, the session will fail and data will not be sent.

Note, however, that the FTP data can go through many different types of media—Layers 1 and 2—on its way to FS1. The devices (switches, routers, PC, and file server) all decapsulate up to at least Layer 2; thus, both sides of each connection between these devices must support the same Layers 1 and 2. For example, if PC1 only supported Ethernet and S1 only supported Fast Ethernet, they would not be able to communicate. Because S1 has an Ethernet port, it can connect to PC1 and then convert the data to send out on its Fast Ethernet port.

Summary

This appendix discussed fundamental networking concepts that form a solid foundation for understanding the design and technology sections in the rest of this book. The following topics were explored:

- An introduction to networks

- A discussion of networking protocols and the OSI model, a key component of networking and the basis of modern protocol suites

- LANs and WANs

- Network devices, including hubs, switches, and routers

- An introduction to the TCP/IP suite and a discussion of the IP, TCP, and UDP protocols

- Routing, including an introduction to routing protocols

- Addressing, including MAC and IP addresses

- A comprehensive example, illustrating the encapsulation and decapsulation processes

This appendix describes how to convert between the binary and decimal numbering systems, and includes the following sections:

- Decimal-to-Binary Conversion Chart

- Decimal Numbers

- Binary Numbers

- Converting Binary IP Addresses to Decimal

- Converting Decimal IP Addresses to Binary

Decimal-Binary Conversion

Binary numbers are used by computers, including routers and switches, for their IP addresses. Thus, when working with and designing IP addresses, you need to understand how to work with binary numbers. People usually prefer to use decimal numbers, so converting between the binary and decimal numbering systems is a useful networking skill.

> **NOTE** In this appendix, the term *IP* refers to IP version 4 (IPv4).

This appendix describes the binary and decimal numbering systems, and explains how to convert between the two.

Decimal-to-Binary Conversion Chart

The easiest way to convert between decimal and binary numbers is to use Table C-1.

Table C-1 *Decimal-to-Binary Conversion Chart*

Decimal	Binary	Decimal	Binary	Decimal	Binary	Decimal	Binary
0	00000000	10	00001010	20	00010100	30	00011110
1	00000001	11	00001011	21	00010101	31	00011111
2	00000010	12	00001100	22	00010110	32	00100000
3	00000011	13	00001101	23	00010111	33	00100001
4	00000100	14	00001110	24	00011000	34	00100010
5	00000101	15	00001111	25	00011001	35	00100011
6	00000110	16	00010000	26	00011010	36	00100100
7	00000111	17	00010001	27	00011011	37	00100101
8	00001000	18	00010010	28	00011100	38	00100110
9	00001001	19	00010011	29	00011101	39	00100111

continues

Table C-1 *Decimal-to-Binary Conversion Chart (Continued)*

Decimal	Binary	Decimal	Binary	Decimal	Binary	Decimal	Binary
40	00101000	71	01000111	102	01100110	133	10000101
41	00101001	72	01001000	103	01100111	134	10000110
42	00101010	73	01001001	104	01101000	135	10000111
43	00101011	74	01001010	105	01101001	136	10001000
44	00101100	75	01001011	106	01101010	137	10001001
45	00101101	76	01001100	107	01101011	138	10001010
46	00101110	77	01001101	108	01101100	139	10001011
47	00101111	78	01001110	109	01101101	140	10001100
48	00110000	79	01001111	110	01101110	141	10001101
49	00110001	80	01010000	111	01101111	142	10001110
50	00110010	81	01010001	112	01110000	143	10001111
51	00110011	82	01010010	113	01110001	144	10010000
52	00110100	83	01010011	114	01110010	145	10010001
53	00110101	84	01010100	115	01110011	146	10010010
54	00110110	85	01010101	116	01110100	147	10010011
55	00110111	86	01010110	117	01110101	148	10010100
56	00111000	87	01010111	118	01110110	149	10010101
57	00111001	88	01011000	119	01110111	150	10010110
58	00111010	89	01011001	120	01111000	151	10010111
59	00111011	90	01011010	121	01111001	152	10011000
60	00111100	91	01011011	122	01111010	153	10011001
61	00111101	92	01011100	123	01111011	154	10011010
62	00111110	93	01011101	124	01111100	155	10011011
63	00111111	94	01011110	125	01111101	156	10011100
64	01000000	95	01011111	126	01111110	157	10011101
65	01000001	96	01100000	127	01111111	158	10011110
66	01000010	97	01100001	128	10000000	159	10011111
67	01000011	98	01100010	129	10000001	160	10100000
68	01000100	99	01100011	130	10000010	161	10100001
69	01000101	100	01100100	131	10000011	162	10100010
70	01000110	101	01100101	132	10000100	163	10100011

continues

Table C-1   *Decimal-to-Binary Conversion Chart (Continued)*

164	10100100	187	10111011	210	11010010	233	11101001
165	10100101	188	10111100	211	11010011	234	11101010
166	10100110	189	10111101	212	11010100	235	11101011
167	10100111	190	10111110	213	11010101	236	11101100
168	10101000	191	10111111	214	11010110	237	11101101
169	10101001	192	11000000	215	11010111	238	11101110
170	10101010	193	11000001	216	11011000	239	11101111
171	10101011	194	11000010	217	11011001	240	11110000
172	10101100	195	11000011	218	11011010	241	11110001
173	10101101	196	11000100	219	11011011	242	11110010
174	10101110	197	11000101	220	11011100	243	11110011
175	10101111	198	11000110	221	11011101	244	11110100
176	10110000	199	11000111	222	11011110	245	11110101
177	10110001	200	11001000	223	11011111	246	11110110
178	10110010	201	11001001	224	11100000	247	11110111
179	10110011	202	11001010	225	11100001	248	11111000
180	10110100	203	11001011	226	11100010	249	11111001
181	10110101	204	11001100	227	11100011	250	11111010
182	10110110	205	11001101	228	11100100	251	11111011
183	10110111	206	11001110	229	11100101	252	11111100
184	10111000	207	11001111	230	11100110	253	11111101
185	10111001	208	11010000	231	11100111	254	11111110
186	10111010	209	11010001	232	11101000	255	11111111

The rest of this appendix introduces and describes how to make this conversion from "first principles," in other words, without the use of a conversion chart like Table C-1.

Decimal Numbers

We first analyze the decimal numbers that we are familiar with. Decimal numbers are known as *base 10* numbers. Within all numbering systems, the symbols used as digits range from 0 up to one less than the base; thus, within decimal numbers, the following ten unique symbols are used as digits:

0 1 2 3 4 5 6 7 8 9

When multiples of these symbols are combined to create a decimal number, each digit in the number is weighted based on its position within the number. The weights used are all powers of 10 (which is what *base 10* means). The rightmost digit, which is the least significant, has a weight of 10^0 (1). The next digit has a weight of 10^1 (10). The next has a weight of 10^2 (100), and so on.

For example, consider the decimal number 5746. Figure C-1 illustrates how this number is interpreted.

Figure C-1 *Interpreting a Decimal Number*

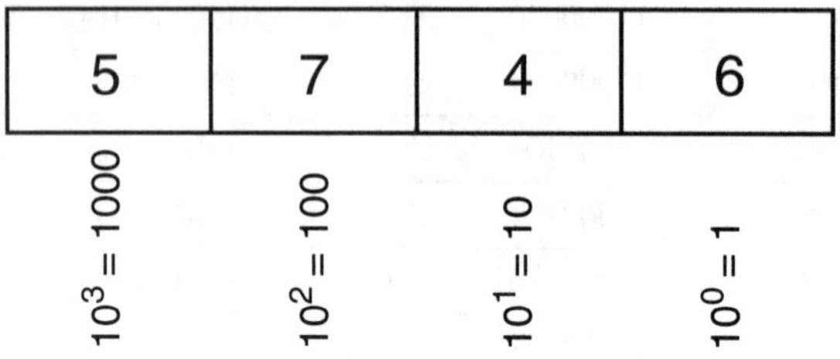

5	7	4	6
$10^3 = 1000$	$10^2 = 100$	$10^1 = 10$	$10^0 = 1$

$$6 \times 10^0 = 6 \times 1 \quad = \quad 6$$

$$4 \times 10^1 = 4 \times 10 \quad = \quad 40$$

$$7 \times 10^2 = 7 \times 100 \quad = \quad 700$$

$$5 \times 10^3 = 5 \times 1000 = \quad \underline{5000}$$

$$\text{Total:} \quad 5746$$

Figure C-1 describes the following points:

- The least significant digit, 6, has a weight of 10^0; thus, it represents $6 * 10^0 = 6 * 1 = 6$.

- The next digit, 4, has a weight of 10^1; thus, it represents $4 * 10^1 = 4 * 10 = 40$.

- The next digit, 7, has a weight of 10^2; thus it represents $7 * 10^2 = 7 * 100 = 700$.

- The most significant digit, 5, has a weight of 10^3; thus, it represents $5 * 10^3 = 5 * 1000 = 5000$.

- The decimal number is the sum of these representations: $5000 + 700 + 40 + 6 = 5746$.

We read this number as "five thousand seven hundred and forty-six."

The next section provides a similar analysis of binary numbers.

Binary Numbers

Binary numbers are *base 2* numbers; within binary numbers, only the following two unique symbols are used as digits:

0 1

Just as for decimal numbers, when multiple binary symbols are combined to create a binary number, each digit in the number is weighted based on its position within the number. The weights used are all powers of 2 (which is what *base 2* means). The rightmost digit, which is the least significant, has a weight of 2^0 (1). The next digit has a weight of 2^1 (2). The next has a weight of 2^2 (4), and so on.

Consider the binary number 11001010. This number is read as "one one zero zero one zero one zero." This representation can get tedious after only a few digits and isn't practical in our everyday decimal world. Therefore, we typically convert binary numbers to decimal numbers.

Converting Binary IP Addresses to Decimal

Routers, being computers, work in binary. For example, 32-bit IPv4 addresses are used throughout the Internet, so you need to understand how to work with IP addresses. Because people usually like to work in decimal, IP addresses are typically written in a format called *dotted decimal notation.* The 32 bits in the address are divided into four 8-bit chunks—these chunks are called *octets.* Each octet is converted into decimal and then separated by dots.

When converting a binary octet to decimal, each binary digit is weighted based on its position, as described earlier. The weights for the eight bit positions in an octet are shown in Figure C-2.

Figure C-2 *Binary Digits Are Weighted Based on Their Position*

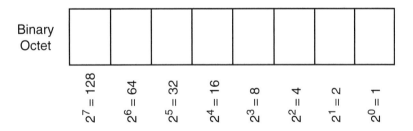

For example, consider the following IP address, written in binary:

10101100000100001000001100001100

Follow these steps to write this binary address in dotted decimal notation:

Step 1   Divide the 32 bits into four octets, as follows:

10101100 00010000 10000011 00001100

Step 2   Convert the first octet into decimal, as illustrated in Figure C-3.

Figure C-3 *Converting an Octet from Binary to Decimal*

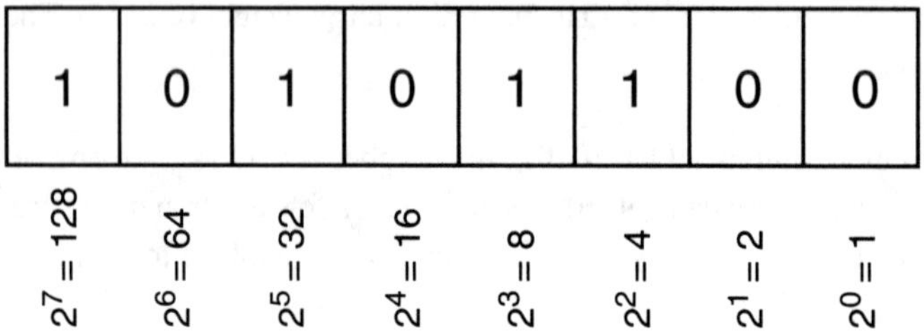

1	0	1	0	1	1	0	0
$2^7 = 128$	$2^6 = 64$	$2^5 = 32$	$2^4 = 16$	$2^3 = 8$	$2^2 = 4$	$2^1 = 2$	$2^0 = 1$

$$0 \times 2^0 = 0 \times 1 \quad = \quad 0$$

$$0 \times 2^1 = 0 \times 2 \quad = \quad 0$$

$$1 \times 2^2 = 1 \times 4 \quad = \quad 4$$

$$1 \times 2^3 = 1 \times 8 \quad = \quad 8$$

$$0 \times 2^4 = 0 \times 16 \quad = \quad 0$$

$$1 \times 2^5 = 1 \times 32 \quad = \quad 32$$

$$0 \times 2^6 = 0 \times 64 \quad = \quad 0$$

$$1 \times 2^7 = 1 \times 128 = \quad 128$$

Total: 172

Note the following points in Figure C-3:

- The least significant digit, 0, has a weight of 2^0; thus, it represents $0 * 2^0 = 0 * 1 = 0$.

- The next digit, also 0, has a weight of 2^1; thus, it represents $0 \text{ x}* 2^1 = 0 * 2 = 0$.

- The next digit, 1, has a weight of 2^2; thus, it represents $1 * 2^2 = 1 * 4 = 4$. The weighted value for each of the other digits is calculated in the same way.

- The most significant digit (on the far left), 1, has a weight of 2^7; thus, it represents $1 * 2^7 = 1 * 128 = 128$.

- Therefore, the binary number 10101100 in decimal is the sum of each of these representations: $128 + 0 + 32 + 0 + 8 + 4 + 0 + 0 = 172$.

Step 3 Repeat this process for the other three octets. The results are as follows:

- 00010000 binary equals 16 decimal.

- 10000011 binary equals 131 decimal.

- 00001100 binary equals 12 decimal.

NOTE You can confirm these results using the decimal-to-binary conversion chart in Table C-1.

Thus, the IP address 10101100000100001000001100001100 in dotted decimal notation is 172.16.131.12.

Converting Decimal IP Addresses to Binary

To convert from decimal to binary, reverse the above process, taking each octet's decimal value and converting it to binary, as follows:

Step 1 Referring to the weighting factors in Figure C-2, find the largest weighting factor that is smaller than or equal to the value of the octet. The binary number will have a 1 in the corresponding bit position and will have a 0 in any bit positions to the left of this 1.

Step 2 Subtract that weighting factor from the decimal octet value.

Step 3 Repeat this process using the new octet value, until the result is 0.

Step 4 Set any remaining bit positions in the binary number to 0.

For example, consider the IP address 192.168.19.255. To write this address in binary, follow these steps:

Step 1 Select an octet to convert. The conversion of the second octet, 168, to binary is shown in Figure C-4.

Figure C-4 *Converting an Octet from Decimal to Binary*

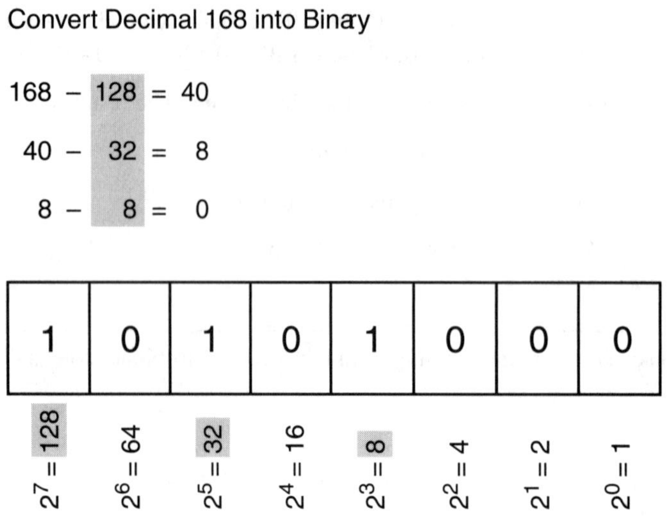

Convert Decimal 168 into Binary

$$168 - \boxed{128} = 40$$

$$40 - \boxed{32} = 8$$

$$8 - \boxed{8} = 0$$

1	0	1	0	1	0	0	0
$2^7 = 128$	$2^6 = 64$	$2^5 = 32$	$2^4 = 16$	$2^3 = 8$	$2^2 = 4$	$2^1 = 2$	$2^0 = 1$

Figure C-4 describes the following points:

- The largest weighting factor that is smaller than or equal to 168 is 128, so the binary number has a 1 in the 2^7 (128) position.

- Subtracting 128 from 168 results in $168 - 128 = 40$.

- The largest weighting factor that is smaller than or equal to 40 is 32, so the binary number has a 1 in the 2^5 (32) position (with a 0 in the intermediary position).

- Subtracting 32 from 40 results in $40 - 32 = 8$.

- The largest weighting factor that is smaller than or equal to 8 is 8, so the binary number has a 1 in the 2^3 (8) position (with a 0 in the intermediary position).

- Subtracting 8 from 8 results in $8 - 8 = 0$.

- The remaining bit positions in the binary number are set to 0.

- Thus, 168 in decimal equals 10101000 in binary.

Step 2   Repeat this process for the other three octets. The results are as follows:

- 192 decimal equals 11000000 binary.

- 19 decimal equals 00010011 binary.

- 255 decimal equals 11111111 binary.

> **NOTE** Again, you can confirm these results using the decimal-to-binary conversion chart in Table C-1.

Therefore, the IP address 192.168.19.255 in binary is as follows:

11000000 10101000 00010011 11111111

This appendix identifies abbreviations, acronyms, and initialisms used in this book and in the internetworking industry.

Abbreviations

Many of these acronyms and other terms are also described in the Cisco Internetworking Terms and Acronyms resource, available at http://www.cisco.com/univercd/cc/td/doc/cisintwk/ita/.

3DES   Triple Data Encryption Standard.

AAA   authentication, authorization, and accounting.

ABR   Area Border Router.

ACD   automatic call distribution.

ACK   1. acknowledgment. 2. acknowledgment bit in a TCP segment.

ACNS   Application and Content Networking System.

ACS   (Cisco Secure) Access Control Server.

ADSL   asymmetric digital subscriber line.

AES   Advanced Encryption Standard.

AF   Assured Forwarding.

ARP   Address Resolution Protocol.

ASBR   Autonomous System Boundary Router.

ASIC   application-specific integrated circuit.

ATM   Asynchronous Transfer Mode.

BE   Best Effort.

BECN	backward explicit congestion notification.
BGP	Border Gateway Protocol.
BGP4	BGP Version 4.
BHT	Busy Hour Traffic.
BPDU	bridge protocol data unit.
bps	bits per second.
BRI	Basic Rate Interface.
CA	certification authority.
CAD/CAM	Computer Aided Design/Computer Aided Manufacturing.
CAM	content-addressable memory.
CAR	committed access rate.
CatOS	Catalyst Operating System.
CBWFQ	class-based weighted fair queuing.
CCITT	Consultative Committee for International Telegraph and Telephone.
CCM	Cisco CallManager.
CCS	1. common channel signaling. 2. Centum Call Second.
CDN	content delivery network.
CDP	Cisco Discovery Protocol.
CEF	Cisco Express Forwarding.
CEO	chief executive officer.
CERT/CC	CERT Coordination Center.
CGMP	Cisco Group Management Protocol.

CIDR	classless interdomain routing.
CIR	committed information rate.
CIS	Catalyst integrated security.
CLNP	Connectionless Network Protocol.
CM	1. cable modem. 2. Campus Manager.
CN	Content Networking.
CO	central office.
CoS	class of service.
CQ	custom queuing.
cRTP	Compressed Real-Time Transfer Protocol (or RTP header compression).
CS	1. common services. 2. class selector.
CSA	Cisco Secure Agent.
CSMA/CD	carrier sense multiple access collision detect.
CTI	computer telephony integration.
CTS	Clear To Send.
CV	CiscoView.
DA	destination address.
DAS	directly attached storage.
DC	demand circuit.
DCE	data circuit-terminating equipment.
DDoS	distributed denial of service.
DEC	Digital Equipment Corporation.

DES	Data Encryption Standard.
DFM	device fault manager.
DHCP	Dynamic Host Configuration Protocol.
DiffServ	Differentiated Services.
DMZ	demilitarized zone.
DNS	Domain Name Service or Domain Name System.
DoS	denial of service.
DSCP	Differentiated Services Code Point.
DSL	digital subscriber line.
DSP	digital signal processor.
DTE	data terminal equipment.
DTS	distributed traffic shaping.
DUAL	Diffusing Update Algorithm.
EBGP	External BGP.
ECN	explicit congestion notification.
EF	expedited forwarding.
EGP	Exterior Gateway Protocol.
EIGRP	Enhanced Interior Gateway Routing Protocol.
ES	end system.
EUI-64	extended universal identifier 64-bit.
FCAPS	fault, configuration, accounting, performance, and security management (five functional areas of network management).

FCIP	Fibre Channel IP.
FDDI	Fiber Distributed Data Interface.
FECN	forward explicit congestion notification.
FIB	Forwarding Information Base.
FIN	Finish (bit in TCP segment code field).
FLSM	Fixed Length Subnet Mask.
FRTS	Frame Relay traffic shaping.
FTP	File Transfer Protocol.
Gbps	gigabits per second.
GLBP	Gateway Load Balancing Protocol.
GoS	grade of service.
GTS	Generic Traffic Shaping.
HAN	home-area network.
HDLC	High-Level Data Link Control.
HIDS	host-based IDS.
HIPS	host-based IPS.
HR	human resources.
HSRP	Hot Standby Router Protocol.
HTTP	Hypertext Transfer Protocol.
HTTPS	Secure HTTP (HTTP over SSL).
HWIC	high-speed wireless interface card.
Hz	hertz.

IBGP	Internal BGP.
ICMP	Internet Control Message Protocol.
ID	identifier.
IDS	intrusion detection system.
IEEE	Institute of Electrical and Electronics Engineers.
IETF	Internet Engineering Task Force.
IGMP	Internet Group Management Protocol.
IGP	Interior Gateway Protocol.
IGRP	Interior Gateway Routing Protocol.
IIS	Internet Information Server.
IM	instant messaging.
IntServ	Integrated Services.
IPCC	IP contact center.
IPM	internetwork performance monitor.
IPS	intrusion prevention system.
IPsec	IP security.
IP/TV	Internet Protocol Television.
IPv4	IP version 4.
IPv6	IP version 6.
IPX	Internetwork Packet Exchange.
IS	1. information systems. 2. intermediate system.
iSCSI	small computer systems interface over IP.

ISDN	Integrated Services Digital Network.
IS-IS	Intermediate System-to-Intermediate System.
ISL	Inter-Switch Link.
ISO	International Organization for Standardization.
ISP	Internet service provider.
IT	information technology.
ITU-T	International Telecommunication Union Telecommunication Standardization Sector.
kbps	kilobits per second.
LCD	liquid crystal display.
LFI	Link Fragmentation and Interleaving.
LLC	Logical Link Control.
LLQ	low latency queuing.
LMS	LAN management solution.
LSA	link-state advertisement.
LSU	link-state update.
MAC	Media Access Control.
MB	megabyte.
Mbps	megabits per second.
MCS	media convergence server.
MD5	message digest algorithm 5.
MGCP	Media Gateway Control Protocol.

MIB	Management Information Base.
MISTP	Multiple Instance STP.
MLS	multilayer switching.
MLSP	Multilayer Switching Protocol.
MLS-RP	MLS route processor.
MLS-SE	MLS switching engine.
MOS	mean opinion score.
ms	millisecond.
MTU	maximum transmission unit.
NAC	Network Admission Control.
NAD	network access device.
NAS	network attached storage.
NAT	Network Address Translation.
NBAR	network-based application recognition.
NBMA	nonbroadcast multiaccess.
NFS	Network File System.
NIC	1. network interface card. 2. Network Information Center.
NIDS	network-based intrusion detection system.
NNM	network node manager.
NSAP	network service access point.
NSF	nonstop forwarding.
OOB	out-of-band signaling.

OS	operating system.
OSI	Open Systems Interconnection.
OSPF	Open Shortest Path First.
OTP	one-time password.
OUI	Organizational Unique Identifier.
PAM	pulse amplitude modulation.
PBX	private branch exchange.
PCM	pulse code modulation.
PDA	personal digital assistant.
PDIOO	plan, design, implement, operate, and optimize.
PDLM	packet description language module.
PDU	protocol data unit.
PGP	Pretty Good Privacy.
PHB	Per hop behavior.
PIM	Protocol Independent Multicast.
PIN	personal identification number.
PIPEDA	Personal Information Protection and Electronic Documents Act.
PIX	Private Internet Exchange.
PKI	public-key infrastructure.
PoE	Power over Ethernet.
POP3	Post Office Protocol version 3.
PPP	Point-to-Point Protocol.

pps	packets per second.
PQ	priority queuing.
PRC	partial route calculation.
PRI	Primary Rate Interface
PSTN	public switched telephone network.
PVC	permanent virtual circuit.
PVLAN	private VLAN.
PVST	per-VLAN spanning tree.
PVST+	per-VLAN spanning tree plus.
QoS	quality of service.
R&D	research and development.
RED	random early detection.
RF	radio frequency.
RFC	Requests For Comments.
RFID	radio frequency identification.
RIP	Routing Information Protocol.
RIPv1	Routing Information Protocol version 1.
RIPv2	Routing Information Protocol version 2.
RM	RF management.
RME	Resource Manager Essentials.
RMON	Remote Monitoring.
ROI	return on investment.

RP	rendezvous point.
RPF	Reverse Path Forwarding.
RSM	Route Switch Module.
RST	Reset (bit in TCP segment code field).
RSTP	Rapid STP.
RSVP	Resource Reservation Protocol.
RTP	Real-Time Transport Protocol.
RTS	Request To Send.
SA	source address.
SAA	service assurance agent.
SAN	storage area networking.
SB	senate bill.
SCSI	small computer systems interface.
SLA	service level agreement.
SLB	server load balancing.
SLC	service level contract.
SMB	small to medium business.
SMTP	Simple Mail Transfer Protocol.
SNMP	Simple Network Management Protocol.
SNMPv1	SNMP version 1.
SNMPv2	SNMP version 2.
SNMPv3	SNMP version 3.

SOX	Sarbanes-Oxley.
SPAN	Switched Port Analyzer.
SPF	shortest path first.
SRST	Survivable Remote Site Telephony.
SSH	secure shell.
SSID	Service Set Identifier.
SSL	Secure Socket Layer.
SSO	stateful switchover.
STP	1. shielded twisted-pair. 2. Spanning Tree Protocol.
SVC	switched virtual circuit.
SWAN	Structured Wireless-Aware Network.
SYN	Synchronize (bit in a TCP segment code field).
TACACS	Terminal Access Controller Access Control System.
TCO	total cost of ownership.
TCP	Transmission Control Protocol.
TCP/IP	Transmission Control Protocol/Internet Protocol.
TFTP	Trivial File Transfer Protocol.
TKIP	Temporal Key Integrity Protocol.
ToS	type of service.
TTL	Time To Live.
UDP	User Datagram Protocol.

USB	Universal Serial Bus.
UTP	unshielded twisted-pair.
VAD	voice activity detection.
VC	virtual circuit.
VIP	Versatile Interface Processor.
VLAN	virtual LAN.
VLSM	variable-length subnet mask.
VMPS	VLAN Membership Policy Server.
VMS	VPN/Security Management Solution.
VoD	video on demand.
VoIP	Voice over IP.
VPN	virtual private network.
VRRP	Virtual Router Redundancy Protocol.
VTP	VLAN Trunking Protocol.
WAP	wireless access point.
WCCP	Web Cache Communication Protocol.
WDS	1. Wireless Domain Services. 2. Wireless Distribution System.
WEP	Wired Equivalent Privacy.
WFQ	weighted fair queuing.
WIDS	wireless intrusion detection system.
Wi-Fi	wireless fidelity.

WLAN	wireless local-area network.
WLSE	wireless LAN solutions engine.
WLSM	wireless LAN service module.
WPA	Wi-Fi Protected Access.
WRED	weighted random early detection.
XML	extensible markup language.

Index

Numerics

A

B

W

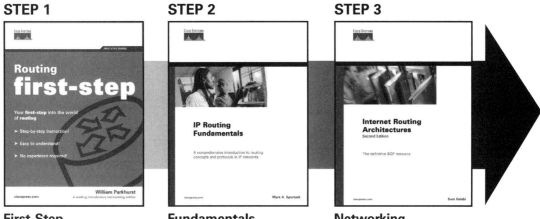

SEARCH THOUSANDS OF BOOKS FROM LEADING PUBLISHERS

Safari® Bookshelf is a searchable electronic reference library for IT professionals that features more than 2,000 titles from technical publishers, including Cisco Press.

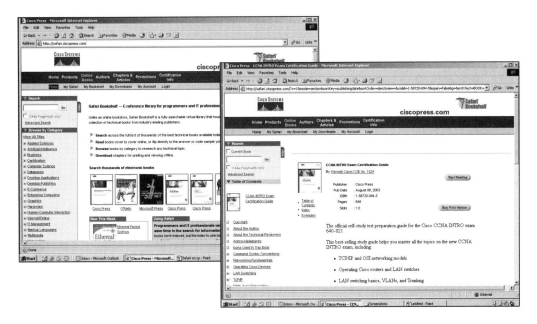

With Safari Bookshelf you can

- **Search** the full text of thousands of technical books, including more than 70 Cisco Press titles from authors such as Wendell Odom, Jeff Doyle, Bill Parkhurst, Sam Halabi, and Karl Solie.

- **Read** the books on My Bookshelf from cover to cover, or just flip to the information you need.

- **Browse** books by category to research any technical topic.

- **Download** chapters for printing and viewing offline.

With a customized library, you'll have access to your books when and where you need them—and all you need is a user name and password.

TRY SAFARI BOOKSHELF FREE FOR 14 DAYS!

You can sign up to get a 10-slot Bookshelf free for the first 14 days.
Visit **http://safari.ciscopress.com** to register.

CISCO SYSTEMS

Cisco Press

FUNDAMENTALS SERIES
ESSENTIAL EXPLANATIONS AND SOLUTIONS

Voice over IP Fundamentals

A systematic approach to understanding the basics of Voice over IP

Jonathan Davidson, CCIE® No. 2560
James Peters

ciscopress.com

1-57870-168-6

When you need an authoritative introduction to a key networking topic, **reach for a Cisco Press Fundamentals book**. Learn about network topologies, deployment concepts, protocols, and management techniques and **master essential networking concepts and solutions**.

Look for Fundamentals titles at your favorite bookseller

802.11 Wireless LAN Fundamentals
ISBN: 1-58705-077-3

**Cisco CallManager Fundamentals:
A Cisco AVVID Solution**
ISBN: 1-58705-008-0

Cisco LAN Switching Fundamentals
ISBN: 1-58705-089-7

Cisco Unity Fundamentals
ISBN: 1-58705-098-6

Data Center Fundamentals
ISBN: 1-58705-023-4

IP Addressing Fundamentals
ISBN: 1-58705-067-6

IP Routing Fundamentals
ISBN: 1-57870-071-X

Network Security Fundamentals
ISBN: 1-58705-167-2

Storage Networking Fundamentals
ISBN: 1-58705-162-1

Voice over IP Fundamentals
ISBN: 1-57870-168-6

Coming in Fall 2005
**Cisco CallManager Fundamentals:
A Cisco AVVID Solution**, Second Edition
ISBN: 1-58705-192-3

Visit **www.ciscopress.com/series** for details about the Fundamentals series and a complete list of titles.

CISCO SYSTEMS

Cisco Press

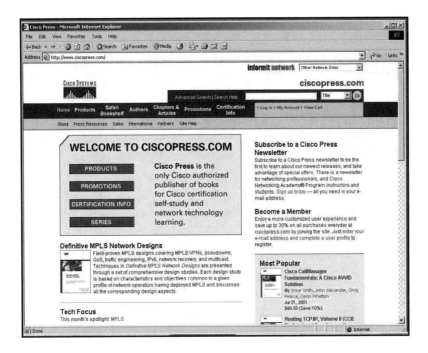
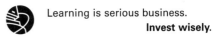

THIS BOOK IS SAFARI ENABLED

INCLUDES FREE 45-DAY ACCESS TO THE ONLINE EDITION

The Safari® Enabled icon on the cover of your favorite technology book means the book is available through Safari Bookshelf. When you buy this book, you get free access to the online edition for 45 days.

Safari Bookshelf is an electronic reference library that lets you easily search thousands of technical books, find code samples, download chapters, and access technical information whenever and wherever you need it.

TO GAIN 45-DAY SAFARI ENABLED ACCESS TO THIS BOOK:

● Go to **http://www.ciscopress.com/safarienabled**

● Enter the ISBN of this book (shown on the back cover, above the bar code)

● Log in or Sign up (site membership is required to register your book)

● Enter the coupon code found in the front of this book before the "Contents at a Glance" page

If you have difficulty registering on Safari Bookshelf or accessing the online edition, please e-mail customer-service@safaribooksonline.com.